I0803147

LUNCH 17

Lunch is a design research journal produced at the School of Architecture at the University of Virginia

Editors: Judy Shao-Yu Chen, Sawyer Davies, Andre Grospe, Eden McCafferty, and Erica Schapiro-Sakashita
Faculty Advisors: Brad Cantrell and Sneha Patel

University of Virginia
School of Architecture
Campbell Hall
PO Box 400122
Charlottesville, VA 22904

Published by Applied Research and Design Publishing, an imprint of ORO Editions.
Gordon Goff: Publisher

www.appliedresearchanddesign.com
info@appliedresearchanddesign.com

ISBN: 978-1-961856-04-2

Printed by Carter Printing Company in Richmond, Virginia

AR+D Publishing makes a continuous effort to minimize the overall carbon footprint of its publications. As part of this goal, AR+D, in association with Global ReLeaf, arranges to plant trees to replace those used in the manufacturing of the paper produced for its books. Global ReLeaf is an international campaign run by American Forests, one of the world's oldest nonprofit conservation organizations. Global ReLeaf is American Forests' education and action program that helps individuals, organizations, agencies, and corporations improve the local and global environment by planting and caring for trees.

Typeface: Bau Pro

TABLE OF CONTENTS

PLAYCRAFT

12 **ContaminantCraft**
Sarah Rivard

20 **A Spatial Tale of Origin for Three Voices: Room One**
Peter Waldman

32 **At Play**
Bailey Briggs

40 **Prompts For Crafting Practice**
Chloe Hawkins

SENSECRAFT

48 **Craft By Extension**
Sasson Rafailov

54 **Behind Hong Kong's Neon Glow**
Celina Qiu

66 **Recrafting Urban Narratives through Body Map Storytelling**
Elizabeth L. Sweet, Sara Ortiz Escalante, Raksha Vasudevan

FIELDCRAFT

82 **Central Valley Accessories**
Dylan Krueger

92 **Made in America**
Anthony Averbeck

106 **Condensation**
Marantha Dawkins

116 **Midwestern Landscapes**
Mike Nesbit

128 **Gravecraft**
Samantha Rosner

PULPCRAFT

144 **The Color of Craft**
Sanda Iliescu, Ailsa Thai, Nita Wareechatchai

152 **Between Place and Thought**
Karey Kessler

158 **Lollygagger**
Eli Sobel

166 **Dog Ear**
Erica Baum

TECHNECRAFT

178 **Tooling Tools & Digital Digits**
Kyle Schumann

186 **Reciprocal Ecology**
Junhong Fu, Elizabeth Needham, Evelyn Saunders, Ehsan Baharlou

200 **SheepCraft**
Theodore Teichman

212 **Preppercraft: Speculative Fiction From the Usable Past**
Kira Clingen

RITUALCRAFT

232 **Test Plot**
Jennifer Jones

238 **Towards the Core**
Larissa Belcic, writing for Nocturnal Medicine

250 **Grow Closer: Prune, Chip, and Stack**
Practice Landscape (Sarah Diamond, Rosetta S. Elkin, Emily Hicks, and Joanna Lombard)

262 Contributors list

RECENTERING CRAFT:
A LETTER FROM THE EDITORS

When the editors of this journal's predecessor, Modulus, chose "Craft and Architecture" as the theme of the 22nd issue (1993), they had little doubt as to how the former related to the latter. To them, craft, deriving from Vitruvius' definition, is a combination of industrial wisdom, a knowledge of buildings, materials, and construction, and a cultural intelligence, coming from a critical engagement with the myths of construction and the ability to further the idea of *homo faber*, or the transformation of the environment through tools and making.

Thirty years later, this editorial board of LUNCH 17 certainly does not have as sturdy a grasp on what "craft" means to architecture. While construction and labor is central to our work, it is rarely the center of the conversation, let alone described as craft. As it's been delivered to us in studio critiques and reviews, craft has been nothing more than a weak compliment to models and drawings that are pleasing to the eye. But where others may bemoan a "loss" of craft within the profession, we see a sea-change in the relationship between design and its tools.

Nearly two decades since Donna Haraway helped introduce the cyborg into contemporary discourse, the relationship between our bodies and the prostheses we use to interact, manipulate, and create with nature have become increasingly entangled and complex; so much so that the synthesis of cultural and technical knowledge embedded in Vitruvius' definition of craft has been completely inverted. Time has continually proven the disastrous effects of the *homo faber* paradigm.

Given the reemerging climatological and ethical issues embedded in design professions, from the carbon footprint of conventional material extraction and assembly to the culture of exploitation and overworking within academia and the profession, the time is right to form a truly crafty response. This comes alongside an acknowledgement and reckoning of the centuries of Indigenous knowledge systems that have been systematically oppressed and erased in the United States and around the world.

While this editorial team doesn't fully comprehend the scale of disciplinary and social shifts happening at the moment, these shifts do seem to constitute a new kind of craft. Thus our call was an open invitation for practitioners, scholars, and students to see craft beyond traditional artisanal labor and the production of objects, instead seeing the world as constructed from the crafty interactions between culture and technology. By giving space, including ______ space on the page to Craft, we hope that readers continue to grapple with what it means to reinterpret rather than rewrite, to regenerate rather than restore.

______craft is empty. open. temporal. dynamic. ready.

Are you?

XO
L17

How do play and improvisation transition into craft?

Can play be deterministic?
Or is it inherently open?

At what point does play become serious?

How do play and improvisation transition into craft?

Can play be deterministic?
Or is it inherently open?

At what point does play become serious?

PLAY

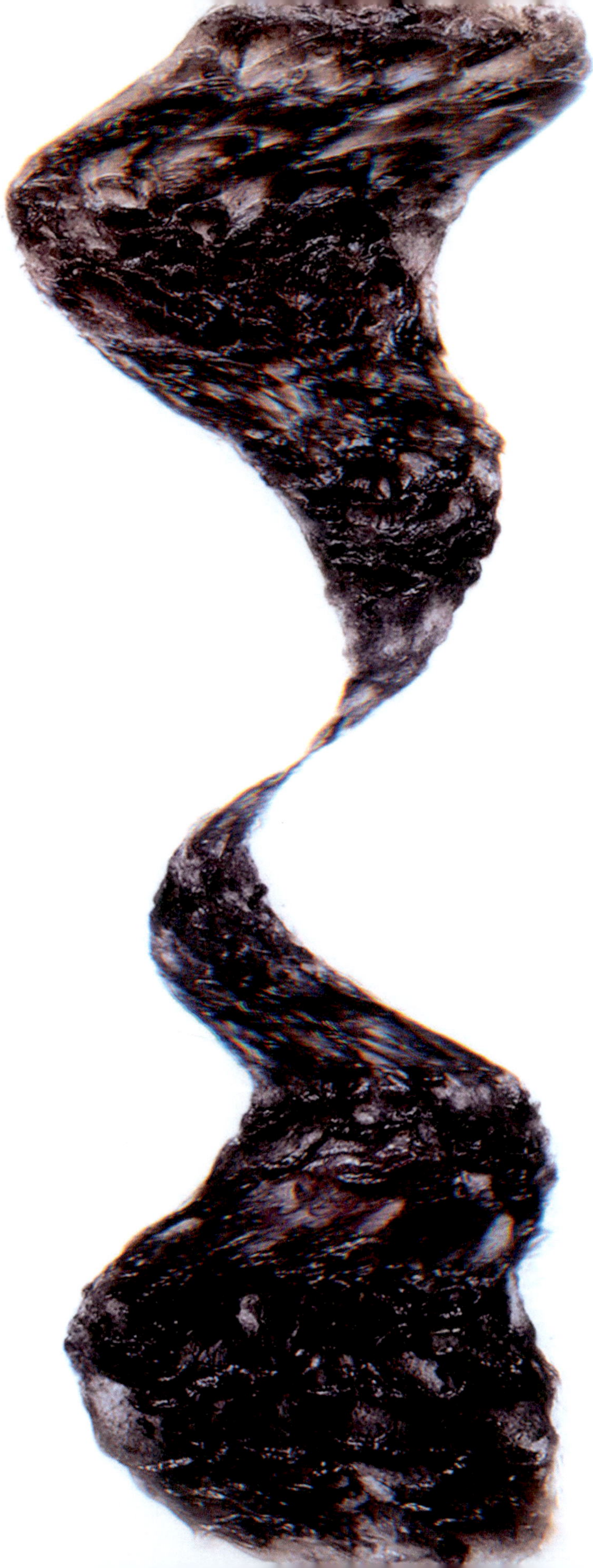

CONTAMINANTCRAFT

Sarah Rivard

Fig. 01 - Source material by Sarah Rivard, image altered by LUNCH editors.

Craft is understood in contemporary terms as both a skill for making, and alternatively, for deception. The duality of this word is captured in this series of paintings.

The shift in method of making from handmade to manufactured drove major shifts in the types of materials used in production. As the way we made things changed, so too did the waste. The waste from chemically synthesized non-biodegradable materials wreaks havoc on the environment and human health.[1] It is contamination.[2] For example, the waste from washing a sweater is now microplastic fiber instead of natural wool fiber as it would have been before the advent of synthetic textiles. Roughly 700,000 plastic fibers can be shed in a single wash cycle![3] The microplastic fibers travel from the washing machine, through the wastewater system into the ocean, and settle with sediments in the seabed. In fact, they settle in the highest densities in deep sea trench beds, leech chemicals over time, and resemble marine snow organic matter that deep sea filter feeders rely on for nutrients.[4] The filter feeders eat the plastic instead of food, which causes them to starve and the plastic to migrate up the food chain.[5] The microplastic fibers contaminate the entire ocean, all lifeforms, and are part of every environment on Earth.[6]

Plastic textiles exemplify craft as deception. Plastic is an excellent imitator and is developed into many different materials including polyester, acrylic, elastane (Spandex), and nylon. Most contemporary manufactured clothing is partially, or entirely, plastic without us even registering that it is derived from petroleum. The cognitive link between the raw material, process, and product is opaque. Further, the tiny plastic fiber waste shed from this clothing is not visible to the naked eye. It is also obscured. The obscurity of these processes is damaging because the mundane act of washing clothes is not recognized as a contaminating act that links extraction,[7] chemical synthesis, manufacture, consumption, contamination, and the deep sea.[8,9]

Can the craft of painting reveal the craft of deception within synthetic textiles? Can it reveal the link between contaminant, where it originates, and where it contaminates?

These ContaminantCraft paintings use a hand-mixed paint of dryer lint and gloss gel medium on canvas. The dryer lint is a combination of synthetic and organic material, and the gloss gel medium is petroleum-derived acrylic. Each ContaminantCraft painting reveals different obscured relationships. Many UVA graduate students donated lint to make these paintings possible, so I would like to thank them for their contribution to this work.

Notes

1. *Eman Abdallah Kamel, "Synthetic Fibers: The Manufacturing Process and Risks to Human and Environment," Owlcation (March 2021): https://owlcation.com/stem/Synthetic-Fibers-The-Manufacturing-Process-and-Risks-to-Human-and-Environment.*
2. *Max Liboiron, "Pollution as Colonialism," Duke University Press (May 2021).*
3. *Laura Paddison, "Single Clothes Wash May Release 700,000 Microplastic Fibres, Study Finds," The Guardian (September 26, 2016). https://www.theguardian.com/science/2016/sep/27/washing-clothes-releases-water-polluting-fibres-study-finds.*
4. *Ian Kane and Michael Clare, "Dispersion, Accumulation, and the Ultimate Fate of Microplastics in Deep-Marine Environments: A Review and Future Directions," Frontiers in Earth Science (April 2019): 2, https://doi.org/10.3389/feart.2019.00080.*
5. *Joe McCarthy and Erica Sánchez, "Even Creatures in The Deepest Ocean Trench Have Eaten Plastic," Global Citizen (February 28, 2019) https://www.globalcitizen.org/en/content/mariana-trench-animals-plastic/.*
6. *Kane and Clare, "Dispersion, Accumulation, and the Ultimate Fate of Microplastics," 2.*
7. *Extraction: Used here specifically referencing extractive petroleum practices such as fracking and drilling to remove crude oil from the Earth.*
8. *Liboiron, "Pollution as Colonialism."*
9. *Damian Carrington, "Microplastic Pollution Revealed "Absolutely Everywhere" by New Research," The Guardian, section Environment, (March 2019).*

Fig. 02 - Wave Cycle, Sarah Rivard.

This painting represents the particle, the washing machine, and the ocean. The density of microplastic in the ocean is increasing exponentially over time. This painting explores a potential future with waves of microplastic and the concept of convergence as the actions of the past impact the future.

Microplastics' impact extends far beyond the ocean due to the overlapping nature of ecosystems. Overlap & Absence continues the visual language of Wave Cycle to suggest that as one contaminated ecosystem overlaps with another, something is lost. Perhaps this loss is time or lifespan, fertility, or even a species. However, this absence also represents room for new life, new thinking, and new modes of relation.

Fig. 03 - Overlap & Absence, Sarah Rivard.

Fig. 04 - Suspended Particle, Sarah Rivard.

This painting examines the convergence of wastewater, the particle, and the trench. The suspended particle is in tension between the two triangles, which represent a funneling from human activity to deep sea environment. This illustrates the tension between Earth's cycles and the overproduction of extractive synthetic materials with microplastic at the center of each.

Fig. 05 - Imbalanced Hourglass, Sarah Rivard.

Imbalanced Hourglass explores the idea of balance and time between human practices and the Earth's cycles. The form invokes the image of a traditional hourglass filled with waves of microplastic fibers and thrown off balance by rounded bases. There is no turning back time on this issue.

A SPATIAL TALE OF ORIGIN FOR THREE VOICES: ROOM ONE

Peter Waldman

All Images courtesy of the Author

A packing crate containing domestic rooms is delivered.
A Totem in uncovered as its steel armature is dismantled.
Eight rectangular plywood sheets are laminated in four-fold layers, twice over to form an eight square.
THE NOMAD OF THE LATE TWENTIETH CENTURY DWELLS IN ONE ROOM.

The Totem records the moments of routine life.
Messages and secrets are stored in the most accessible drawers
And in the most hidden of compartments.
The Totem is transformed into a Cabinet.
Two arcs are projected onto this square, and then cut out
as the first maps of the land.
Steel belts tether these concentric laminations in place.
THIS ROOM HAS COUNTLESS EYES BUT ONLY ONE GREAT PORTAL.

One day at a time, the Cabinet yields its mysteries.
A Garden unfolds.
The Tomb—or parquet floor—assembles landscapes yet to be told.
This cabinet has a back, two sides and a front.
They shield themselves in armor while enlisting one hundred eyes to keep watch from behind.
The front unveils itself only at its head.
THIS ROOM IS BOURNE ON TWO CONCENTRIC CARRIAGES,

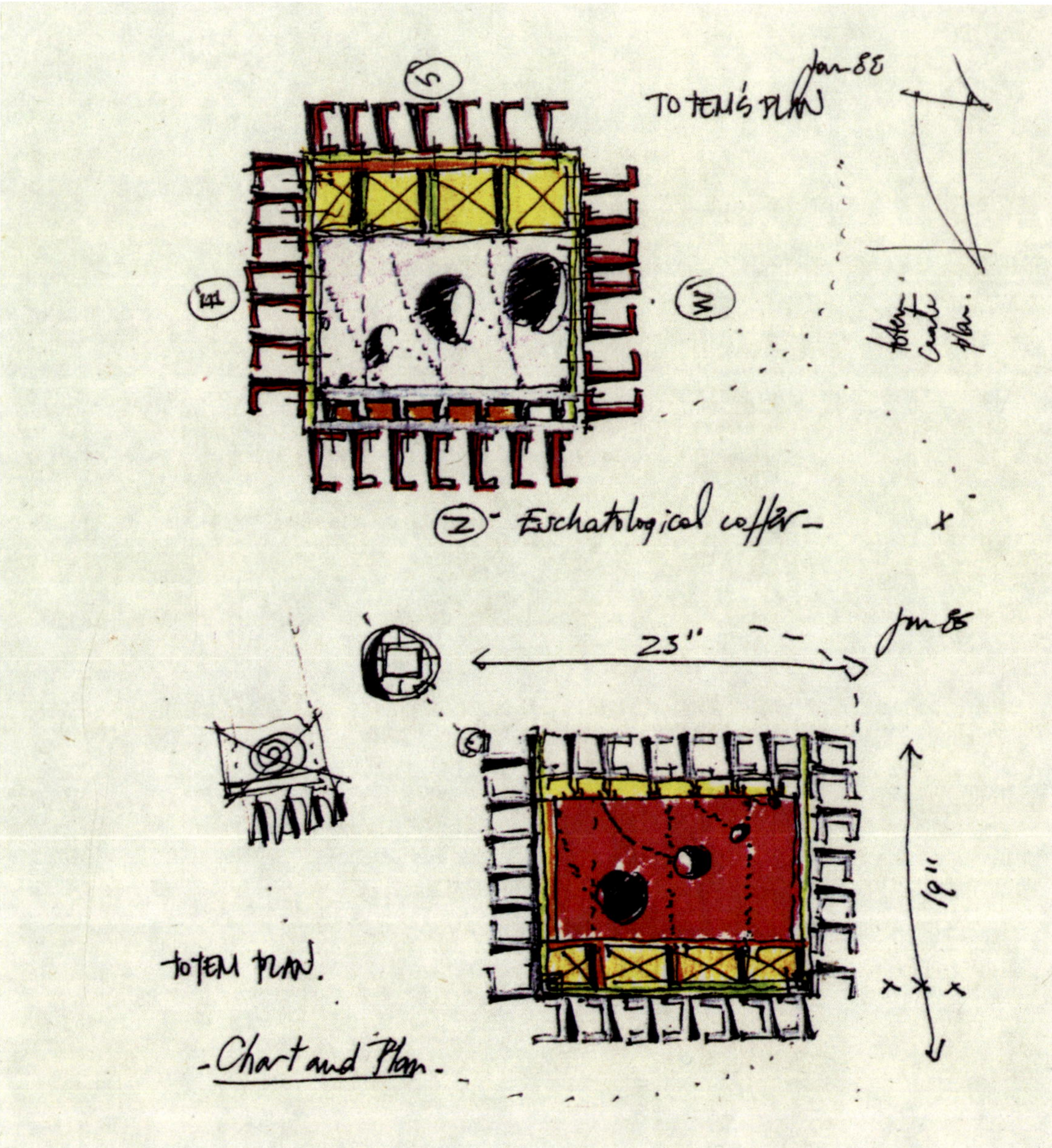

WITH WHEELS WHICH MEASURE THE WORLD OVER AND OVER
WITH THE AID OF ASTRONOMERS AND LUNATICS ALIKE.

From Totem to Tomb, an eschatological manual is proposed.
This text of endings marks the surface of the space with
the imprint and the shadows of its inhabitants.
In this rectangular Room, time measures itself by the interrupted
brutality of its own cyclic topography.
During the journey the wheels become scarred, burned and used by
the frictional aggregations of time.
THIS IS THE SPATIAL TALE OF ORIGIN OF ONE VOYAGEUR.
ONE VOYEUR TO THE NOMADIC CONDITION OF THE NEXT
MILLENIUM.

In the fall of 1987, while I was teaching at Rice University in Houston, Texas, I was one of four North American architects invited to assemble a team to submit a "Speculation on the Relationship of Architecture and Craft" for the American Craft Museum in New York City. As an exhibition criss-crossing the Continent over three years, it was critical to consider the Packing or Shipping Crate as generative.

This pragmatic imperative suggested that Architecture as a Wheel (Vehicle) was now relevant as a modest Nomadic Encampment (Container) tentatively rolling over the earth to be deeply stained by time. Our project became immediately the Gerund of Crafting— a transformation of plywood sheets and steel sections. These orthogonal materials were reduced to circular panels and joints to record the Passage of Time while evidencing lingering Fingerprints in the Act of Making.

I invited Professor George Smith, a steel fabricator in Rice's Studio Art Department, and Chris Genik, a recent graduate from Rice's M. ARCH. program, as my primary collaborators. I had been Chris's Thesis Advisor on *Spatial Tales of Origin as Specifications for Construction* in 1983, thereafter collaborating and winning a series of urban design competitions. We took on this dimensionally smaller challenge in the light of the previous vast urban work, now with the idea of One Good Room which was A Packing /Shipping Crate as an easily Transportable Wheel to be rolled from our Rice Studio onto a truck to reach New York, Montreal, Los Angeles, Chicago, Cincinnati, Denver and finally back to Houston acquiring the patina, blisters, and

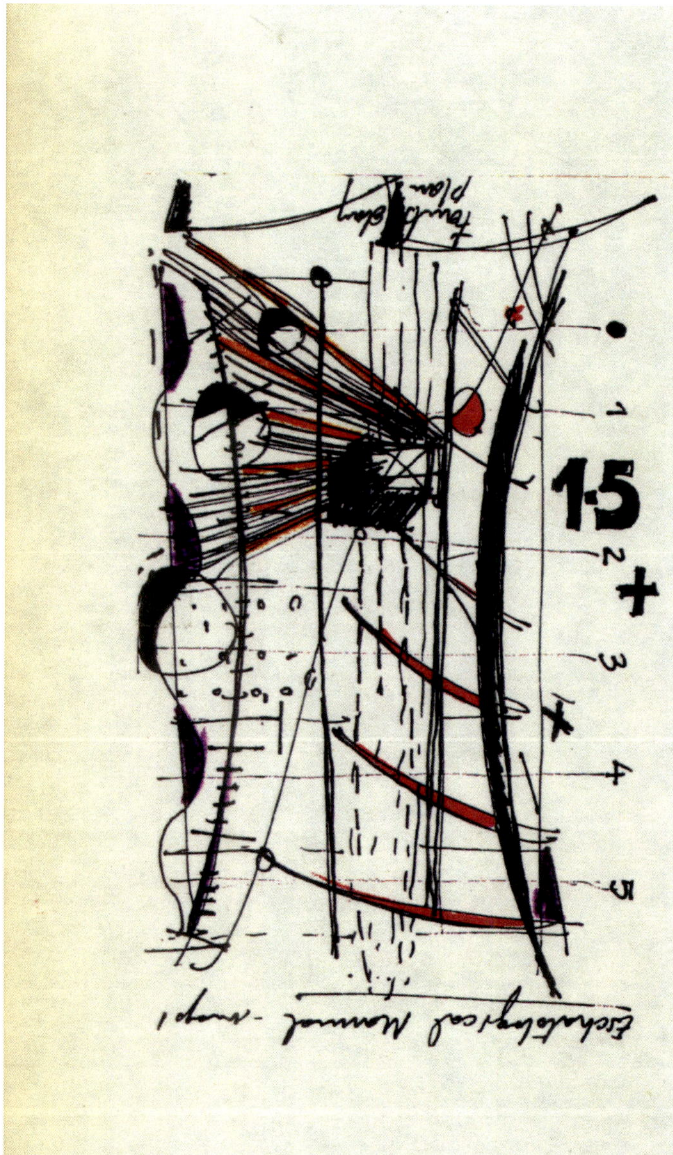

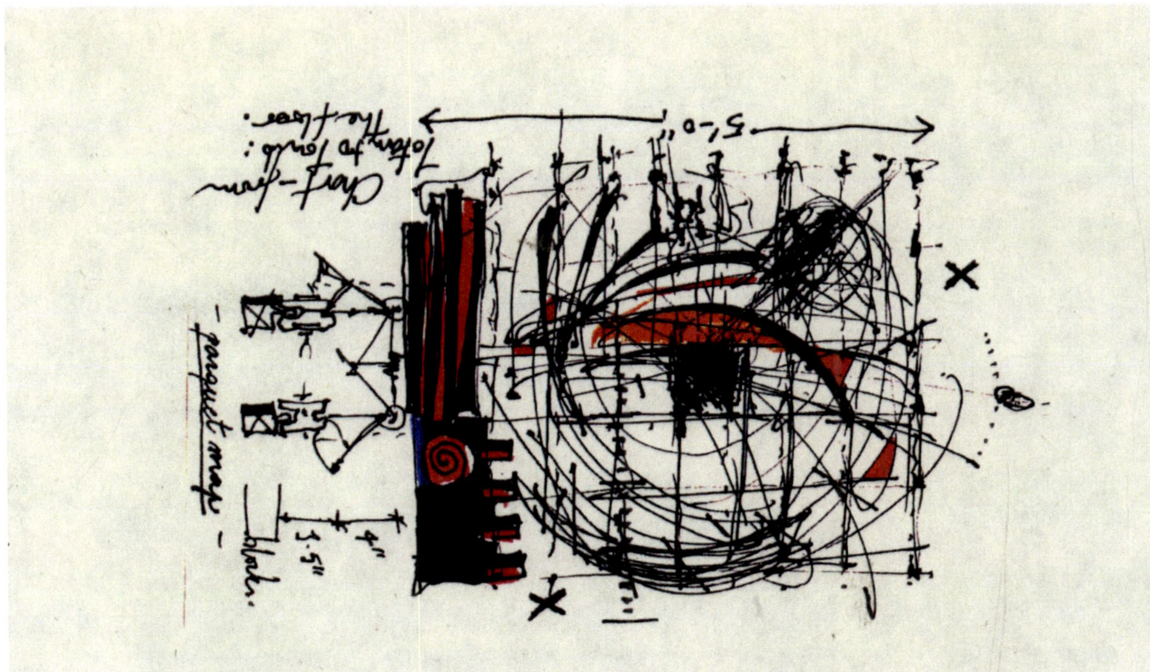

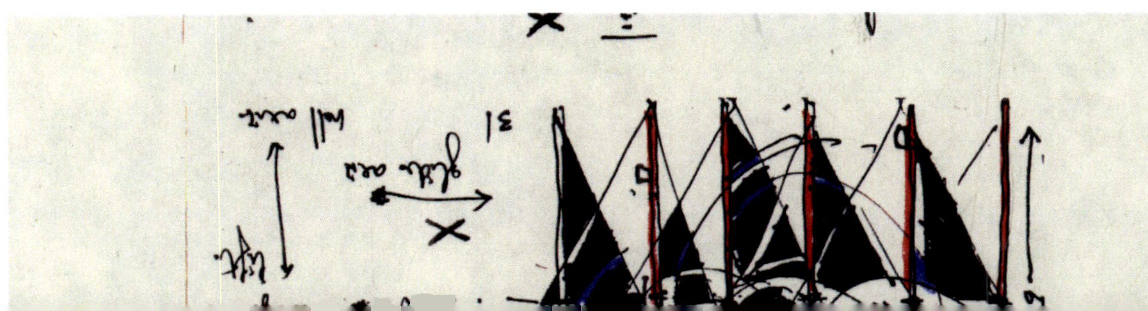

scars of this shipping process in the hands of perfect and imperfect strangers along the way.

With a modest budget of $6,000.00, this team of three constructed the armature over four months in the spring of 1988 in the Woodworking and Steel Fabrication Shop of the Fine Arts Faculty at Rice. We knew we wanted to explore the presence of the singular human figure in a project that appeared to be simultaneously the scale of the larger universe itself, both a pantheon and cenotaph. The proposition was to make a Compass to hold the human figure as an idea in dialogue with the enduring diagrams of DaVinci and Le Corbusier. We made many basswood models over two weeks in January, delighting in time lag exposures as we spinned it in multiple configurations.

None of us were systematic critical linear thinkers, but rather delighted in what some call circumstantial play, reveling in both upside-down and inside-out. Determined that at each exhibit venue the Project of Crate now Wheel containing a Crafted Reliquary Chamber within would take on this obligation to unfold or deconstruct into distinct landscapes. After the first two weeks with only 14 weeks remaining until shipping time, we decided to purchase the final material inventory as a commitment to crafting from the logic of a step-by-step process; to transform the Orthogonal Character of Rectangular 4'X8' Birch Plywood panels into a Kaleidoscope of Circles framing the Passage of Time.

We purchased 16 sheets of 4'x8" Plywood panels, ¾" thick and laminated them four to a panel, and then aligned them side by side to yield two 8x8 panels which would be transformed into the Two Wheels to support the Carriage.

Now with two overall Squares of 8'X8', we cut two eccentric Arcs, the outer edge 8'-0" in diameter but subtracting the inner Arc 6" on the top and 12" on the bottom, to yield in plan a perfect circle on the outside and eccentric ellipse on the inside.

We drilled and bolted 8" o.c. each of these 4 ply laminates together and placed 1/8" steel plate banding screwed into the outer end grain to toughen this emerging Packing Crate.

With the remainder of the subtracted curvilinear panels, we made the Carriage or Chariot which had now four subtractive remnants of wooden wheels to ride in the grooves of the larger layered Wheels.

Thus, we had one composite Wheel of two eccentric panels with a Carriage riding on four wheels with now circumstantially necessitated welded steel plates bolted in turn to wood infill panels, using all the available resultant pieces. There were never to be left over pieces as we were bricoleurs at heart.

We cut out five circular apertures in each of these five wheels to give us grip holes to correspond to our four hands of five digits each.

Finally, George was catalytic to stabilize this middle carriage with first orthogonal and then diagonal rods of steel as structural struts.

This Packing Crate was now complete as an Architectural Frame Transformed from Square to Circle whose primary intention was to move on from here and now to then and there. It could take on the scars of weathering and celebrate generational endurance. The Protagonist of Craft was waiting in the wings. We intended to offer an intimate space for human habitation as small as a casket or was it a pregnant uterine profile, a Caryatid of sorts, Totem or Tomb, some would say a Torture Rack, derived from one panel of Baltic Maple 1X2 meters (approximately 40"X80"), thus smaller than the 16 Birch panels of 48"X96".

We constructed a box from this unblemished resource, two sides and a back, and an open drawbridge front door panel. The enclosing flanks and back were protected then with galvanized sheet metal, providing armor for us wishing the Maple would never be stressed.

These were installed delicately with marine wing screws as it would be secured with Texas rawhide tie-down straps. The front of this Caryatid chamber door was made of thin ½" maple laminates and dowels as a bas-relief with a chrome piano hinge on the bottom and left unveiled on the upper part.

Within this Tomb or Totem, the back was punctured with 48 apartment door ID pinholes, see-through tubes (we wanted 100 but the hardware store had a supply chain problem). Within, we installed on the top two marine sail braces which appeared to us as uterine pelvic bones to suspend the sandbag derived from medieval sand clock technologies. In each exhibit the sand would be loaded up in the morning and drain out over a 12-hour day leaving the cloth sagging and a new spillover mountain trespassing onto the gallery floor. Attached to the inner part of the front door panel were three etched copper plates indicating the itinerary maps of the routes by truck, train, and finally air to connect each destination city and finally to return home to Houston. We did not want our Wheel/Carriage/Caryatid/Chariot to be lost in Solnit's Blue of Distance.

Late one afternoon in April, after studio crits, when we were just about finished, I returned to the Art Program Workshop to fulfill my daily obsession to sand off Chris's notations on the Birch and Maple wood components as my way of keeping the project virgin, pure, perhaps abstract until its Odyssey to travel away from this protected womb on its way Up East. Chris was there apparently annoyed by my obsession to wipe off his fingerprints in the act of making. He was awaiting in ambush as I entered and then started to fire up the welding torch and to burn, blister, and to scar the assembled wood components. He said this Wheel needed to grow up, to get scarred by life before it received the marks of strangers. I was horrified, but not paralyzed, and then intuitively applied handfuls of Turtle Wax onto the smoking wood. Chris then fought back and brushed blue and red paint onto these smoldering waxed surfaces. As I was waxing, he then took a rough textured file and scored random scars to complete this selfish rush into pock-marked adolescence. The larger outer wheels, now toughened up for shipping, then bore Chris's signature, supporting the more delicately crafted and refined Carriage of my more nurturing if not complex appetite for connective tissues if not iridescence.

We agree that the slender Totemic Maple box would remain the Crafted Figure so armored and sheltered that resilient generations may find it as a nurturing Oasis. Over three decades even these galvanized shields have become blemished by the passage of time. I have learned the Gerund of Crafting is never an Idealized Stabilized Condition but positively displays Vulnerability. JB Jackson, in The Necessity for Ruin, has the last word.

References

1. Solnit, Rebecca. A Field Guide to Getting Lost. New York: Viking, 2005.

2. Jackson, John Brinckerhoff. The Necessity for Ruins, and Other Topics. Amherst: University of Massachusetts Press, 1980.

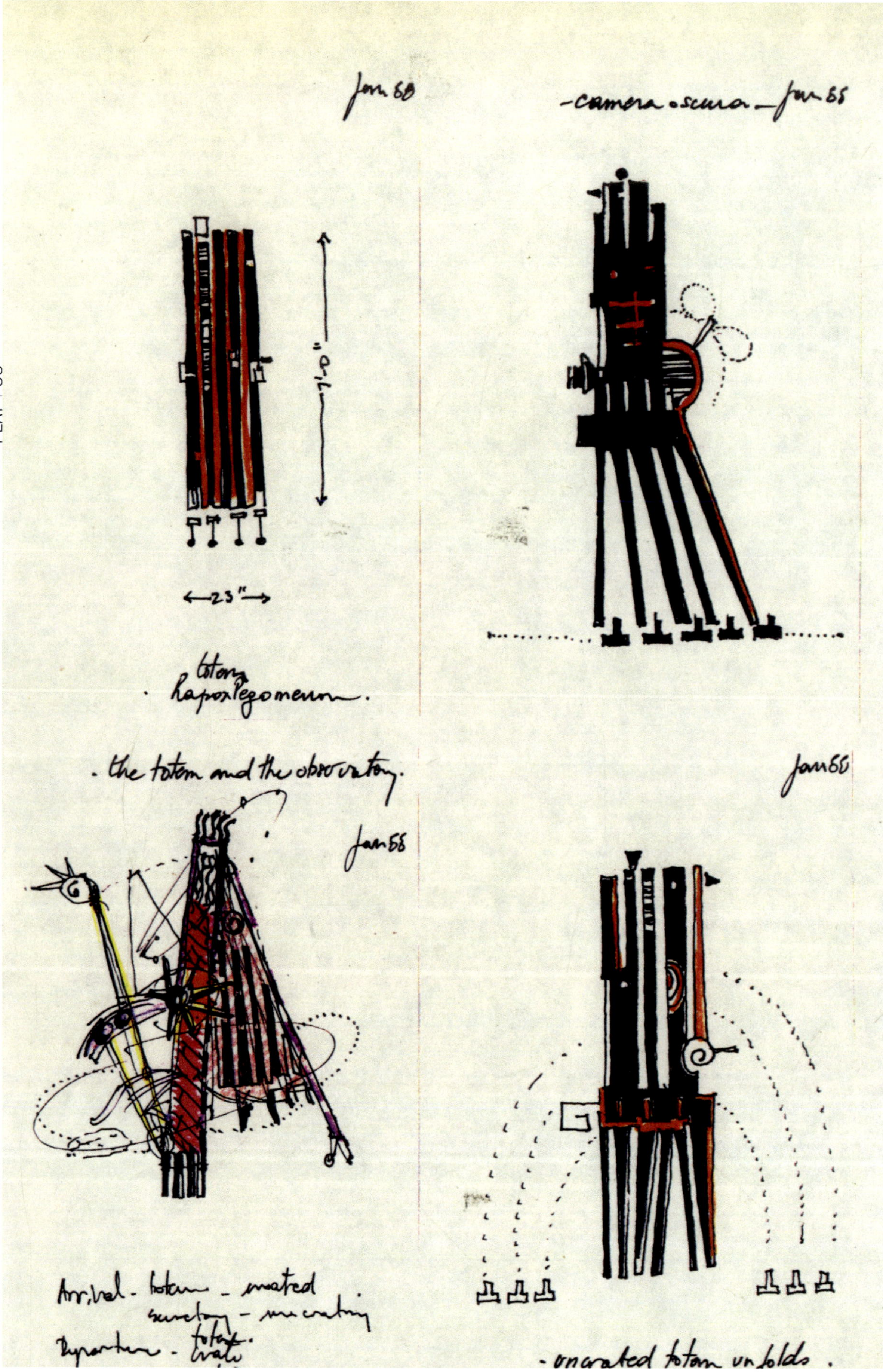
Jan 68
-camera obscura- Jan 68
7'-0"
←23"→
totem
hapaxlegomenon.
. the totem and the observatory.
Jan 68
Jan 68
Arrival - totem - created
sanctuary - uncreating
Departure - totem
crate
- uncreated totem unfolds.

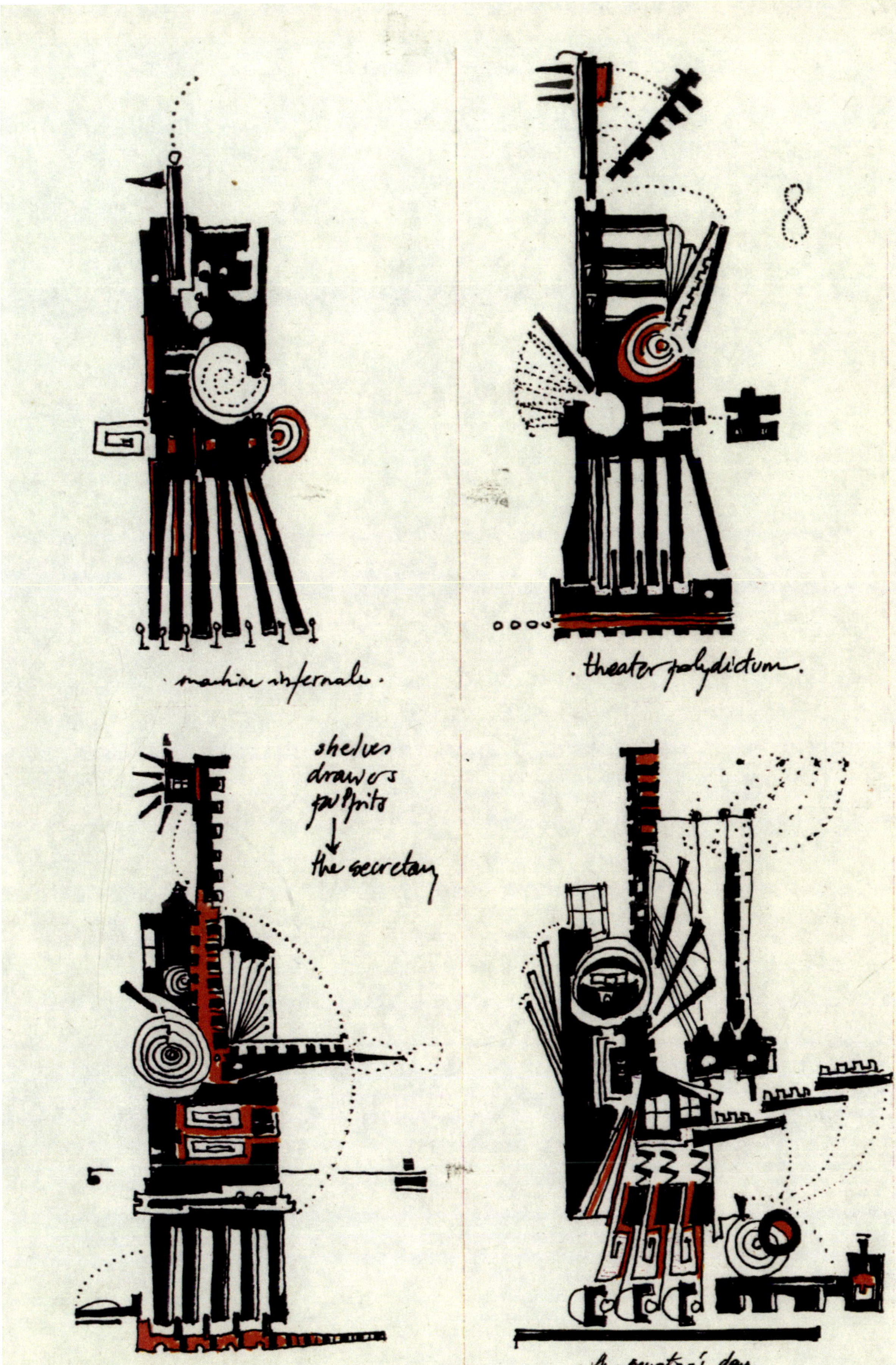

8
. machine infernale .
. theater polydictum .
shelves
drawers
pulpits
the secretary
. the secretary's day .

AT PLAY

Curated by Bailey Briggs

Fig. 01 - Charcoal Tracks, Bailey Briggs.

Physical, aesthetic and dynamic attributes of water were explored through "Drawing Water," a course taught by Associate Professor of Landscape Architecture Brian Davis. Students were first introduced to multiple hydrodynamic processes of water and its movement, in tandem with readings and conversations about artworks by Vija Celmins, Hiroshi Sugimoto and Sol LeWitt, and the ideas of philosophers and scientists like John Dewey and Nicolaus Copernicus. This foundation inspired experimental studies on a geomorphology table to manipulate and 'play' with the fluid *techne* of landscape. 'Play' can be defined as "unstructured exploration within a bounded space."[1] Establishing boundaries without an end goal allowed the process of drawing and representation to lead experimentation through materials, influence and interface. Selection of tools and materials were the first creative choices. The geomorphology table, photogrammetry, pencil, ink, food coloring, and string, among others, allowed for the journey of learning through play to be implemented. This resulted in a diverse series of artful compositions within the limits defined by each individual.

Notes

1. *Brian Davis and Alexander Robinson, "From solution space to interface." In Codify, ed. Bradley Cantrell and Adam Mekies (London: Routledge, 2018) 155-68.*

A custom framework of strings tied at even intervals within a frame were suspended into water multiple times at different periods to capture the direction and velocity changes of water flowing down a river. A series of photographs documented the changes and then were traced to recreate the essence of the water's changing movement.

Fig. 02 - Direction and Flow, Ailsa Thai, Colored pencil.

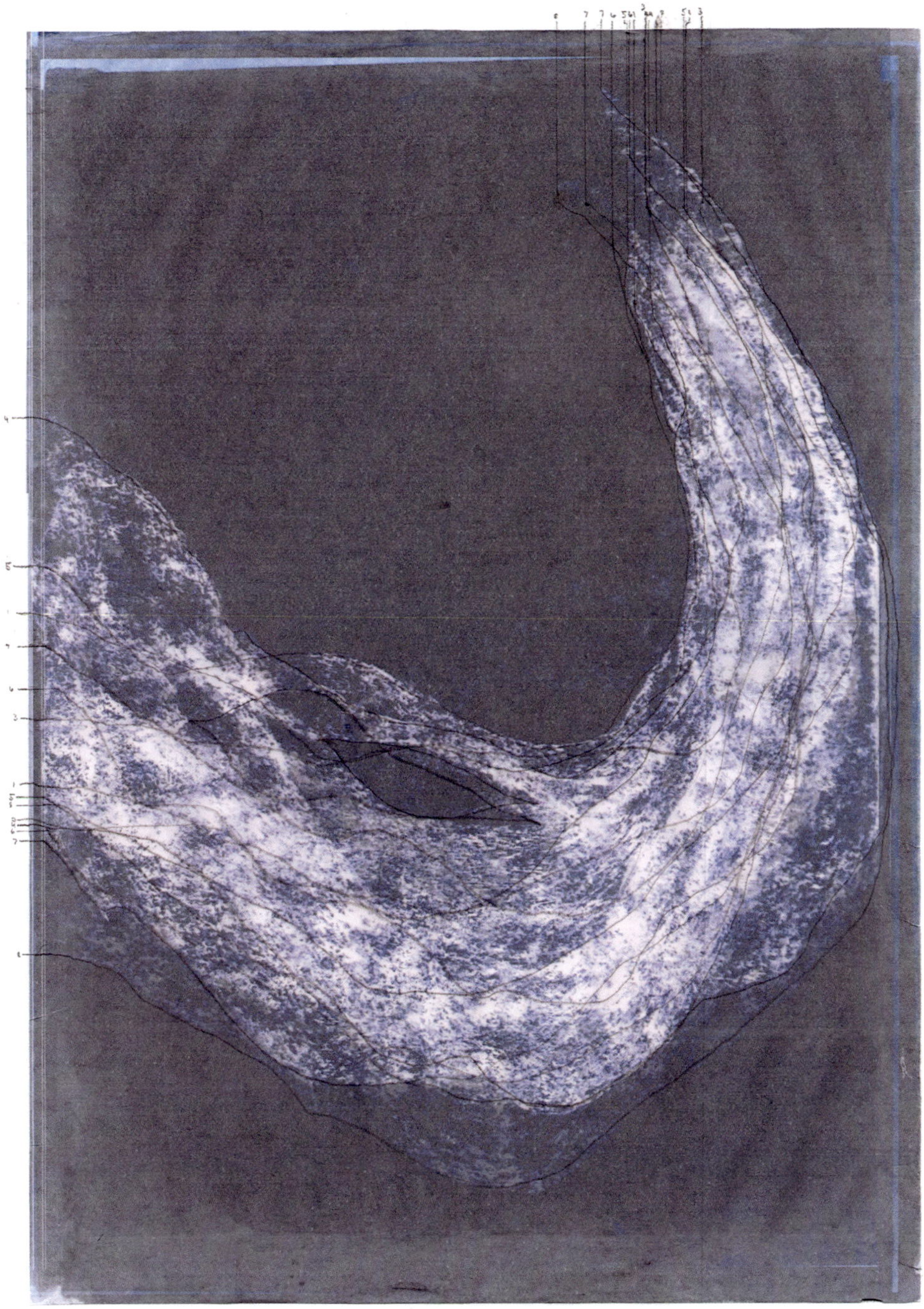

Fig. 03 - Point Bar, Andre Grospe, Cyanotype paper.

A series of cyanotype papers were exposed on the surface of the water flowing through an eddy periodically during its formation. Each sheet was layered to show this change over time. The drawing emulates the ephemeral nature of water and sediment moving together infinitely.

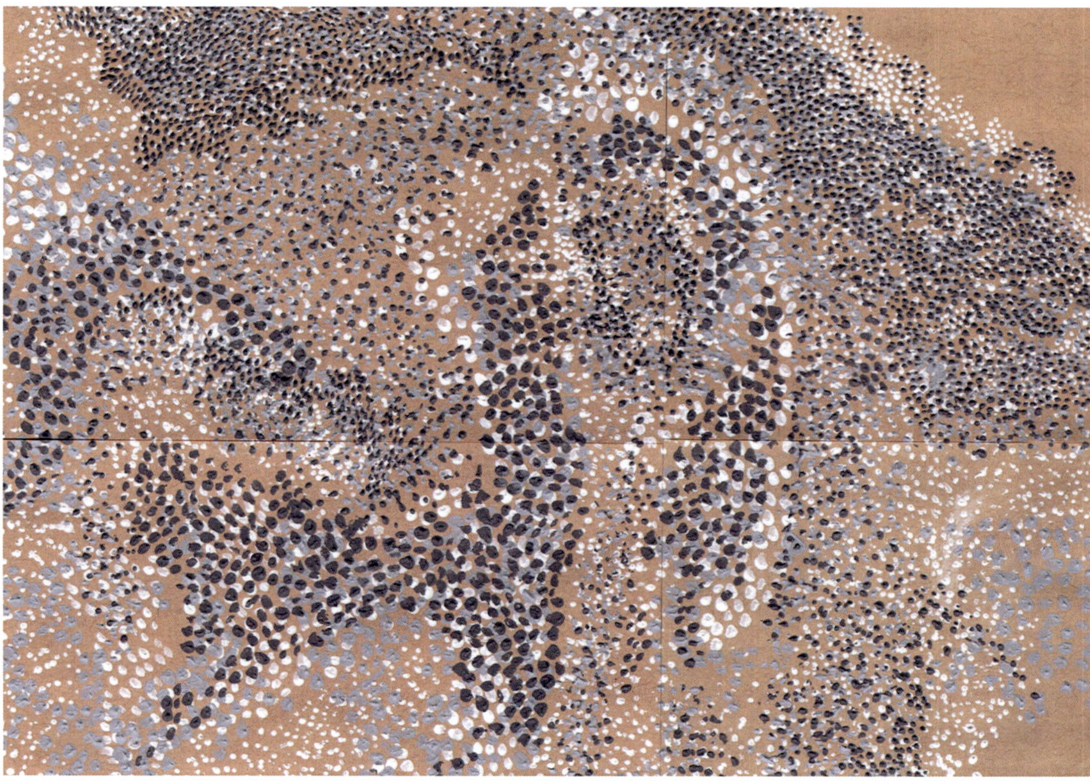

Stipples mimic the strand lines of sediment that suggest the ebb and flow of wave action over time. Different colors represent stages in the ebb and flow process, while the stipple sizes represent different sediment sizes interacting with the system.

Fig. 04 - Strand Lines, Bailey Briggs, Acrylic paint.

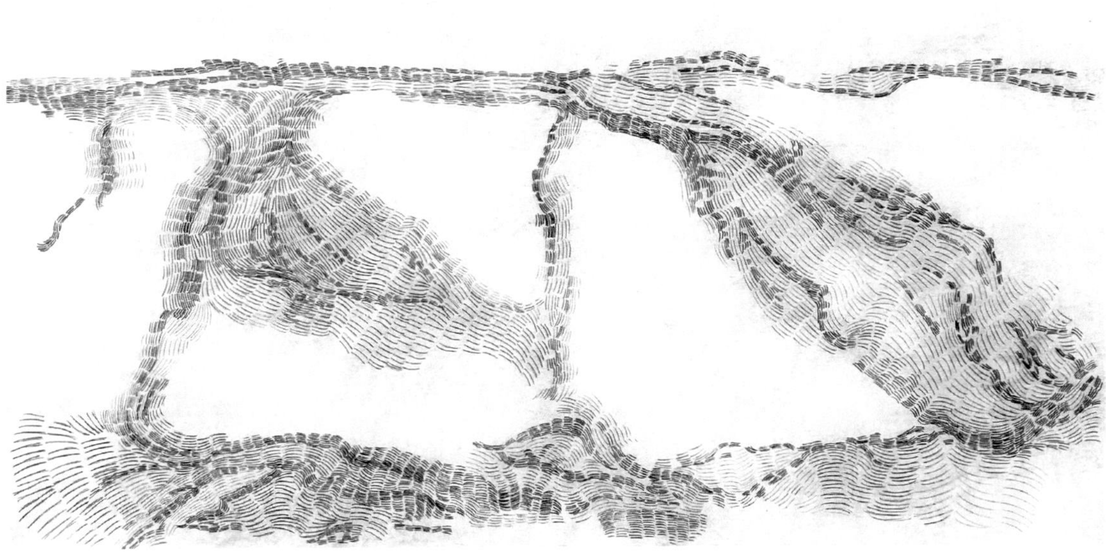

Fig. 05 - Quiver Plot, Leah Li, Graphite.

Directional hatches indicate the movement and speed of water across a geomorphology table's sediment landscape. Visual and photographic studies documented the drawing that was generated within these boundaries.

Water movements choreographed by small rock piles on a geomorphology table were captured by introducing ink up-river, then laying paper on the surface to capture the hydrological tendencies of a river system. Individual pieces come together to create a series that freezes the surface flows in time.

Fig. 06 - Surface Flows, Nita Wareechatchai, Paper, ink, water.

Fig. 07 - Strands and Riffles, Sawyer Davies, Graphite.

Sediment formations were captured at unique and aesthetically pleasing moments to portray the migration and dynamism of sediment flows influenced by moving water on a geomorphology table.

PROMPTS FOR CRAFTING PRACTICE

Design is a big game of pretend. We observe what is here and imagine what isn't here but could be. We use our own senses and many tools to register, understand and interpret the complexity of our surroundings. We use drawings to communicate.

These exercises present drawing routines to craft a way of practicing that supports skills of hand, mind and imagination. They are inherently embedded in the work we do as designers, but are intentionally separated here from design production. At the heart of these prompts is the conviction that doing anything with care leads to an ability to bring care to any pursuit and that taking care is foundational to sustaining creative work. These prompts invite you to freely and regularly draw; to move your bodies; to develop judgement without being judgmental; to love something that someone else made; to closely observe, be curious, record and interpret your environments; to condition yourselves to be inquisitive; to develop care-fullness in creative work and to make for the joy of making.

THE IMPORTANCE OF DRAWING

Drawing is proof of concept of craft—that ability can be developed through practice. Drawing by hand immediately proves that transformation is possible—the marks you make in

Figs. 01-06 - Drawings & Photographs, Chloe Hawkins.

the first minute after you begin will always differ from the marks you make in the last minute before you stop. You change—your body warms up, the connection between mind and body is clarified and your inner and outer worlds brought together as you improve your control of your drawing tools. Drawing is like any language—the more you practice, the better you can communicate, express yourself and connect with others.

THE IMPORTANCE OF STRUCTURE

Though simple, each of these prompts has some structure—whether it is limiting the task to a single subject or proposing a particular sequence of events. While there is a role for free drawing, these are intentionally organized to support improving your craft of practicing and allows for the opportunity, with repetition, to gauge personal change and establish a framework for organizing and referencing your own ideas.

HOW TO USE THESE PROMPTS

These exercises are purposely simple. They can be as elaborate or as plain as you make them and endlessly repeated with different results. They are adaptable to individuals, groups, skill levels and creative pursuits and not specify a medium, though are intended to be done by hand. The word "draw" can easily be replaced with "model" or "sculpt." They can be done alone or together, applied to straightforward or complex subjects and be completed in a few minutes or in a day. Do them for fun, to facilitate a studio critique, as a creative warm-up or as a break from work. However you practice, start these from a place of enjoyment and affection—draw what you are drawn to.

Chloe Hawkins

FIND YOUR HAND

Your hand is a part of your bodythat you leave behind in the marks you make. Draw the way that only you can—with your own handsaw to find your hand, as a part of you, as the part of you that stays on the page. Try different materials—pencil, charcaol, ink. Try different ways of moving your drawing hand —from your shoulder, elbow, wrist, and fingers. Give yourself some structure—a single subject—on which to try your hand. Be minimal and be maximal.

Fig. 01

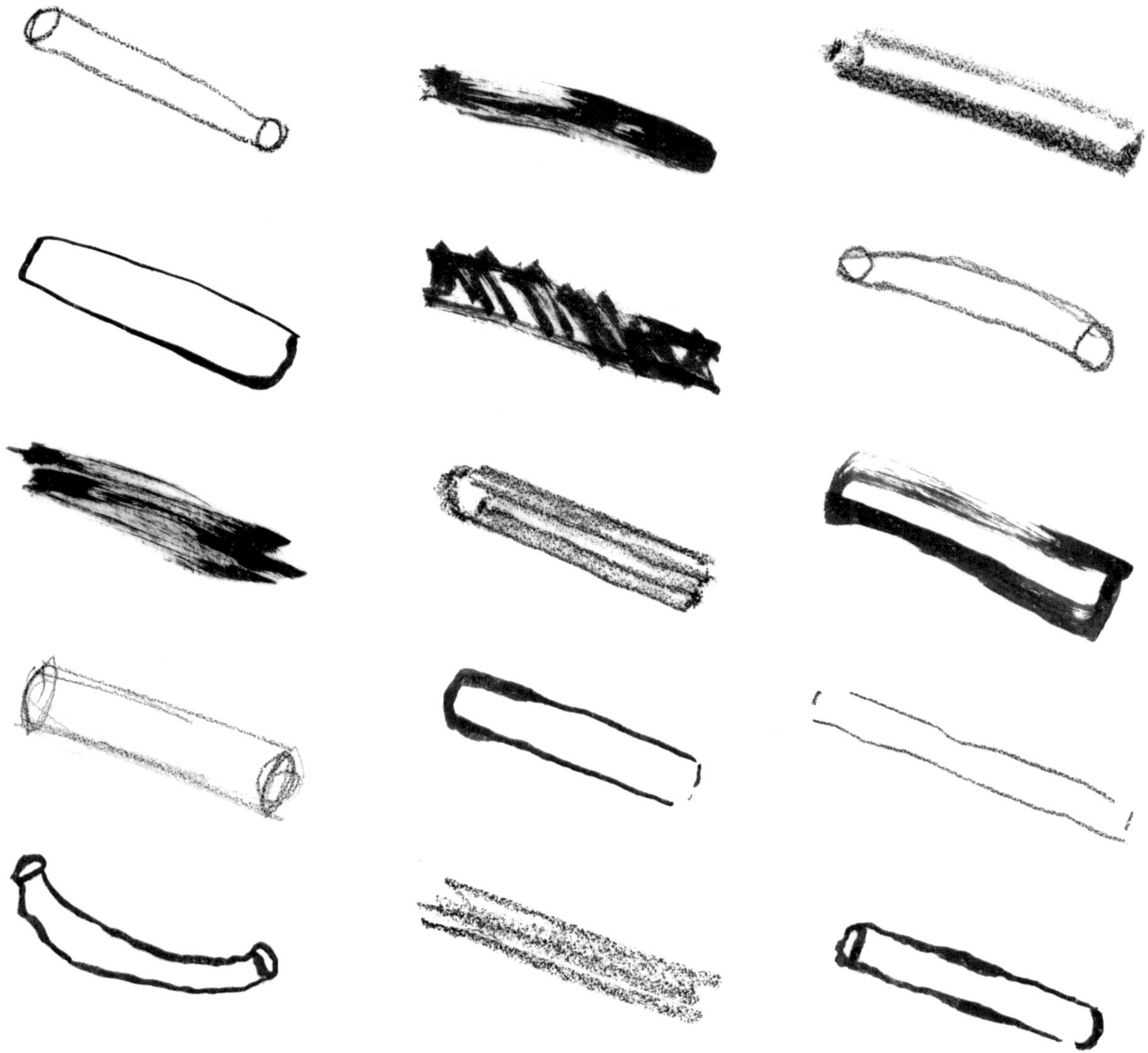

How does intuition, the sixth sense perhaps,
relate to the senses?

Is sensitivity a framework for craft?

When we rely on the unseen–emotion, intuition,
flow–can craft transcend beauty?

How does intuition, the sixth sense perhaps,
relate to the senses?

Is sensitivity a framework for craft?

When we rely on the unseen—emotion, intuition,
flow—can craft transcend beauty?

SENSE

CRAFT BY EXTENSION

Sasson Rafailov

Fig. 01 - Source material from The Association of Cultural Properties, image altered by LUNCH editors.

Craft implies an extension of human consciousness into the realm of earthly materials. It is an evocation of spirit through knowing hands and sharp tools which comes to have some influence on the world beyond the limits of our flesh. As an immaterial process, craft is meditation: it extends the mind and spirit through time and place in pursuit of a common interest among peoples of every ilk. In its embrace of material, craft pushes beyond the human: it creates cyborgs at every stroke of the brush and strike of the chisel;[1] it attaches an isolated body to an interconnected planet; it allows us to inhabit a world outside our own. Understood in these terms, craft is a posthumanist practice which simultaneously augments our consciousness and preserves the traces of our being through time in flesh which often outlives our own. By connecting concepts of craft across these physical and spiritual planes, we create the potential for a new ontology of hybrid objects to emerge and position the human in a more genuine relationship with their environment.

Contemporary conceptions of craft do well to frame it as an all-encompassing ideology,[2] one which makes it difficult to distinguish between human and world; but by committing to such an abstract position, these theorists sacrifice their ability to analyze the material relationships which join the two together. It is in this realm that writing from philosophy of technology makes greater strides, for while they might rely on a mediating force to bridge the gap between object and subject, authors in this field also understand that such a coalescence essentially represents the birth of something new.[3] The term *embodiment*, as developed by Don Ihde in "A Phenomenology of Technics," (2007) is fundamental to this concept because it gives us a starting point for understanding the physical elision of space between a human being and the tools they use to manifest their crafts.[4]

A simple example of this phenomenon can be seen in the experience of a person wearing a pair of eyeglasses: given its natural transparency, the "tool" disappears in the mind of its user so long as it functions as it should. Though a malfunction might invoke Heidegger's concept of the tool present-at-hand,[5] bringing the glasses back as a distinct entity separate from their user, "normal" use implies that they join the body and become invisible extensions of human

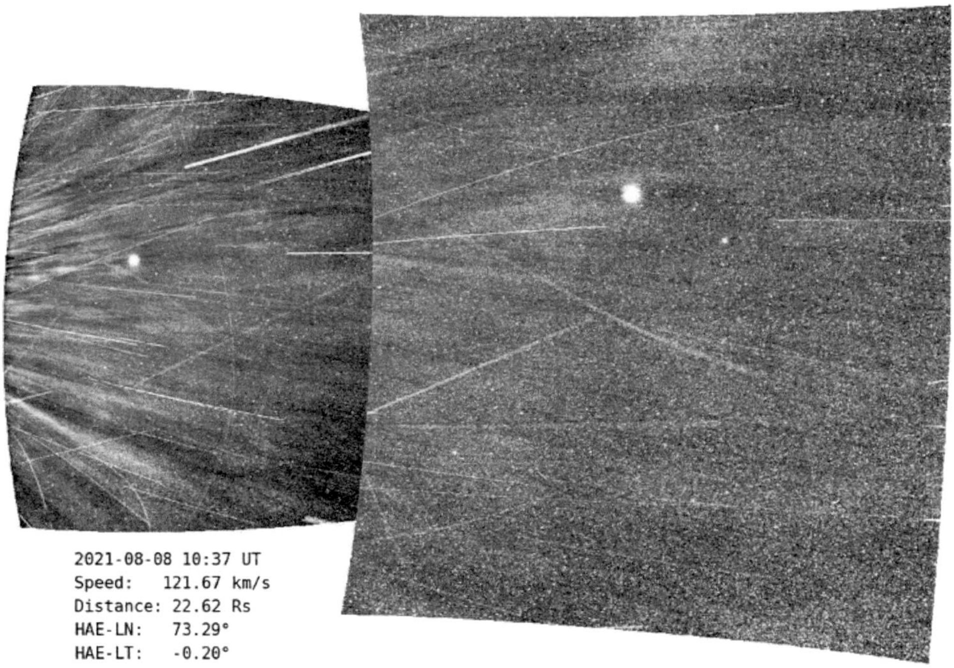

Fig. 02 - Parker Probe WISPR visualization, NASA.

perception. And embodiment is not simply limited to objects which remain in physical contact with our bodies: a more cutting-edge example from NASA's Parker Solar Probe demonstrates that we can feel ourselves flying through something as unfamiliar and distant as the sun's atmosphere, so long as the data from the vessel's sensors is visualized in first-person perspective (Fig. 02).[6] Even in this case, where the tool is millions of miles away from us in physical space, it is still perceived as an extension of the human body, inseparable from its conscious understanding of the world–the only reason we continue to make a distinction between the two entities is because the tool is made of flesh that is different from our own.

The difficulty in translating this theory into the world of craft is that the concept of embodiment is not typically extended beyond the relationship of a human and their tools. But if these tools become part of our being, why should the connection stop once that embodied consciousness makes contact with another material? And if the tool itself emerges from the workshop of a craftsperson, doesn't that mean their consciousness is already bound to it; that it does not need added human activation to garner some ontological dignity? By circumventing the tool in this analysis and examining a craft practice which does not always depend on a third body to mediate between human and world, we may begin to establish a model for such connections which can then be applied to understand other, more tool-intensive, crafts.

Among the more ancient crafts still practiced today, pottery lends access to a posthumanist and, at times, mystic understanding of material being. Though it is not always the case in contemporary studios, potters can dig up clay and form it into something useful without relying on anything other than their bare hands. Given the potential for such a direct engagement with the work, it would be inconsistent to claim that the human could extend their bodies through the tools they use in their studios, but could not be embodied in the clay if they choose to form it with their hands alone. Embodiment is surely experienced differently in this case than it is with a pair of glasses but, fundamentally, it is the same concept: the clay being worked is an extension of the hands working it; the potter's senses of touch and sight are augmented and redefined as they try to build the material up into some coherent form. And just as the potter's life is embodied in the clay at the tips of their fingers, the clay takes on the life of the potter: once released, this material bears witness to that moment of embodiment in its flesh; the life given can only be taken away by the destruction of that material and physical memory. For potters, the "birth" of a new piece is a phenomenon so ingrained in their work that it begins to take on anthropomorphic qualities, as the anatomy of a pot is often described using human terms like foot, lip, belly, and shoulder.[7]

Life in clay takes on more than just a formal significance, however. The Japanese potter Ken Matsuzaki, whose work emerges both geographically and intellectually from the Mingei folk tradition, says of his pots "I want to feel [the] cosmos within the Chawan bowl, and among the ones I've created, I want to pick one that has my world within it."[8] For Matsuzaki, the object of his work holds greater meaning than a simple extension of his life force; the chawan (Fig. 03)[9] becomes a spiritual object, one which represents the very potential for life in the vastness of the cosmos. In this sense, once

Fig. 03 - Kizaemon tea bowl, produced by an unknown Korean potter in the 16th-17th c., The Association of Cultural Properties, Japan, 1952.

the tea bowl is given life by the potter, it becomes its own life-giving entity–a material which is the product of geological development, typically taking place over the course of millennia, suddenly adopts an ontological status normally reserved for biological life. The great power in this transformation is that the material remains of a geological sort, so its hybridity essentially extends the life of its maker beyond its biological limits.

One aspect of ceramic production is missing from this analysis, however: a tool in the form of a kiln is required to transform wet earth into ceramic, but the status of this particular mechanism, even in modern potteries, warrants separate treatment. Though it is a tool entirely contrived and operated by human hands, there is a mysticism that surrounds kilns in both traditional wood-fired processes as well as in their more modern, electric equivalents. This force is often referred to as the "kiln gods," and some potters believe in their power to such an extent that they will offer ritual sacrifices to these beings before firing their kilns.[10] If the firing is a success, the potter feels a sense of gratitude. If not, they do not take the failure out on themselves because they were not the only agent in this process. The kiln gods are a mystic force in this context: their influence can be capricious, and their identity poorly understood, but they are revered and feared by craftspeople all the same. Kilns, then, are not only ontologically valid beings occupying a plane that is level with ours, but their status is bound to a divine order beyond our comprehension.

My purpose here is not to determine whether these beings exist in some universal, empirically demonstrable way, but to ask if there is value in seeing the world and the things which comprise it as bearing life and agency similar to our own. Is the belief that we can impart life into inert matter just a romantic notion, or simply the product of an overgrown ego? Is a potter's sense of gratitude at the end of a successful firing meaningful or beneficial to their craft? Hubert Dreyfus and Sean Dorrance Kelly discuss the place of gratitude towards fortune in an ancient Greek context in their *All Things Shining*: "Indeed, gratitude is more than simply the appropriate response in Homer's world; it is essential to a well-lived life."[11] Perhaps the most compelling reason to believe in the agency of inert matter is that, like the Greeks of antiquity, we are never truly in control of our surroundings.[12] We might not attribute good fortune to our standing with the gods in the same way Homer's heroes did, but it might enrich our lives to conceive of the materials in our world as bearing some responsibility for our standing in it. In this sense, the statement which began this essay needs reformulation: it is disingenuous to say that the movement of life goes from the human into the world; instead, we should ask what in this world gives us life, and we should work to find our place in the craft of engaging with that matter.

Notes

1. *Donna Haraway, "A Cyborg Manifesto: Science, Technology, and Socialist Feminism in the Late Twentieth Century," In Philosophy of Technology: An Introduction (Malden, MA: Blackwell, 2007), 610-30.*
2. *Richard Sennett, The Craftsman (New Haven: Yale University Press, 2009).*
3. *Haraway, "A Cyborg Manifesto," 610-30.*
4. *Val Dusek and Don Ihde, "A Phenomenology of Technics," In Philosophy of Technology: An Introduction (Malden, MA: Blackwell, 2007), 539–60.*
5. *Martin Heidegger, The Question Concerning Technology (New York: Harper Colophon Books, 1978).*
6. *Miles Hatfield, "NASA Enters the Solar Atmosphere for the First Time," NASA, December 13, 2021. https://www.nasa.gov/feature/goddard/2021/nasa-enters-the-solar-atmosphere-for-the-first-time-bringing-new-discoveries.*
7. *Bernard Leach, A Potter's Book (London: Unicorn, an imprint of Unicorn Publishing Group, 2016), 46.*
8. *Goldmark Gallery, "Ken Matsuzaki: The Intangible Spirit," YouTube, December 8, 2018. 34:16. https://www.youtube.com/watch?v=r9clFHIrv4E&t=1455s&ab_channel=GoldmarkGallery*
9. *Association of Cultural Properties, "Ido Chawan Kizaemon," Portfolio of National Treasures Volume 1st: Tokyo, March 30, 1952. https://upload.wikimedia.org/wikipedia/commons/b/b5/Ido_chawan_Kizaemon.jpg*
10. *Hubert L. Dreyfus and Sean Kelly, All Things Shining: Reading the Western Classics to Find Meaning in a Secular Age (New York: Free Press, 2011), 64.*
11. *Jane Bennett, Vibrant Matter: A Political Ecology of Things (Durham, NC: Duke University Press, 2010).*

BEHIND HONG KONG'S NEON GLOW

Celina Qiu

Fig. 01 - Source material by chankalun, image altered by LUNCH editors.

There is a scene in Clifton Ko's 1986 film *Devoted to You* in which a pair of lovers share a passionate kiss against giant red glowing letters that read "TDK." Here, a Canadian visitor and a local secondary school student find themselves, within a fleeting moment, their sexual desires and the jet black sky set ablaze by neon lighting. These gas-filled glass tubes effortlessly capture the energy of their electric attraction and the dynamic zeitgeist of Hong Kong. Cascading along street corners and alleyways, haphazardly superimposed, the city's uniform blocks are subverted under a cacophony of visual noise, calling out the entrepreneurial spirit of the city's consumerist ambitions. They obscure the concrete jungle into a kaleidoscopic spectacle and demonstrate the complexity of Hong Kong's hybrid identity wrestling between the influences of global economic powers.

Stripping their practical function as advertising mediums and systems of communication, this article will cast a spotlight on the locals' influence on the neon streetscape. This involves the public spectators who navigate under the illuminated signage, the craftsman who diligently twist the glass into calligraphic symbols, and the contemporary artists who sustain the vernacular practice as a creative artform. By revealing the various relationships that weave between people and artifacts, we can recognize neon lights as inseparable from the identity and image of Hong Kong. A medium of place-making and memory, a spectacle, a way-finder, a visual language and a vernacular practice, neon signs hold many identities

whilst simultaneously encapsulating a metropolis on the precipice of transformation. They not only illuminate streets but shape the experience of place, embedded within systems of artisanal labor and as an opportunity for creative expression that is intrinsically contributing to the everyday visual and imaginary perception of the city.

Fig. 02 (right) - A scene in Clifton Ko's 1986 film Devoted to You depicts an intimate moment shared by the main characters, Lee and May, embracing each other under the glow of a gigantic "TDK" red neon sign that ignites their passionate love affair.
image courtesy: @2010 Fortune Star Media Limited.

Originally a European invention that finds its early applications in Parisian opera houses and American highways, neon lights were popularized in Hong Kong in the 1950s alongside a post-war immigration boom and rapid economic growth.[1] Stimulated by influences of Western visual culture combined with the creativity of recently immigrated Shanghainese artists, a novel aesthetic of neon arts emerged that fused the pictorial language of art deco with Chinese calligraphy.[2] This visual language exemplifies the city's east and west hybrid identity, zhongxi hebi (中西合璧), negotiating between popular culture and Chinese vernacularism and materialized through an informal craft involving intimate observation and life-long commitment by neon masters, Si Fu (師傅).[3] To sustain a competitive drive for businesses to adopt larger and more innovative signs to impress potential clients, they experimented with colors, typography, symbology, layout, and structural frameworks that contributed to a plethora of elaborate messages that dominated the streetscape.[4] Appearing chaotic and overwhelming, it represents a portrait of collective talent, ambition, and everyday life; a *laissez faire* urban sensibility of disordered textual accumulation that personifies the vibrancy of Hong Kong's creative class.

At its height, 80,000 unique neon signs dotted Hong Kong's streetscape and within 40 years, that number had dwindled to less

Fig. 03 - An intersection in Mong Kok neighborhood illuminates with neon lights, activating nightlife that is occupied by street vendors and urbanites strolling the city at night. image courtesy: Val Viajero, @valviajero.

than 10,000.[5] The phantasmagoric scene of dazzling banners that once greeted foreign visitors to 'the pearl of the orient', began to be associated with the seediness of informal work alongside 1960s urban decay.[6] As they cantilevered above sidewalks on metal scaffolding, safety concerns also ensued over their structure and demanded the Buildings Department to regulate informal architectural additions.[7] Following a strict guideline that straitjackets the legality of acceptable signage in examinations of distances, dimensions, and potential risks, the insensitive erasure of cultural practices for aesthetic coherency leads to a monotonous streetscape that plagues many contemporary globalized cities.[8] Local businesses are replaced by chain stores, tenement blocks are razed for glass skyscrapers, and neon lights are substituted by mass-produced LEDs. Spontaneity and diversity, which are the inherent values of Asian urbanism, become eroded for promoting a modern city.

PART I: THE PUBLIC SPECTATORS

Layers of superfluous street advertising beam up at night, activating the nocturnal rhythm of the streets, transforming a space of frantic hustling into a place of spontaneous interaction. Street hawkers, buskers, food vendors, and political activists colonize traffic routes encouraging others to pause and gather. Participants become both spectators and agents in the city's metamorphosis, expressing a common desire to both access and contribute to the multi-sensorial experience of the public realm. Medium is the message, neon signs activate life. The image of the city is less defined by building forms but more by informal practices, lives, and activities that overlap within the interstitial spaces in between, adding meaning to the conception of locality through involvement. Finding shelter under a canopy of neon signs, they appropriate streets to become a multi-functional environment assuming the roles of marketplace, convivial space, and performance stage simultaneously.

As rooftop emblems, shop plaques, or projecting overhangs, neon lights follow a "decorated shed" typology,[9] demanding attention from dazed pedestrians and luring them to potential destinations of interior services. It suggests a dialogue manifested through the physical articulation of messages displayed as overlapping signage which conceals raw building surfaces to emphasize a culture of consumption. By reading the city through neon signs rather than building form, we can also identify the lives of society's inhabitants and their patronage: the master chef who makes the city's best Peking duck, the judo master who trains local kids, and the mom and pop who run the pawn shop. Informal mix-use buildings combined with visual communication blur the boundaries between inside and outside, connecting patrons to customers and unifying citizens through a process of way-finding. Every sign is uniquely designed and handcrafted for a specific business, and when read, locates their service within the physical and imagery network of the city. Each individual emblem becomes a landmark in itself, orienting citizens through the perceptibly chaotic streets of Hong Kong. While buildings act as massive and fragmented containers for people and services, neon signs contribute as communicative mediums and connective devices, strengthening the image of the city and asserting a more interdependent society.

PART II: THE CRAFTSMAN

In a dusty workshop, an elderly man stares at the glass rod he holds in his hands, calculating the exerted pressure applied by the flame torch and strategizing his next bend. Surrounded by his apprentices, he demonstrates the act of being engaged, sensitively heating up the fragile material and intuitively comprehending the limits of its

Fig. 04 - In another piece by chankalun, 香港 (Hong Kong) is drawn out calligraphically as a neon sign and traces the penmanship of Tsang Tsou Choi, a self-proclaimed "King of Kowloon" and infamous graffiti artist who's "urban poetry" can be found inscribed across the city. image courtesy: @chankalun.

malleability. It is due to this human touch that neon signs hold an aura that cannot be met by the advent of industrialization. Mass production for the sake of speed and efficiency loses the intimate connection that fosters within the choreography between head and hand, thinking and practice, perception and execution. Driven by the craftsman's commitment to the craft,[10] it involves decades of experience to master material consciousness, understand the response of fragile materials to heat and pressure, and manipulate the curves without cracking.

> "To bend a simple circle might require the knowledge and skill of twenty years' shop experience."
> —Rudi Stern

Regardless of the low wage and hazardous conditions, the craftsman is dedicated to this back-breaking work, pursued by the pride in one's work and as a way of life.

The production of neon lights is deeply enmeshed in the practice of the local culture, involving a high degree of informality and subjectivity which reinforces the identity of the arts community. Without professional training or education, neon artists acquired their technique through apprenticeship (shituzhi, 師徒制), shadowing Si Fus who passed their knowledge through close guidance, hands-on imitation, and constant repetition.[11] With a wave of fine arts educated craftsmen arriving from Shanghai or Guangzhou to escape the 1960s Cultural Revolution, Si Fu's were initially skeptical, preferring to maintain technological secrecy against younger or foreign newcomers but eventually admired them for their diverse skill set and perseverance.[12] Working tenaciously together in clandestine conditions, their relationships flourished to be close-knit and familial, generating a thriving environment of cross-cultural innovation. Strong geometric shapes, lines, and patterning frame hand-scripted characters dynamically painted with energetic brushstrokes, laid out hierarchically and in proportion to maximize legibility and dominate our visual perception. The most compelling feature is usually the text drafted by a skilled calligrapher who can render it with an energetic aura. Typically depicting the Beiwei Kaishu (北魏楷書) style, which finds its origins in the Northern Wei Dynasty, its asymmetrical construction, unexpected angles, exaggerated beginnings, inflection points, and endings add a sense of dynamism to an ordered framework.[13] First, hand-drawn with gouache paint on paper, then, used as a plan to execute the bending and blowing of glass, the bold yet lively style cannot be replicated by digital fonts.[14] The bricolage of styles condensed on one sign is not only ambitiously harmonious but reveals the contextual story about human relations, knowledge, and material transfers intersecting within the everyday life of Hong Kong's creative society.

Fig. 05 - A step-by-step process of how neon lights are created in a local Hong Kong workshop that involves intimate knowledge of glass behavior and attachment with mechanical apparatus, Celina Qiu.

HOW TO CREATE HK'S NEON LIGHTS

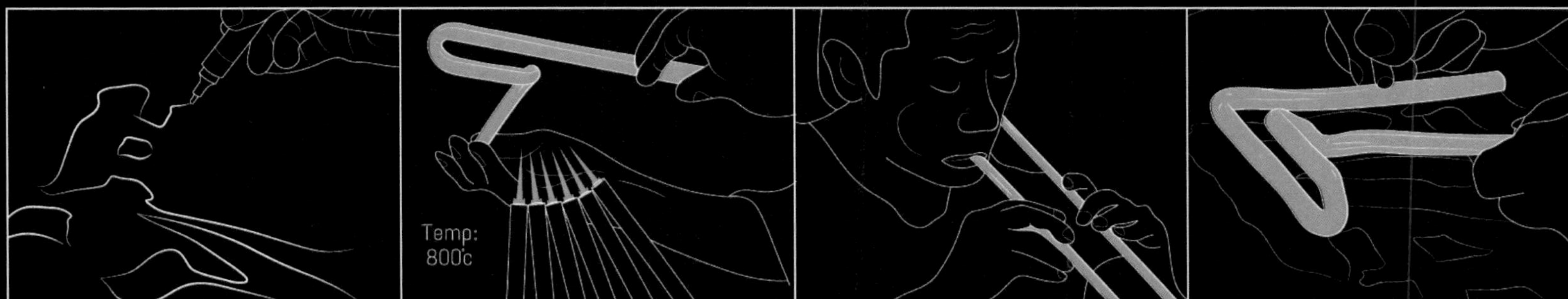

1. Sketch scaled drawing for tracing
2. Melt and bend tube over flame
3. Blow through tube to expand joint
4. Check drawing and mark next bend

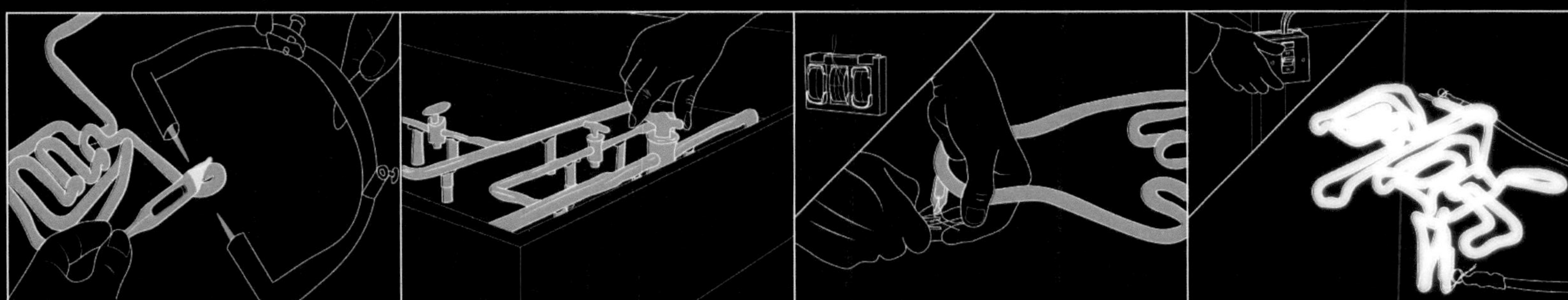

5. Attach electrode to one end
6. Vacuum out impurities and add gas
7. Connect to transformer
8. Switch it on!

PART III: THE CONTEMPORARY ARTISTS

Through the market streets of Causeway Bay, a schoolgirl hurries home. Weaving in between pedestrians and dodging murky puddles, she pauses to observe the aurora of lights flickering above her. As the 1990s wore on, she passes by the same streets but becomes disoriented as the neon fades along with long-established family businesses hesitantly tearing down their signs. Wanting to revive the endangered craft, she set out on the unfavorable task of persuading one of Hong Kong's last remaining Si Fu's, Master Wong Kin-wah, to mentor her on the art of neon signage.[15] With harsh words and minimal instruction, she has felt the sharp burn of an open flame and the cuts from crystalline edges as the weight of the glass rod anchors her shoulders. Persistent and ambitious, today, Karen Chan is the only female neon light designer in Hong Kong, dedicated to pushing the boundaries of a traditional craft by collaborating with international glass artists to experiment with its contorted formwork and integration with multimedia elements.[16]

Persevering under the strenuous tutelage of Master Wong, Chan understands that the real threat to the disappearance of the vernacular craft is not the dismantling of signs but the lack of recognition of the skilled Si Fu's and their unyielding reluctance to pass on their knowledge. Desperate to preserve the knowledge, she has also taken the initiative to record her experiences in an upcoming book, hosted workshops for curious creative folks, and showcased her artworks in festivals and exhibitions across the world.[17] By expanding the cultural influence of a naturally insular group of neon artists to a global audience, she hopes to not only preserve a traditional craft that was once emblematic of a city's bright promise but also integrate experimental pieces into the city that could reconnect people in alternative ways.

Fig. 06 - The first neon art piece Shhh (樹) designed by CeeKayEllo, the art-was displayed after Typhoon Mangkhut in 2018 at the design studio founded by chankalun. The piece involves an interactive embroidered installation that lights up when touched by participants creating a closed circuit that calls to action the need for citizen participation and collaboration to revive Hong Kong's natural scenery and infrastructure after it was destroyed. image courtesy: @chankalun and @ceekayello.

The gradual erasure of neon lights from the everyday streetscape sparks nostalgia amongst Hong Kongers for a period in history when the city seemed like a perfect melting pot bustling with commercial and cosmopolitan vitality and before political tensions began threatening the sense of place. Apart from its heritage value, neon lights also hold cultural importance as tokens of memory that encapsulates the grassroots perseverance, adaptability and solidarity that make up the Lion Rock Spirit, (獅子山精神),[18] a collective determination hardwired in Hong Kong people. Through ongoing demonstrations against an atmosphere of uncertainty, the eradication of neon signs provokes an emotional trigger that contributes to the anxiety over losing familiarity with their homeland. It also calls into question who is excluded from the post-handover development of the urban landscape which has been largely defined by transnational financial elites and puppet state authorities. With their work and advocacy, artists, conservationists and architectural historians are addressing an urgent need to value, embrace, and protect neon crafts. Whether as artifacts or a skill to pass on, their pursuit to keep the art alive and relevant is a preservation of Hong Kong's identity.

Notes

1. *"Tomorrow's Neon: A History | NEONSIGNS.HK 探索霓虹," accessed February 28, 2023, https://www.neonsigns.hk/neon-in-visual-culture/tomorrows-neon-a-history/?lang=en.*

2. *Brian Sze-Hang Kwok, "Vernacular Design: A History of Hong Kong Neon Signs," Journal of Design History 34, no. 4 (December 1, 2021): 349–66, https://doi.org/10.1093/jdh/epab017.*

3. *Chan Shao-yi, "From Neon Signs to Skyscrapers: The Spectacle of Fluidity in Hong Kong's Post/Modern Cityscape," n.d.*

4. *Brian Sze Hang Kwok, "The Imageable City–Visual Language of Hong Kong Neon Lights Deconstructed," The Design Journal 23, no. 4 (2020): 535–56.*

5. *Kwok, "Vernacular Design," 2.*

6. *"Tomorrow's Neon: A History | NEONSIGNS.HK 探索霓虹."*

7. *Emily Verla Bovino, "Neon Crisis in Hong Kong," ARCHITECTURAL REVIEW, no. 1484 (2021): 56–61.*

8. *"Neon Fades Out | NEONSIGNS.HK 探索霓虹," accessed February 28, 2023, https://www.neonsigns.hk/neon-in-visual-culture/neon-fades-out/?lang=en.*

9. *Robert Venturi, Denise Scott Brown, and Steven Izenour, Learning from Las Vegas, Revised Edition: The Forgotten Symbolism of Architectural Form (MIT press, 1977).*

10. *Sennett, Richard. The Craftsman. New Haven: Yale University Press, 2008*

11. *Kwok, "Vernacular Design," 7.*

12. *Kwok, "Vernacular Design," 7.*

13. *"Sign Maker and Calligrapher Keeps His Art Alive, Architects Preserve Old Signs as They Are Stripped from Hong Kong Streets | South China Morning Post," accessed February 28, 2023, https://www.scmp.com/lifestyle/arts-culture/article/3094348/sign-maker-and-calligrapher-keeps-his-art-alive-architects?module=perpetual_scroll_0&pgtype=article&campaign=3094348.*

14. *"The Architecture of Communication: The Visual Language of Hong Kong's Neon Signs | NEONSIGNS.HK 探索霓虹," accessed February 28, 2023, https://www.neonsigns.hk/neon-in-visual-culture/the-architecture-of-communication/?lang=en.*

15. *"How the Only Female Neon Artist in Hong Kong Is Reinventing the Craft | Tatler Asia," accessed February 28, 2023, https://www.tatlerasia.com/lifestyle/arts/female-neon-artist-hong-kong-karen-chan.*

16. *"How the Only Female Neon Artist in Hong Kong Is Reinventing the Craft | Tatler Asia."*

17. *"Chankalun the Young Master Who Keeps Hong Kong's Neon Heritage Alive," accessed February 28, 2023, https://zolimacitymag.com/young-master-chankalun-keeping-hong-kong-neon-heritage-alive/.*

18. *"The 'can Do' Attitude That Defines Hong Kong - BBC Travel," accessed February 28, 2023, https://www.bbc.com/travel/article/20220515-the-can-do-attitude-that-defines-hong-kong.*

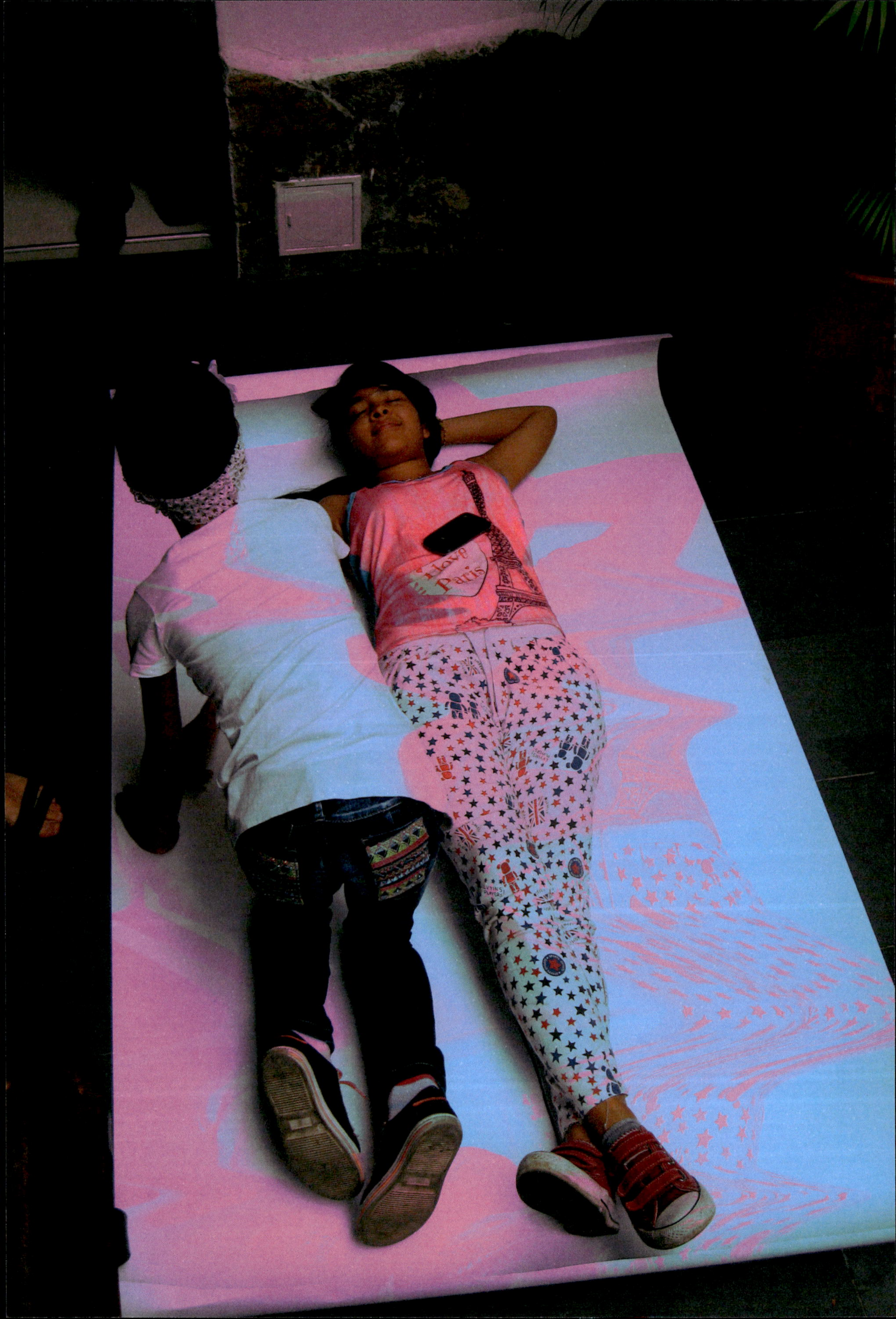

RECRAFTING URBAN NARRATIVES THROUGH BODY MAP STORYTELLING

Elizabeth L. Sweet, Sara Ortiz Escalante, and Raksha Vasudevan

All images are provided by Elizabeth L. Sweet, Sara Ortiz Escalante, and Raksha Vasudevan, with consent from the participants and original authors.

Fig. 01 - Source material provided by the authors, image altered by LUNCH editors.

Body maps (re)work embodied experiences in space onto butcher block paper, which is then re-inscribed into the imaginations of the receivers. The process between CRAFTER and CRAFTING invokes the senses, unveiling and creating new (dis)connections, pulling together ideas, information and experiences in different ways. Drawing, cutting, coloring and collaging leave space to reveal violence, and challenge racial, spatial, and gender logics. Data and knowledge are co-created between CRAFTER and facilitator into a visual representation of a body, as the first territory impacted by Design. Centering humanity and corporeality that is silenced in urban narratives, body map storytelling reveals alternative possible futurities by reflecting about the past.

WHAT IS BODYMAP STORYTELLING?

Urban planning and its relatives (architecture, engineering) have relied heavily on expert knowledge to develop and (often violently) impose spatial logics that tell us where we can move and how we can move through a city. Such an androcentric and ethnocentric approach to planning, architecture and design has resulted in epistemological and ontological orientations that prioritize and give power to rationally-driven, 'scientific' methods and data that reproduce oppression. Tools, such as cartographic maps, grids and modeling are used to articulate a controlled, singular and ordered narrative of the urban, its uses, and intentions.

Body map storytelling as a CRAFT serves as a counterforce by literally and visually documenting bodies as geographical spaces that consistently experience and resist these violent impositions.

Body map storytelling enables planners to consider various dimensions of power in planning practice as well as various scales of analysis (body-community-city-territory) simultaneously. The process of body map storytelling centers around a particular issue(s) that a group wants to explore+document+process. This could include almost any phenomena facing a community or group: gender-based violence, migration processes, community health, gentrification, lack of transportation options, housing shortages, economic challenges, political abandonment, etc. Let's take a group of neighborhood residents concerned about climate change as one example.*

Group members help each other draw a silhouette of themselves on a large piece of paper or cardboard. Using art supplies, participants respond to guided questions about how climate change impacts their body... If you are concerned about climate change, where on your body do you feel the stress? What colors would you use to represent this stress? How does climate change impact your daily life (at home, work, school, etc.)? What senses are invoked when thinking about climate change? What other stressors do you have in your daily life that add to/enhance your stress about climate change- how would you represent them on your body? What kind of work do you do in your daily life to advocate/fight for climate change/climate justice?—mark that on your silhouettes. What words come to mind when you think of climate change?

Participants are able to reflect on experiences and emotions as a central way of knowing, understanding, navigating and imagining the city. The use of symbols, patterns, shapes, colors, three dimensional objects, and some words are typical attributes of body maps. Once the questions are answered, each mapper shares with the group the story of their map and describes the attributes on their map. Body map storytelling is useful in two aspects: on the one hand, adding colors, shapes, and objects creates an important space of reflection and processing that typical planning processes do not account for. On the other hand, the creation of an artistic product raises curiosity and engenders conversation amongst participants.

Acknowledging the body as a scale and site of experience is critical to challenge the oppressive

Figs. 02&03 - Dominican women collectively reflect on climate change and infrastructure in Salem, Massachusetts.

dualisms (male/female, public/private, rational/emotional) that have long persisted in design practices.

Body-map storytelling can expose/document the personal and often unspoken daily impacts of racism, sexism, ableism, classism, and other embedded and embodied inequities, and allows for nuances in the range of experiences and feelings that participants might have about particular spaces+places. For a workshop we conducted during the Design Futures Forum in 2021 we wanted to work through what it was like to experience remote learning. We framed the workshops as follows.*

> *Since remote learning has fundamentally changed the 'classroom' experience and learning for students and teachers during this past year, we will facilitate a body map storytelling activity about participants' experiences in their virtual and physical space during remote learning and teaching. We will ask participants to draw on a piece of paper with a silhouette of their body on it, the following questions as a means to illustrate how body map storytelling can work. Can you draw how the remote learning space/place has*

impacted your body? Draw what emotions, feelings, and sensations you have had during remote learning/teaching? Where do you feel these emotions on/in your body? Draw where on/in your body you have developed ways to survive and thrive during remote teaching and learning. Reflect on and then draw on your body map the ways in which your intersectional identity (race, gender, age, etc.) has impacted and been impacted by this experience. Are there specific objects in your physical and/or virtual space that have played a major role in your learning?

We have included three body maps from the Design Futures conference (Figs. 04-06), with permission from the participants. First, note the diversity of resulting body maps, the variation in use of colors and symbols in representing experiences, and the range of artistic 'skills' that the participants employ. Second, the body silhouette itself but also around it provide visual cues of how remote learning is being felt on/in bodies. For planners these kinds of data are often absent or intentionally ignored. We contend that decision making should not only be based on about "facts" but also experiences, emotions and sensation that are corporal in their nature. More points of reflection would make planning more resonant with more community members, more complete and more comprehensive.

Figs. 04-06 - Natalie Johnson (upper left), John Kraus (lower left), and Xioran Zhang reflect (right) on the impact of virtual home-learning during COVID-19.

BODY MAP STORYTELLING AS PLANNING __CRAFT

We have used this technique extensively in our own work. Sara Ortiz Escalante facilitates workshops for Col·lectiu Punt 6 in combination with other community mapping strategies to analyze planning issues from a feminist perspective at different scales: body-community-city-region.[1] Elizabeth L. Sweet facilitates body map storytelling workshops for professionals (community members, librarians, women's support organizations, and administrators), as well as faculty and students in planning and policy schools. Raksha Vasudevan facilitated body map storytelling exercises with young people in her dissertation work and facilitates workshops as a guest teacher. Here we share our personal experiences and appreciation for this CRAFT in our work.

RAKSHA

Although I have worked with young people for many years, learning about and employing body map storytelling has been one of the most effective tools to center young people as experts in cities. Specifically, the use of non-verbal tools to complement interviews, participant observation, and surveys has been an important method to pay attention to 1) more subtle experiences of the city that young people may have trouble verbally communicating and 2) young people's experiences moving through the city (with pauses) that is not built for them. In design professions we have been fixated on developing

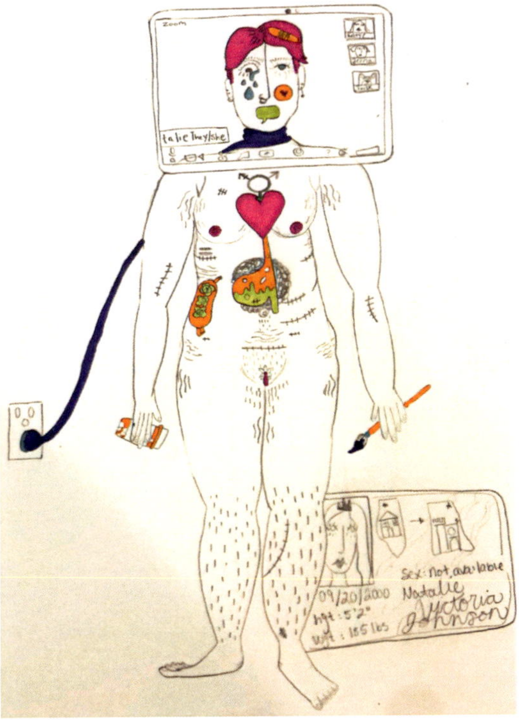
Zoom
Sex: not available
09/20/2000
Natalie
Victoria Johnson
hgt: 5'2"
wt: 165 lbs

energy source
coffee
depressing
slower
anxiety
sitting for too long
begin to exercise
eat better
become lazy

place-based or mobilities approaches to understanding city life; by starting at the scale of the body we are able to accommodate both to build a multi-scalar understanding of city experiences. This felt critical during my dissertation in Santo Domingo, Dominican Republic where young people experience persistent colonial logics in all aspects of their everyday lives, as well as in my more recent work with young climate activists who similarly feel the burden of climate change and related topics in many different facets of city experience. Betsy and Sara's seminal work for planning was critical in helping me think through how I would develop and adapt body map storytelling to varied contexts such as informal settlements or virtual platforms, where resources, access to materials, and power relationships might be different.

BETSY

Body map storytelling as craft and for craft has provoked a huge shift in my thinking and practice in planning. Most of my work has been on gender and race as markers that have the most impact from vulnerability to violence and injustice. But also, as a tool to help craft new relationships and awareness. My own work regarding violence against immigrant women in the US has taken on new meaning for me by including body map storytelling. The gift of creating craft has opened new opportunities for often marginalized and maligned communities to show themselves and show their strength. Body map storytelling is central to more in-depth storytelling. It has reaffirmed

Fig. 07 - Collaborating during the project Nocturnas by Col·lectiu Punt 6.

Fig. 08 - Youth participate in safety audit in Cali, Colombia.

voice, body and mind in a way that is hard hitting and softly elegant. I have worked with journalists and theater arts faculty to show the deep impact of racism on campus through crafting body maps. Those maps were used in a play that emotionally touched the core of everyday racism, the violence of everyday racism and the strength of communities to fight for their dignity. The aspect of craft central to body map storytelling is its collaborative and collective process—a process that is full of hard emotions but buttressed by community support, care, and love.

SARA

I started to use body map storytelling with Betsy, searching for visceral and feminist methods that could help to understand better the impact of gender-based violence on women's use of the city. We realized that planning has systematically ignored bodies as a scale, and in particular the bodies of those non-White heteronormative groups. In my practice, I have used body-map storytelling with women night-shift workers to locate the impact of planning policies on women's bodies, and to address women's exclusion from the public space. Using body mapping enabled gathering information about embodied lived experiences at different scales, and women nightshift workers' bodies were analyzed not only as a biographical space, but also a space of resistance. Body mapping helped women reclaim their bodies, the most intimate space, to be able to take ownership of other territories: the home, the neighborhood, the city, the country. We also combined body mapping with everyday life maps and collective mobility maps, to examine the interconnection and continuum between bodies and the space of the home-neighborhood-city to "reveal feelings and sensations people have as part of space, in particular related with safety" and how bodies and land are simultaneously reconnected.[2]

Fig. 09 - drawings done by the Xioran Zhang(top), Natalie Johnson(middle), and John Kraus(bottom). Image altered by LUNCH editors.

**The above exercises are examples of the types of prompts that can be used with body map storytelling. However, we share these with a cautionary note: developing body mapping prompts and facilitating these exercises requires a commitment to creating a community where participants feel safe to share their experiences, some of which may be heavy, painful, and/or violent. It also may require the development of additional facilitation, arts-based and mediation skillsets which have not typically been discussed in planning. Therefore, while body map storytelling as planning __craft has the opportunity to transgress some of the violent impositions of planning, it also poses the danger of reproducing those violences if not done with a careful and critical reflection on facilitators' skills and their positionality.*

Notes

1. *"Nocturnas (English) by Col·lectiuPunt6 - Issuu," November 17, 2017, https://issuu.com/punt6/docs/nocturnas_eng.*
2. *Elizabeth L. Sweet and Sara Ortiz Escalante, "Engaging Territorio Cuerpo-Tierra through Body and Community Mapping: A Methodology for Making Communities Safer," Gender, Place & Culture 24, no. 4 (2017): 594–606.*

Additional References

Denise Gastaldo et al., Body-Map Storytelling as Research: Methodological Considerations for Telling the Stories of Undocumented Workers through Body Mapping (Toronto, 2012).

Elizabeth L. Sweet and Sara Ortiz Escalante, "Bringing Bodies into Planning: Visceral Methods, Fear and Gender Violence," Urban Studies 52, no. 10 (2015): 1826–45.

Sara Ortiz Escalante, "Planning the Everyday/Everynight: A Feminist Participatory Action Research with Women Nightshift Workers" (University of British Columbia, 2019).

Raksha Vasudevan, "The Potentials and Pitfalls of 'Art in Research'Methodologies: Foregrounding Memory and Emotion in Planning Research," Planning Theory & Practice 21, no. 1 (2020): 58–75.

Sofia Zaragocin and Martina Angela Caretta, "Cuerpo-Territorio: A Decolonial Feminist Geographical Method for the Study of Embodiment," Annals of the American Association of Geographers 111, no. 5 (2021): 1503–18.

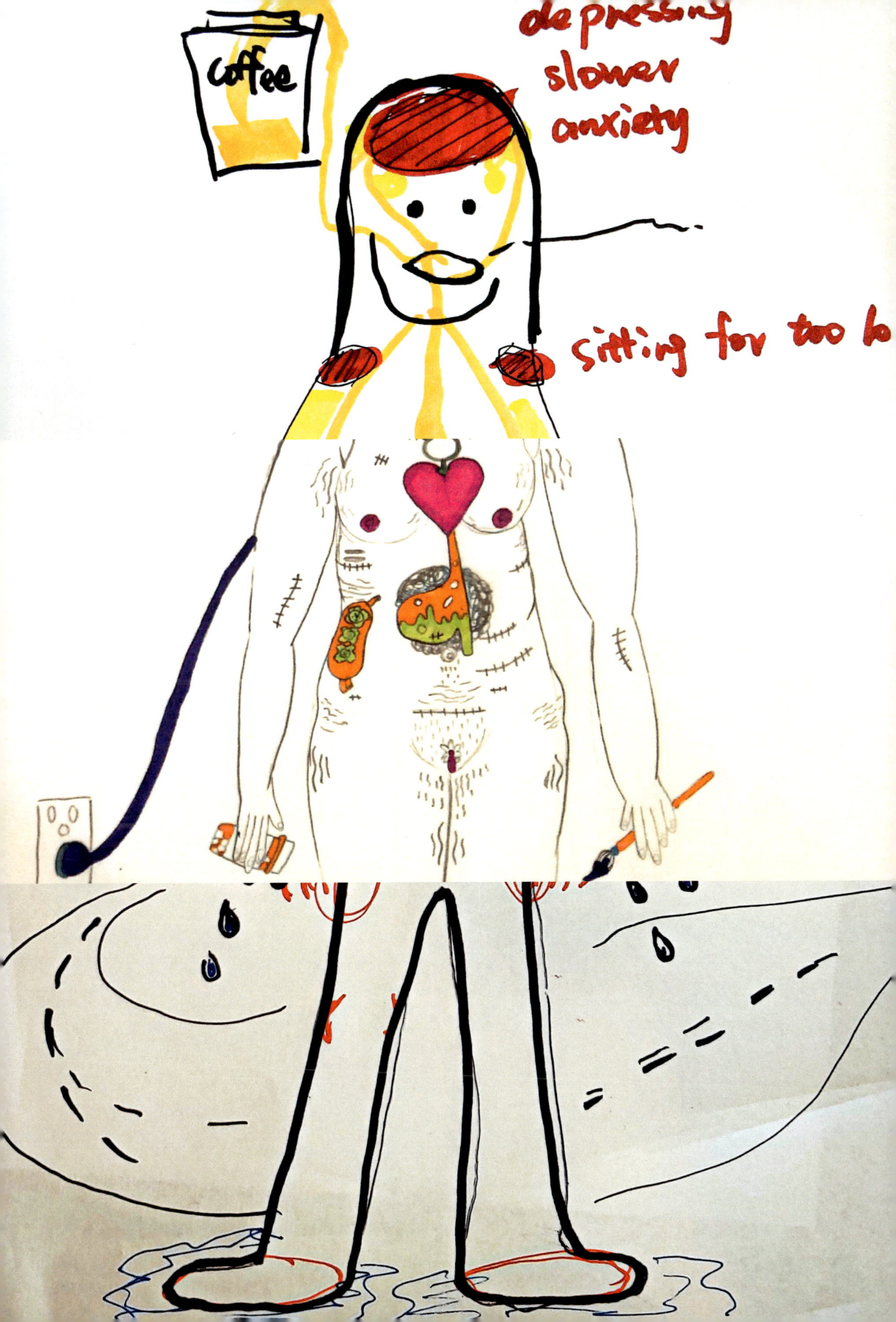

coffee
depressing
slower
anxiety
sitting for too lo

SEE CHANGE

Draw a transformation. Regularly observe and document a subject that is changing over time. A plant poking up from the ground in spring. A sunlit room. The Sky. Draw as a serial or layer each new obersvation over the previous observation

Fig. 02

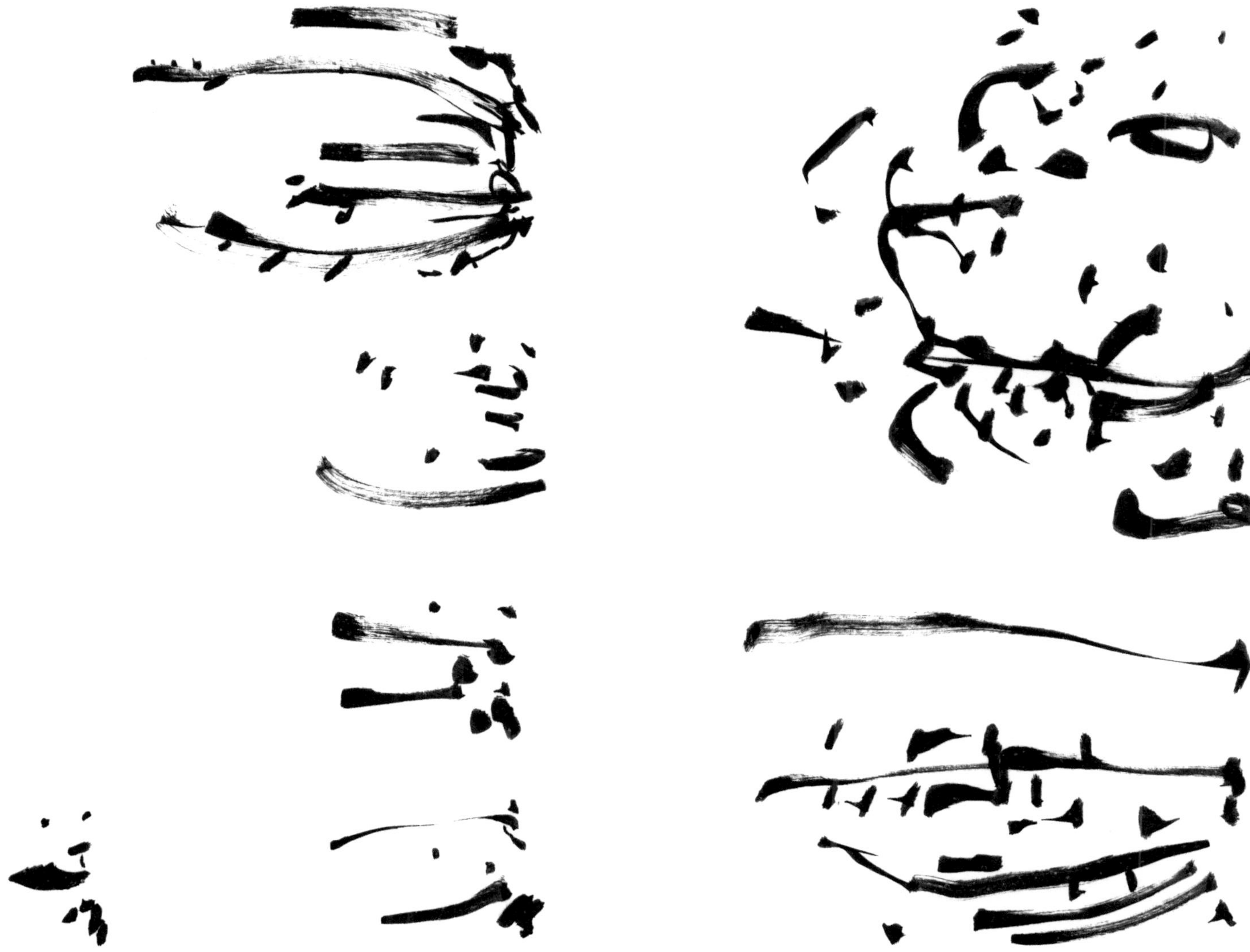

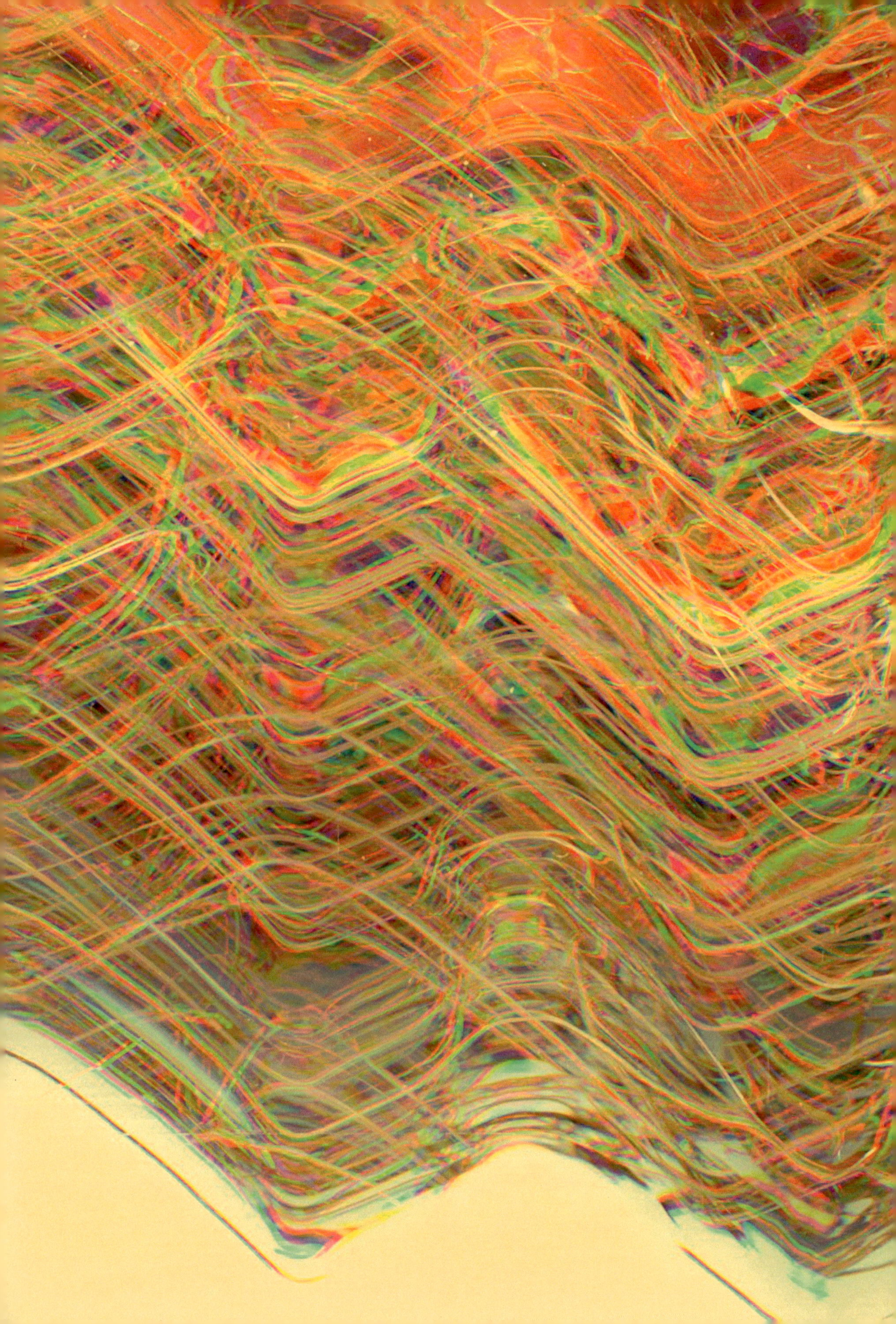

How do you perceive and experience a field?

What gives a place, space, or atmosphere definition?

What is the last field you moved through?

How do you perceive and experience a field?

What gives a place, space, or atmosphere definition?

What is the last field you moved through?

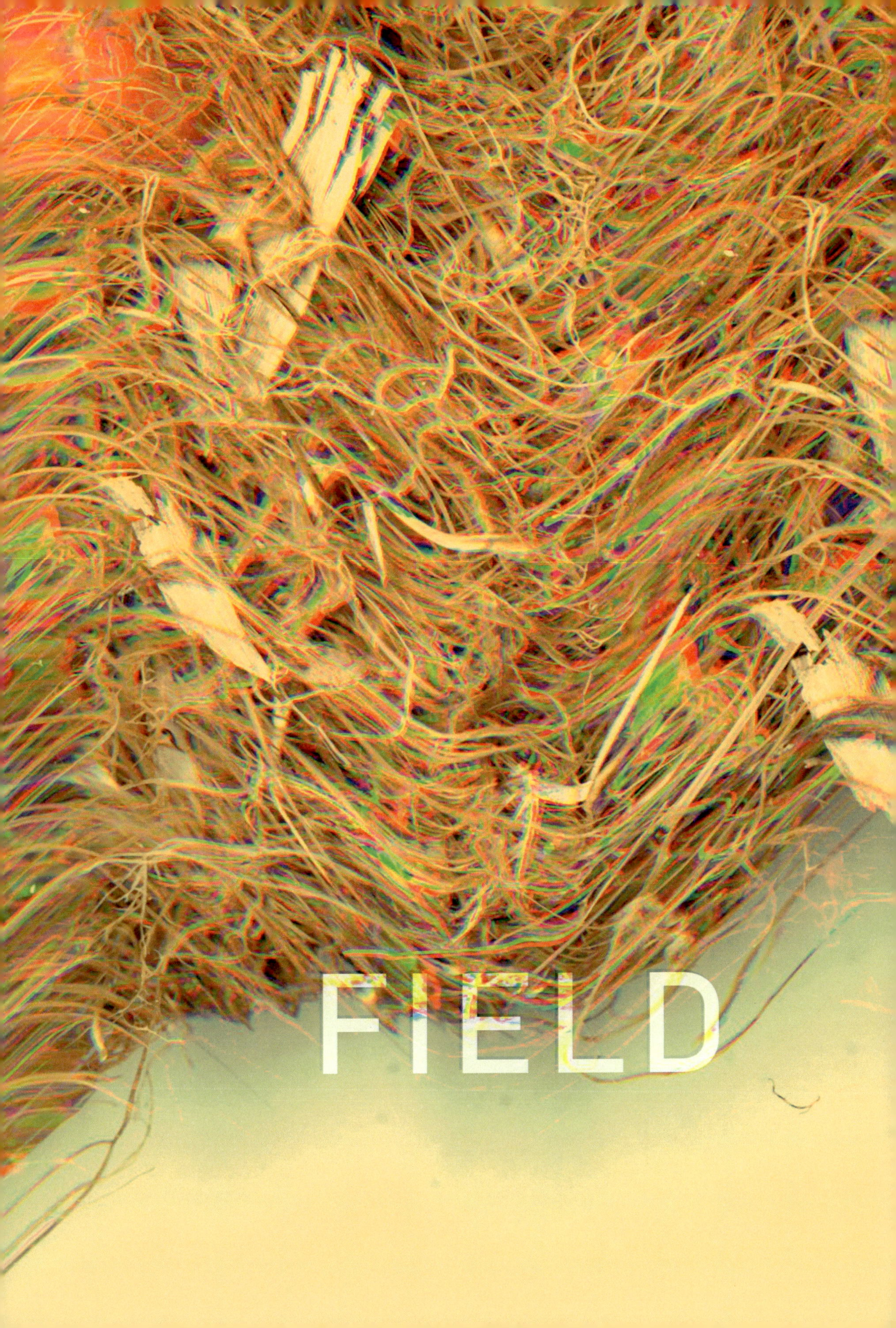
FIELD

CENTRAL VALLEY ACCESORIES

Dylan Krueger

Fig. 01 - Photograph of a utility shack near Lemoore, California, Dylan Krueger.

You may know of California's Central Valley because you passed through it on your way to Yosemite National Park. Perhaps it is because of the famed Sun Maid California Raisins television commercials and subsequent Emmy-winning blues group—or maybe you just eat a lot of almonds.

You probably do not know the area's architecture. In addition to the physical artifacts of agricultural production, the Central Valley is occupied by sheds, barns, warehouses, garages, shacks, stall, stables, coops, lean-tos, silos, among others forms that supplement the physical context of the Valley. I term these architectures as Accessories. Their presence in the locale is immense. In an otherwise dense array of crop and orchard contours, Accessories are the only semblances of built landmarks in California's Central Valley.

Despite their scale, Accessories are monumental manifestations of their own locational context. Their typological strength is rooted in their record of place. Their pragmatic yet charismatic presence positions Accessories as a legible part of their contextual landscape.

I concede that Accessories aren't visually dazzling by standard architectural metrics. However, they should be acknowledged as valuable to our field. Central Valley Accessories make a cohesive typological group—their scales, forms, materials, colors, and programmatic uses provide a consistent visual language worth

Fig. 02 - Drawings of assorted Accessories located in California's Central Valley, Dylan Krueger.

noting. As a typological series, Accessories have definable qualities: mute, modest, rude, dull, subdued, blunt, humble, unassuming, somber. We can evaluate the group using a common set of terms, producing a catalogue of quotidian forms that challenge the values of contemporary architectural discourse.

Acknowledging the value of architectures outside of our established consideration fosters diverse participants represented in our exclusive dialog—something most would contend as a necessary change for our historically insular community. If we gaze at these Accessories through an objective lens, their significances are comparable to the architecture we cherish.

These buildings, photographs, models, and drawings encourage exchangeable legibility. Alone, each representation presents a subject to a singular audience. Together, collective representations present a subject to multiple audiences. Productive conflictions arise as a drawing enters the context of a model, or as a model enters the context of a building. Multivalent representations necessitate diverse interpretations.

During a lunch break, consider the possibilities of Accessories and architectures alike.

Fig. 03 - Framed photograph of red shed near Tulare, Dylan Krueger.

Notes

Model fabrication credit: Jack White

Fig. 04 - Relief models of drawings of Central Valley accessories, along with scattered clutter, Dylan Krueger.

Fig. 05 - Framed photograph of tall barn near Merced, California, next to beige fabric armchair, Dylan Krueger.

Fig. 06 (previous page) - Accessories from assorted locations in California's Central Valley, Dylan Krueger.

Fig. 07 - Relief model of a drawing of a green warehouse near Hatch, California, Dylan Krueger.

Fig. 08 - Wallpaper drawing from brown coop interior in Twin Rivers, California, Dylan Krueger.

Fig. 09 - Framed photographs of a barn and a shed near Modesto, California, Dylan Krueger.

MADE IN AMERICA

How Common Design and Landscape Making Shape American Space

Anthony Averbeck

Fig. 01 - Source material by Glacier National Park, Montana, image altered by LUNCH editors.

American space is immense. Its scale defies categorization and bewilders professional designers and intellectuals into the indolent othering of the rural and otherwise non-metropolitan territories that comprise 97% of the continental landmass and 20% of the population, while feeding the country and contributing to the national GDP.[1] Described as "bigger than big" by Manifest Journal of the Americas; a cartesian mosaic of small towns, crossroad junctions, homesteads, ranches, national parks, roadside attractions, military bases, tribal lands, and server farms comprise a vast American interior beyond urban centers often dismissed as "flyover country"—often excluded from much of academic discourse that tends to fixate on the exotic while disregarding the ordinary, and mostly outside the journalistic purview of the New York Times. Nonetheless, such territories are the product of settler colonialism, displacement, and extraction logics that have enduring epistemic and physical effects on the land and its indigenous people. Only recently has this history been acknowledged by institutions of power. American space has been and remains the site of complex, volatile, and transformative practices of American land-shaping, common building, placemaking, capital investment, political movements, and cultural development. As the pressures of technological change, telecommuting, and their resultant social reconfigurations mount, and as society progresses further into the networked age, the access to data, knowledge and information will only further undermine the centralization of power and institutional authority in major urban centers—opening new territorial possibilities for seemingly "peripheral" places receiving little attention today.

In the context of a vast country, the shaping of land is fundamentally an everyday practice. "Landscape making" is what scholars in the tradition of J.B. Jackson and John Stilgoe have long argued is a common practice, based on orally and example-transmitted traditions.[2] Each individual creates landscape, they argue, not only by the actual moving of earth, erecting of buildings, or felling of forest. The privileged class might own the land, but the "observant walker in time," as Stilgoe describes it, "owns the landscape."[3] The power of observation and its resultant actionability on available land is therefore critical to this understanding of landscape. When Indigenous peoples and later settler colonialists, enslaved peoples, and migrants shaped the American landscape out of wilderness, they did so largely unbeholden to the disciplinary expertise of professional design. Instead, common knowledge and observed traditional practices undergirded the establishment of indigenous settlements, the platting of the first New England towns, and later the cow towns and railroad junctions of the westward-moving frontier. In many ways, little has changed. The cartesian grid of the Public Land Survey System that blankets the continental landmass west of the Appalachians allows for the projection of infinite desires onto the landscape. This article outlines six key thematic aspects of American common design and landscape-shaping (Bigness, Grid, Nomadland, Stead, Framing, Frontier). Collectively, they challenge traditional narratives around authorship, agency, and power in relation to American land; and in the process, reveal an awareness of the socio-spatial dynamics that undergird the places designers urgently need to learn about in a rapidly changing world—places that certain politicians and capital investors already understand well enough to hedge their personal fortunes on. "Made in America" seeks to understand what undergirds common, rather than professional, crafting of American space. This understanding empowers the designer and intellectual to approach territories outside of global cities and metropolitan centers not with dismissal or indignation, but with the kind of sustained scrutiny that such places of immense power, influence, and potential truly merit.

I. Bigness

Despite bewilderment from onlookers and the casual tourist, American landscape makers and common designers (hereafter referred to as simply "Americans" for simplification) understand the latent potential of spatial immensity to subtly (and sometimes not-so-subtly) shape local, regional, continental, and global forces. The psychogeography of American vastness is only fully comprehended by those who inhabit it. Abundance of space begets scalar bigness. These landscapes are defined by sprawling homesteads, 5,000 square-foot McMansions, big-box stores and various "junk-space"

Fig. 02 - Marion Post Wolcott, Mountains seen from the highway. Glacier National Park, Montana. 1941. Library of Congress Prints and Photographs Division.

accumulations of architectural debris frequently sitting underutilized or vacant, organized by interminable spreads and densities of synthetic groundcover.[4] Scalar bigness in the physical realm perhaps precipitates the kind of imaginaries that design the virtual spaces of the internet, spurs fantasies about metaverse futures, and have for centuries dreamt what lies beyond the natural realm in celestial and mythological places (look no further than America's religious landscape or the American farmer's perpetual dependence on astrological folklore when dutifully subscribing to the "Old Farmers' Almanac.")

Americans build big because they can. They have space for excess; they take advantage of repositories. Americans frequently buy household products and food at bulk discounts, only to be stored away; saved for an indeterminate future in oversized cellars and walk-in pantries. They store information in colossal data centers out of sight in the Utah desert.[5] Americans produce knowledge anywhere and everywhere; manifested urbanistically in "innovation districts" that have exploded in recent years, from Boston to Silicon Valley, taking advantage of an abundance of underutilized urban, suburban, and exurban space. They prefer to keep open space open. Americans build cities with concentrated CBD's while dwellings set among trees lie just beyond the requisite urbanity.

II. Grid

Following the Land Ordinance Act of 1785, rationalized wilderness and a formalized agrarian republic spread rapidly westward; a resultant checkerboard superimposition of township and range lines now blankets the continent west of the Appalachians. One might readily argue that, in its territorial completeness, the American grid embodies today the vision that Jefferson first formalized in the Academical Village at the then-periphery of the town of Charlottesville—a frequent topic of Peter Waldman's musings on the fundamental acts of constructing place; the "word made flesh."[6] Mostly invisible on the ground until it fails or is interrupted by correction lines, the American grid allows for the infinite projection of individual desires.[7] Rem Koolhaas posits in *Delirious New York* that the Manhattan grid represents a conceptual speculation that, despite its apparent neutrality, "implies an intellectual program for the island; in its indifference to topography, to what exists, it claims the superiority of mental construction over reality."[8] Perhaps American space west of the Appalachians represents a macrocosm; the original if not more exemplary manifestation of the island as the basic building block of American space. Private property organized by the homestead unit—affording each individual just enough land to cultivate, to dwell, and to support a family—became the basic building block of a continental network of towns, county seats, crossroad junctions, schoolhouses, township halls, and other collective program. After seventeenth century enclosure laws in England erased common pasturage in favor of private property held only by those of higher social orders, the early American settlers would desire such a piece of the wilderness to own and inhabit for themselves; the basis for "American dream" mythos. Throughout the nineteenth century, the size of the section would decrease in intervals, subdivided to make land affordable for more than just speculators. Towns and cities of the American West would then form their urban grids from this national survey; subdivided from the one-mile square section down to the half and quarter-sections; or in the case of incorporated settlements, the urban block. Such scalability is reflective of a certain visual and practical self-similarity. The homestead seems to be conceptually scaled not from the collective to the individual, but from the individual to the collective. American cultural values reflect this spatial order, leaving foreign observers often disconcerted by a "rugged individualism" so unfamiliar in places where land and society are organized differently.

Fig. 05 - U.S. Geological Survey, Cherokee County, Iowa. 2016.

III. Nomadland

Fig. 03 - Peter Sekaer, Trailers for Defense Workers at Vultee Aircraft Plant. Nashville, Tennessee, 1941. Library of Congress Prints and Photographs Division.

"Americans broke the ties of attachment to their native soil long ago, and have not formed new ones since," observed the French aristocrat and philosopher Alexis de Tocqueville in 1848, intending to study prisons, but somehow happening upon the essence of American democracy and social order.[9] John Stilgoe aptly notes the Frenchman's awe for the significance of geographic mobility in the New World, concluding that in his missives and publications, Tocqueville clearly "understood how a restless spirit, immoderate desire for wealth, and an extreme love of independence—all passions Europeans considered great social dangers—contributed to the strength and peacefulness of the Republic."[10] The American obsession with spatial mobility engendered the decentralized settlement patterns that would come to characterize American space. Without such "restless passions," perhaps the population would have been concentrated around fewer places. Americans have thus always been, and remain so, geographically mobile makers. They actively shape space out of wilderness, making and remaking their collective and individual domains. Inherently nomads, many Americans own private mobility vehicles that are effectively extensions of themselves. They drive diesel pick-up trucks and pull fifth-wheel campers, trailer-loads, and car-trunks full of cargo across town and continent. Automobile culture—from "cruising" Main Street to the peculiar retirement-age obsession with restoring the dream cars of one's youth, remain synonymous with American culture. Eighty-three percent of Americans today drive a car "frequently."[11]

Automotive entrepreneurs Henry Ford and Elon Musk have achieved a degree of sainthood in the American consciousness, while railroad tycoons and airline founders tend to fade into relative obscurity. The automobile, unlike the locomotive running on "train time" for instance, offers a freedom of movement in the landscape that is regarded as almost sacred to Americans. This will be very difficult for reformers to disregard in the search for preferred transit futures. Moreover, twenty million Americans live in mobile homes sited just far enough off the road to conveniently back them in and though rarely, back out to another lot.[12] Today, factory-built modular homes are constructed in single, double, and triple-wide dimensions, loaded onto "oversize-load" tractor trailers that precariously lumber down freeways alongside commuters, motorcycle enthusiasts, and cross-country vacationers, before being assembled on site. Americans still memorialize Thoreau's Walden experiment and Buster Keaton's two-reel silent comedy by dwelling in self-constructed "tiny homes" on wheels, often parked at the edges of civilization and nature.

IV. Stead

Thomas Jefferson envisioned a nation of "yeoman farmers"—self-sufficient, free from the "corruption and discord" of cities, and resistant to tyranny.[13] This ideal has persisted in the American imaginary and leaves its imprint on American space. In much of the country outside of metropolitan centers, the homestead is physically and conceptually the basic unit of American domestic life—self-reflected and scalable from homestead to township to county to

Fig. 04 - Arthur Rothstein, Using a hand tractor for cultivation. Falls City Farmstead, Nebraska. 1936. Library of Congress Prints and Photographs Division.

state to country. Suburban middle landscapes offer house lots for the crafting of homestead in miniature, as Stilgoe describes it—the garage a facsimile of the barn; the ornamental fruit tree reminiscent of the orchard; the vegetable garden in remembrance of the crop field; and so on. The nuclear family was of course once essential to this model, and in much of the country, remains so (sixty-six percent of Americans resided in two-adult family households at the time of the 2010 census). Just over seventy percent of Americans today live in houses (attached/detached or mobile homes), with the remaining minority living collectively in apartments, condominiums, co-living, group homes, and other such dwellings.[14] The American single-family home was of course borrowed from types familiar to early settlers transplanting themselves from European towns and hinterlands—in the same way that American democracy and social order itself was appropriated from Western European Enlightenment thinking.[15] Americans embrace national ideals, but adapt them constantly to individual whims, real estate considerations (their homes are often their largest assets), and regional necessities, i.e. locally-available building materials, knowledge of construction methods, topographic and climatic conditions. This is reflected in the typological diversity of the American single-family home itself—Colonial, French Colonial, Dutch Colonial, Cape Cod, Georgian, Adobe, and so forth—themselves variants on a basic type; regional in distribution and distinct both stylistically and performatively, yet united in a common national ideal of homemaking that dates to the founding of the country; thereby formalizing the domestic unit as the basic building blocks of a nation.

V. Framing

Americans prefer small bets, and when possible, to build things themselves. This entrepreneurial predisposition is reflected in how they build towns and cities. In frontier outposts, settlers first constructed temporary wood-framed structures. If the nascent town and its speculators were successful, these structures would be replaced with ones of greater permanence, often of brick or stone.[16] Americans tend to build with speed, simplicity, and economy at the fore; with a comparative disregard for such values as architectural longevity or the disciplinary prestige of professional design that emerged in eighteenth century European cities. Knowledge of building materials, structural engineering, and vernacular fabrication methods were historically passed on through oral tradition and learned experience. Settlers built homes and other structures from locally available materials; from sod houses in the treeless prairies to adobe structures in the desert and the rough-hewn log cabins erected in the country's many forested regions. They rarely did so with professional assistance, though also not alone. House

Fig. 06 - Alfred T. Palmer, War Housing, Erie, Pennsylvania. 1941. Library of Congress Prints and Photographs Division.

and barn-raisings, as they were called, would bring neighbors together out of necessity to construct each other's domains. The American landscape, argues Lewis Mumford, embodies the "a collective effort" to live a private life. The Industrial Revolution led to dramatic changes in the nineteenth century—with technology enabling the standardization of elements and increasing the speed of construction. Rapidly supplanting timber frame construction, light wood framing has since dominated the American construction industry. Buildings across scale, architectural expression, and program are today "stick built"—light wood frames constructed on site. According to the National Association of Home Builders, more than 90% of new houses in the United States today are framed using dimensional lumber. Out of this redundance in material and method, American common design is revealed. Wood framing's adaptability, approachability, and relative egalitarianism extends beyond its cost and ease of construction. In its commonness, one could argue that light wood framing reflects the expansiveness of the American character; the extent to which knows few practical limits when it comes to making. And if anyone with land, a few tools in their shed, moderate physical strength, and a little know-how can build using what is now a decades-old construction system, one cannot help but ponder whether 3D printing might soon enable every American with a bit of software knowledge to construct the physical environments of the future from the comforts of home, without a professional in sight.

VI. Frontier

Americans reside comfortably at the edge conditions of urbanity and nature. Wilderness often lies just beyond Main Street. Henry David Thoreau retreated to Walden Pond not in any sort of permanent hermitage; he hiked just two miles into town regularly to visit family and friends, lecture, and attend to business.[17] The historian Frederick Jackson Turner contemplated the “closing of the American frontier” as the unsettled areas of the continent were increasingly closed in

on by isolated settlements in 1893.[18] What he failed to recognize was that the frontier is personal, in flux, and would survive in the American imaginary through an evolving territorial "beyond"—from the abandoned railway behind a childhood backyard to the indefinite horizons of oceans and outer space, to the ever-expanding realms of virtual and augmented reality. Crafting the edges of civilization and wilderness, human and nature, the known and the unknown, are what American makers do best. Americans persistently make and remake their own domain and re-draw its limits in the process. A country defined by spatial immensity, the United States is an incubator of spatial innovation through common design and landscape-making. Unlike the professional design and planning that regulates the physicality of global cities, the spatial and formal logics that define most of American space are undergirded by profoundly common practices enabled by the existence of loose, often invisible territorial frameworks. American social form is reflected in its built form. The economic, political, and cultural forces of globalization and neoliberalism appear to threaten the social and physio-spatial order of peripheralized places beyond global cities; all the while regionalism and the particularities of place stubbornly persist. "Planetary urbanization" and other such universalizing alter-urban theories that propose new territorial logics rightly challenge the city's centrality, but many astute critics note that they effectively erase the embodied milieu of region and place particularities. Meanwhile, in turning his attention to the countryside, Koolhaas oversimplifies the global rural and its regional complexities into a generic "non-urban," arguably perpetuating the othering of the countryside, while fetishizing rural ruins, remote server farm anomalies, placeless neoliberal territorialism, and exploitative "agri-tourism" industries. Understanding, and more pointedly, harnessing the latent potential of the American territory beyond its centers of perceived power and influence—a landscape that is vast, distinctive, complex, regional, grounded in place, and worthy of study in its own right; would better serve professional designers than continuing to zero in on 4% of the "urban" landmass while significant territorial transformation is afoot beyond.

Fig. 07 (previous spread) - U.S. Geological Survey, Bombay Beach, California, 2012. USDA Farm Service Agency.

Notes

1. U.S. Census Bureau, "New Census Data Shows Differences Between Urban and Rural Populations," December 8, 2016.

2. John R. Stilgoe, Common Landscape of America (New Haven: Yale University Press, 1982), p. 29.

3. John R. Stilgoe, What is Landscape? (Cambridge: The MIT Press, 2018) p. 51.

4. Rem Koolhaas, Junkspace (Rome: Quodlibet, 2006), pp. 132.

5. NSA Domestic Surveillance Directorate: Utah Data Center, https://nsa.gov1.info/utah-data-center/ Accessed January 2022.

6. Peter Waldman, Lessons from the Lawn (New York: ORO Editions, 2018)

7. Every automobile operator in the rural Midwest knows to be aware when driving on otherwise straight country roads that dogleg every twenty-four miles to achieve such spherical corrections; see Gerco de Ruijter's 2018 short film "Grid Corrections."

8. Rem Koolhaas, Delirious New York (Oxford: Oxford University Press, 1978) Introduction.

9. Alexis de Tocqueville, Democracy in America, p. 283.

10. John R. Stilgoe, Borderland: Origin of the American Suburb, 7.

11. Gallup, "Poll of American's driving habits and attitudes toward cars," April 23-29, 2018.

12. U.S. Census Bureau, "Manufactured Housing Survey (MHS)" 2020.

13. Thomas Jefferson, Notes on the State of Virginia (Philadelphia: Prichard and Hall, 1785)

14. U.S. Census Bureau, Census 2010 Summary File 3

15. Virginia McAlester, A Field Guide to American Houses (New York: Knopf, 2013)

16. Richard Lingeman, Small Town America: A Narrative History 1620-Present, especially Chapter 3.

17. Henry David Thoreau, Walden (Boston: Ticknor and Fields, 1854)

18. Frederick Jackson Turner, "The Significance of the Frontier in American History" in The Frontier in American History" (New York: Henry Holt and Company, 1921), Chapter 1.

CONDENSATION

Marantha Dawkins

Figs. 01-03 - Examples of new cloud types. Marantha Dawkins.

Clouds are funny, puffy things—masses of liquid droplets, frozen crystals, and other microscopic matter. Their ethereality lends them to metaphor and myth: the ubiquity of digital technology's growing record of everything, global conspiracies to chemically alter the atmosphere, disease and modernity blackening the skies of industrializing cities. Their materiality means that when they get thick enough, they drop rain, swirl into weather systems, and make airplanes shake when flying through them. Cloudiness, here, is a way of discussing statecraft and narrative craft: from real clouds, to fake clouds, brain fog, clouds of data, and finally condensation as a paradigm for coherence.

Clouds are statecraft in this age of climate change. Their emergence as a cooling agent has been strange. Though dismissed by the climate science community in official reports as too risky or ethically complex, every year fake clouds feel a little bit more plausible as a potential climatic intervention. New experimental runs of climate models come out, new parameterizations help define the climatic impact of clouds a little better, think pieces are published, and fake clouds enter the ends of talks and presentations as hypothetical exercises. These clouds would be made from aerosols like sulfates, alumina, calcite, or salt injected into the atmosphere; particles small enough to suspend in air. In 2018 the Intergovernmental Panel on Climate Change (IPCC) noted that there is "high agreement that stratospheric aerosol injection could limit warming to below 1.5°C"; a level that is

impossible with mitigation techniques (like emissions reductions) alone.[1] The term 'high agreement' describes the fact that aerosols are one of the few mechanisms that have been researched enough, that are understood well enough, and that are either already naturally present (e.g., sulfate aerosol) or that we have a history of producing (e.g., industrial smog) that we are fairly certain can have a significant effect on the positive radiative forcing that causes global temperatures to rise. Earth receives more incoming energy from sunlight than it radiates back to space and this net gain of energy causes warming. The premise behind cloud-based solar radiation management is that blocking some of this incoming energy will have a cooling effect. These new clouds—artificial masses of matter injected or sprayed up into the atmosphere—would reflect solar energy upwards and away from earth's surface (Figs. 04-05).

Figs. 04-05 (above) Cirrus homogenitus. George Anderson. (below) Cumulus homogenitus. Jarmo Koistinen. From the International Cloud Atlas.

Some of the new cloud types spotted around the earth are very beautiful (Figs. 01-03). The newest edition of the *International Cloud Atlas*, published in 2017, added five new, "special" cloud classifications including the volutus roll cloud, the asperitas, and human-made clouds like contrails. Contrails, or aircraft condensation trails, are classified as Cirrus homogenitus—cirrus clouds formed due to human activity. The homogenitus species has been also assigned to the Cumulus, that form above nuclear power plants. It is unclear what geoengineered clouds would look like, and the risks and bureaucracy involved in 1:1 experimentation means it is also unclear how they would perform in the real world. The engineered clouds are always illustrated in diagrams and drawings as heavy, clunky things but described as precision feats. They would have to be precisely engineered for optimal particle size. This is because there are complex, site-dependent, and even cloud-dependent microphysics at play. If particles are too large or small, or too many or few, they can work against conditioning the planet for livability by clumping into violent storms, producing anomalous weather and drought, leading to resource shortages, etc. Effects would not necessarily remain local. The temperamentality associated with the unknowability of clouds is notoriously difficult to model and would likely lead to their becoming wild, uncontrollable, and highly charged political tools. These are risks that are stripped of their resonance by scientific proofs and bureaucratic language.

Fig. 06 - Marine brightening field trial, March 2021. Credit: Brendan Kelaher/SCU.

The process of spraying salty mist over marine systems is called 'brightening' because when the clouds become more reflective, from above they look brighter. But from below, everything turns gray.

One of the ways we know about clouds as a mechanism for geoengineering is our experience with the climatic effects of volcanic eruptions. In the summer of 1991, Mt. Pinatubo erupted in the Philippines in a 22-mile-high cloud of ash. 20 million tons of sulfur entered the atmosphere. These particles reflected enough sunlight to push global temperatures down by around 0.5 degrees Celsius over two years.[2] More than a hundred years earlier, in 1815, Mt Tambora's four-month eruption led to "The Year Without a Summer." Accounts describe feet of ash in the sea around Indonesia and cold, wet, dark conditions over Europe and North America. Crops failed and snow fell. Mary Shelley's 1816 "wet, ungenial summer" holiday at Lake Geneva was spent indoors telling ghost stories rather than boating and riding.[3] She began to write a story about a man possessed by technology that was brought to life in a storm. Our darkness would be more permanent than Shelley's summer: if we imagine climate has

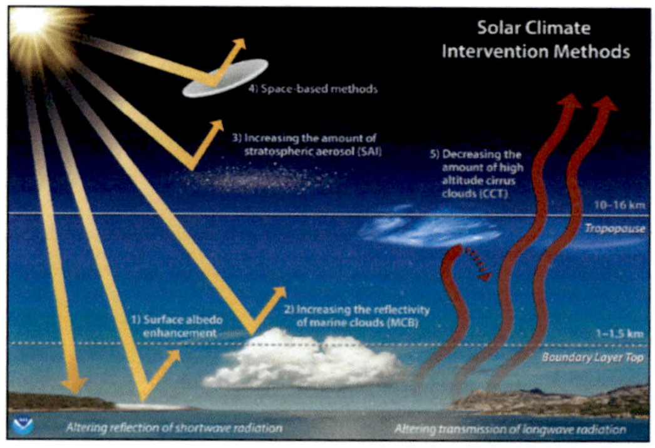

to be controlled, a future of increasing carbon dioxide concentration looks ominously cloudy. Just as Frankenstein was borne of darkness, powerful technology, and strange weather, a new mood, a new mentality, a new consciousness will emerge from a dark, gray future.

A new kind of cognition is already beginning to develop now that the air is thickening, invisibly, every day. Since the 1815 eruption, atmospheric carbon dioxide has risen 50% on average.[4,5] It has increased steadily since the darkened skies of the Industrial Revolution and is at levels that exceed 417 parts per million.[6] Human brains function differently under the duress of all of this new atmospheric mass, allegedly. This is a truly modern condition—cognitive impairment due to carbon dioxide saturation atop the cognitive dissonance of mass production twinned with mass extinction. By 2100, the IPCC predicts outdoor carbon dioxide levels could climb to 930 ppm. Karnauskas et.al., have developed a model relationship between outdoor and indoor carbon dioxide that suggests indoor concentration could rise to 1400 ppm. More research is needed, but there is evidence that levels this high induce significant cognitive impairment: high-level processes like decision making and complex strategic thinking may be cut by 25 and 50%, respectively.[7] So these clouds of matter are climatic but also cognitive.

Carbon dioxide's assault on cognition is exacerbated by the growing

Fig. 07 - (above, left) Lithograph of clouds pouring from the volcano on Krakatoa, from The Report of the Krakatoa Committee of the Royal Society (1888). Parker & Coward (Photo by Hulton Archive/Getty Images).

Fig. 08 - (above, middle) A diagram of cloud radiative performance. NOAA.

Fig. 09 - (above, right) Eruption of Mount Pinatubo, June 12, 1991. NOAA/NGDC, K. Jackson, U.S. Air Force.

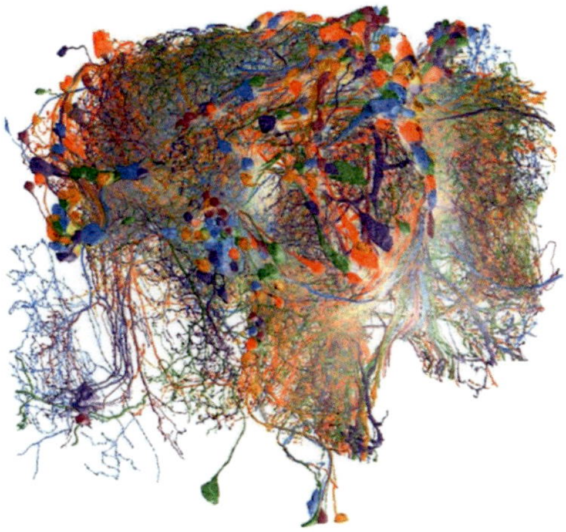

Fig. 10 - (above, left) Inverted picture of a fly brain. Marantha Dawkins.

Fig. 11 - (above, right) A picture of a data network. Marantha Dawkins.

concentration of data stored in decentralized server farms that are the anonymous backend of what we call the Cloud: the ubiquitous network of hard and software storing and producing data at increasing rates and in so doing creating another kind of immaterial haze.

The accumulation of carbon dioxide and information are parallel processes. In both cases the particulate matter possesses an immensely strong reproductive drive. Carbon dioxide begets more carbon dioxide and data begets more data. They clump and morph in manners very similar to one another. These productivities and behaviors feel like they are distinctly twenty first century afflictions, but acute symptoms have been around for almost a century. The "burden of this vast mass [of information]" was decried by Bernal in 1939.[8] He explains that the uncontrolled proliferation of scientific publication meant that there was too much information, most of it useless, but beyond its uselessness it was a handicap to the advancement of research. Data continues to handicap but the burden has become much more democratized.

Making sense of clouds of information stored in the Cloud in this age of collective brain fog requires dramatic narrative craft. Density has overtaken directness as an authorial choice. In some part this has to do with the atemporality of digital space, within which information has lost most forms of linearity. But I think that density reigns because the cloudy qualities of volume, thickness, and unstable immateriality are undeniable.

Density, in a drawing, coheres things about the future that directness cannot. Here one could discuss emergence or agency, but these issues are relatively semantic in the face of density's virtual, vibrational, condensational forms of truth. The figures that emerge from thousands of points and lines are hypothetical, and this hypothetical form has a unique kind of power. This power is 'scientific,' or of value to research, in that these hypothetical forms can become questions rather than flat prescriptions. But there is also something about condensation that requires a shift in sensibility. Condensation forces matter to cohere. There is an emphasis on intensity over figuration.

At their best, drawings like this can read like garbled prophecies. Enchanting, mystic, slippery, opaque. At their worst they stand for nothing. But the duality is kind of interesting. Walter Benjamin says the most perfect divine text would be universally translateable but also untranslateable and that in its perfect abstraction it would become transcendent. It is essential that clouds be fuzzy. This is one of the ways computation has become an interesting tool for thinking and drawing—for fuzz. Running simulations, for example, is about more than aggregating iterations of an outcome. It allows for the chance to find the edges of something richer than a straight answer. In my work it allows me to form questions that can be experimentally interesting. This is because the way that contingency is built into an algorithmic process means that results can be directional rather than definitive. Contingency and directionality are the main ways in which the obsessive and dense work of this kind of drawing can be different than other methods for handling volumes of information and aggregating them into versions of truth—methods like statistics or overlay. Statistics creates norms based on probability and uses this knowledge to constitute intelligibility from massive quantities of information. The insights that emerge from statistical processes are correlative and decidedly not generative. They look backward rather than forward, and consequently probabilistic knowledge is far better suited to management than to invention. Statistics can prescribe and predict within a closed, known world. Overlays tend to create territories of suitability, averaging their constituents into singularities that can be perfect specimens or ideal tools for recommendation. Statistics rely on the past and overlays rely on the average. Probability and suitability are very unmagical compasses.

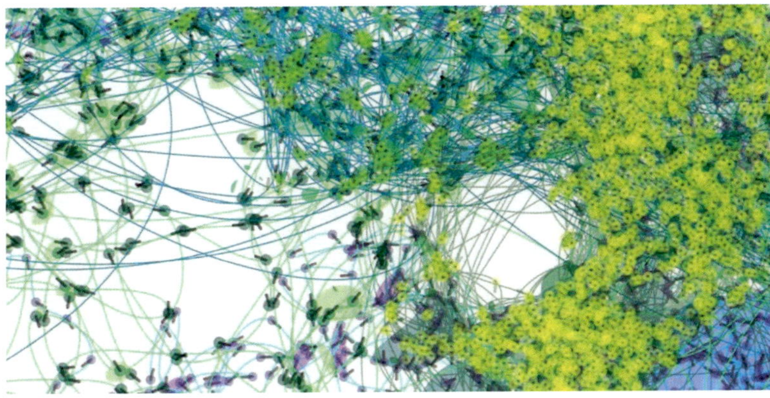

Fig. 12 - (above left) Dense clouds of data. Marantha Dawkins.

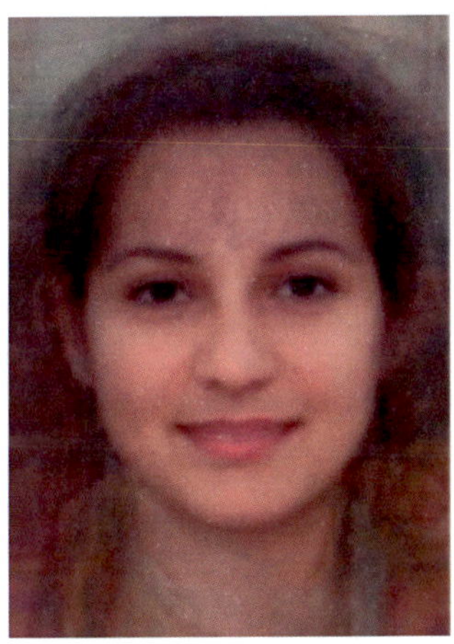

Fig. 13 - (center left) - 'Average' Romanian woman. Marantha Dawkins.

Fig. 14 - (Center right) Vector fields. Marantha Dawkins.

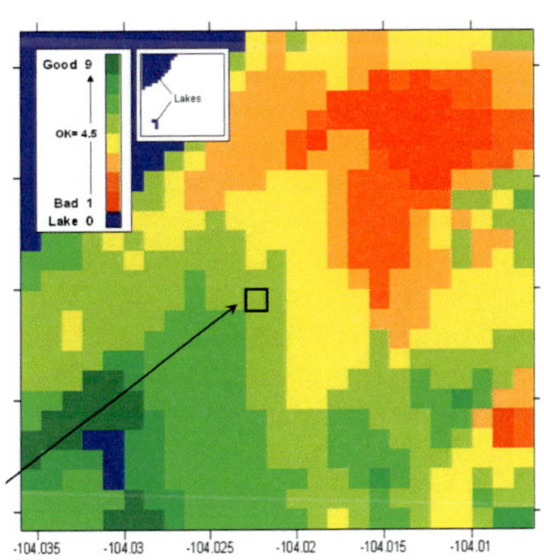

Fig. 15 - (Bottom left) Suitability map. Creative Commons License.

Fig. 16 - (Bottom right) 'Average' Czech man. Marantha Dawkins.

Fig. 17 - Wilding Trajectory. Marantha Dawkins & Nicolas Azel (2020).

Notes

1. *"Chapter 4 — Global Warming of 1.5 ºC." Intergovernmental Panel on Climate Change, 2018. https://www.ipcc.ch/sr15/chapter/chapter-4/2018/. : 349-350*

2. *Brian J. Soden et al., "Global Cooling after the Eruption of Mount Pinatubo: A Test of Climate Feedback by Water Vapor," Science (New York, N.Y.) 296, no. 5568 (April 26, 2002): 727–30, https://doi.org/10.1126/science.296.5568.727.*

3. *Mary Shelley, "Frankenstein [1818]." New York: Oxford (2001).*

4. *C. D. Keeling et al., "Exchanges of Atmospheric CO2 and 13CO2 with the Terrestrial Biosphere and Oceans from 1978 to 2000. I. Global Aspects," Scripps Institution of Oceanography, June 1, 2001, https://www.semanticscholar.org/paper/Exchanges-of-Atmospheric-CO2-and-13CO2-with-the-and-Keeling-Piper/7a58734f92f697f8623e49779431d7b585bf2b98.*

5. *C. MacFarling Meure et al., "Law Dome CO2, CH4 and N2O Ice Core Records Extended to 2000 Years BP," Geophysical Research Letters 33, no. 14 (2006), https://doi.org/10.1029/2006GL026152.*

6. *Mauna Loa CO2 Observatory, Dr. Pieter Tans, NOAA/GML (gml.noaa.gov/ccgg/trends/) and Dr. Ralph Keeling, Scripps Institution of Oceanography (scrippsco2.ucsd.edu/).*

7. *Kristopher B. Karnauskas, Shelly L. Miller, and Anna C. Schapiro, "Fossil Fuel Combustion Is Driving Indoor CO2 Toward Levels Harmful to Human Cognition," GeoHealth 4, no. 5 (2020): e2019GH000237, https://doi.org/10.1029/2019GH000237.*

8. *Bernd Frohmann, Deflating Information (University of Toronto Press, 2004), https://doi.org/10.3138/9781442673779.*

Fig. 01 - The Blues,
Mike Nesbit Studio 2018,
photo by Dan Schawlm.

MIDWESTERN LANDSCAPE

Mike Nesbit

the mound piles up
erasing the thing before it
another way of thinking
letting go
moving forward
don't forget about the shadows
remember the landscape
it's the end of autumn
the leaves fall towards winter

a cut through the landscape
a generational process
about time
about the seasons
about patience
appreciate delayed gratification

to recognize an object forgotten
a readjustment of context
value within cracked paint
texture of stucco
open to the light
bring in the landscape
more than a cut
an abstraction of an object
a discovery

not thinking deeply about it
tools for the day
a circular saw
a pickax
a crowbar
not to over complicate this
just open the roof to the sky
bring the light in
it's dark in here

I came across this shed in the landscape
it peaked out through the trees
don't forget about me
I have use
there is more to me

the moment between things
to cover
to remove
maybe an opportunity
an appreciation for something else
the transparency of material
a composition
a dark shadow
nothing to do with the objective ahead
he just wants to work

light and shadow
bring in silence
a moment to recognize
an unintentional composition
drywall mud and a door left open
the cut seems to reinforce this
a metaphor of light and consciousness

thin and light for one context
yet heavy for another
a piece of concrete
lifted effortlessly
the shadow seems to be heavier
don't look down

slightly hidden
underestimated
an underdog of sorts
most needed
can't do it without you

leaving something
finding something
objects in the landscape
placing new objects
next to old objects
a collage of objects
a distraction of sorts
the snow enters
the great unifier

can't really draw it up
we try
we think we know how to do it
but we don't
means and methods
the beauty in letting go
the power of trust
Morrison comes to mind

at first glance
it might not seem important
it's still captured
you revisit it another day
years later
intuition tells you something
a drawing or a sculpture
a collage
why is the shadow at a diagonal

not much of anything aligns
layers build up
alignment becomes irrelevant

the corner can be a confrontation
the corner can be a problem
dust always finds itself in a corner
but this corner has no top
and the bottom is earth
morning light finds its way through
it always does

Fig. 02 - The Blues,
Mike Nesbit Studio 2018,
photo by Taiyo Watanabe.

Fig. 03 - 12:38,
Mike Nesbit Studio 2020,
photo by Mike Nesbit Studio.

to be surprised
not even sure of scale
the clouds help
remove the sky for a moment
forget about the ground
think about it again

monumental moments are fleeting
they matter but they don't
a marker to reference
look at the trees in the background
the slope of the landscape
the colors of the season
late fall
maybe early winter
seems like a lifetime ago

a brief moment at 12:38
it made sense
the intention was changed
a couple weeks later
daylight savings ends
11:39
the sun sped up
or maybe we slowed down

sometimes you commit to a color
and it's all around you
Miles did it
Kind of Blue
If you think about a color all the time
maybe you can understand it for a moment
maybe it will find you

a cut or frame looking out
a composition that brings you in
scale and repetition
the cold of winter
text and silos
take one step back
appreciate the landscape

black and white seems to push abstraction
things that might be different become similar
value systems become questioned
wander into a space of gray tones

the moment something rusts
time seems to speed up
a recognition of movement
an optimism for change
held together by duct tape

the edge of everything is not refined
tethered
textured
an allowance for difference

a bone yard of sorts
an equal playing field
it's all discarded
another glance
it's all precious

nostalgia and anxiousness
the accident becomes a savior
intention in the unintentional
captured and left for truth
light through a window
casted on a wall

Fig. 04 - Flood,
Mike Nesbit Studio 2017,
photo by Dan Schwalm.

Fig. 05 - The Blues,
Mike Nesbit Studio 2018,
photo by Dan Schwalm.

maybe that's what the snowfall does
blankets
except the trees
without their leaves they stand alone

Fig. 06 - Shed,
Mike Nesbit Studio 2019,
photo by Dan Schwalm.

how do you get things to float
it takes some steel
why do you want things to float
it enforces the sublime
why do we need the sublime
it allows us to ask questions

light bends around a corner
it becomes spatial
not flat at all
not invisible
the shadow helps

not an echo here
push the corner
it will move
and if it moves
so will the light
so will the shadow
so will the window beyond
so will the building outside
none of it's still
and yet there is silence

digging is a primitive act
a child digs
we dig in the end
the dig reveals something hidden
the dig opens the landscape above
to dig is to discover
home can be taken for granted
we leave it
we remember it
we want to have it back

Fig. 07 - Dig,
Mike Nesbit Studio 2021,
photo by Mike Nesbit Studio.

to cut through it
an opening of a memory
let the landscape in

the sky
often light
seems to be heavy
weighing down the objects below
pressed into the ground
compression
and yet still plenty of room to breathe

technique and finish
process
beginning and end
expectations
it's finished now
walk away
your day is done

you dig
you think about down
you think about deep
you dig
you dig
you dig some more
you dig to the bottom
did you dig enough
you look up
can you dig out the sky
earth and concrete
makes sense
one and the same
the concrete was earth
as it anxiously sets to get back

trying to catch blue
trying to catch the sky
trying to catch the landscape
trying to catch the sublime

it's not work
it's art
it's not art
it's work
make it look easy
act like you're making
the work is not seen
it falls to the back
it looks effortless
it disappears
it never happened

objectifying the landscape
sit there long enough
the object forgets

Fig. 08 - Flood,
Mike Nesbit Studio 2017,
photo by Anna Finocchiaro.

Fig. 09 - The Blues,
Mike Nesbit Studio 2018,
photo by Dan Schwalm.

MAJOR JESSE SNEAD
REAL
DAUGHTER
SOLDIER
1812
WAR OF
1812
HAGAR
Faithful
Servant
OF THE WORLD
FAIRFAX
TAYLOR
B. F. FICKLIN
BORN
1952
CARE

GRAVECRAFT

Reflections on a Downtown Municipal Cemetery

Samantha Rosner

All Images courtesy of the author

Fig. 01 - Graphite rubbings.

Cemeteries are a strange mirror of their home cities. Charlottesville, Virginia's Maplewood Cemetery is the town's subterranean utopian double: neatly ordered, filled with multi-generational family units, and kept in peaceful adjacencies without quarreling about density. Through Maplewood Cemetery one passes markers bearing names such as Brown, Fry, Massie, Michie, Meade, and Venable—the same names one might see driving through the Charlottesville region. Many of the forebears of the town are buried on this 3.6 acre tract of land northeast of downtown. Their plots are divided into neat grids arranged in small subterranean neighborhoods forming a town within a town.

I first read about Maplewood in a thread on a local message board discussing the appropriate-ness of off leash dogs in downtown graveyards and whether or not the cemeteries were acting as "de facto dog parks."[1] On neighborhood forums, questions about off leash dogs are always a popular topic to get people to share their strong opinions, but this post seemed to capture an ongoing debate about what should be the proper use of municipal graveyards and what kind of respect is due. One resident called the cemetery "the last shitty gated community" and another said that if it's a public space then it belongs to the public and another chimed in that they didn't expect the "residents to complain." While some claimed that it was a disrespectful use, many more saw it as an enlivening of what they considered to be "dead space."

Fig. 01 - Maplewood municipal cemetery context plan, in Charlottesville, Virginia.

The nineteenth century saw a wave of public cemeteries which popped up in cities and towns throughout the United States. Prior to the 1800s, many cemeteries were more private affairs—churchyards, family plots, or town commons set within American cities and towns. They had complicated reputations, seen as both a necessity for the ceremonial rites of the city's deceased and as potential hazards for outbreaks of communicable diseases such as cholera and smallpox. Urbanization and industrialization reshaped the nineteenth century city and created a need for more space for the living denizens. By the 1830s ideas such as shifting cemetery grounds to the outskirts of the city gained traction and the rural cemetery movement was underway. Mount Auburn Cemetery in Cambridge, Massachusetts is credited as being the first public cemetery in the United States. Its design includes spacious grounds that enable multiple generations to be buried in family plots that are set in a "naturalistic" park setting. While one may picture a cemetery as an orthogonal affair, Mount Auburn rejected the grid and allowed the topography of the site to determine the flow of the graves. One walks among ponds, meadows, and groves which are dotted with marble markers and mausoleums, some engulfed by organic vines, some covered with the marble likeness of creeping oak. This approach of public grounds would become popularized by the work of Frederick Law Olmstead almost 30 years later.

While on a vastly smaller scale, Maplewood Cemetery is an early adopter of the rural cemetery movement. Though its location today

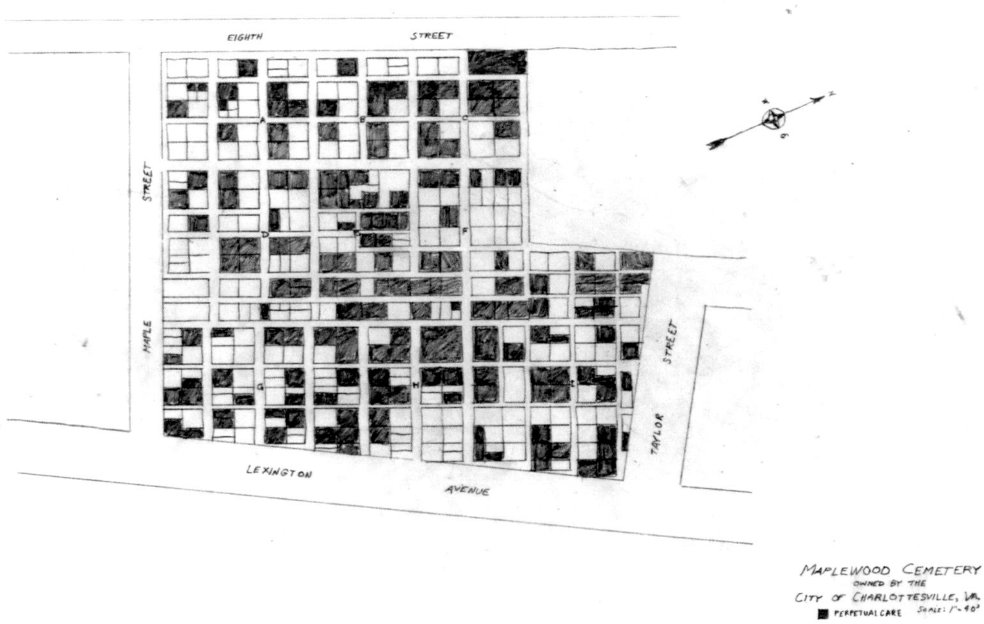

Fig. 02 Maplewood Cemetery plan of plots with perpetual care.

could hardly be considered marginal, at its creation in 1827, due to sanitary restrictions, Maplewood was set slightly outside of the city limits on land appropriated from a nearby plantation.[2] Plantations of this area typically hosted their own graveyards. They would have one plot for the family, marked by formal engraved stones, and a smaller, more informal plot usually set within a clearing in a glade for the enslaved community to bury their own. Graves dating from the late eighteenth century, which were originally buried nearby, were exhumed and relocated to their new home within Maplewood where they joined their more recently deceased neighbors and friends. Initially proposed as a segregated white cemetery, restrictions due to race were not strictly enforced and by the end of the nineteenth century, mostly lifted. Charlottesville itself would not be considered an integrated city until 1959, nearly 60 years after Fairfax Taylor, civil rights activist and freedman, was interred at Maplewood. Despite his storied lifetime, his inscription simply marks his birth year as 1816, when he was born into servitude, and his death year 1895, when he died a free man. He was survived by his son, James T.S. Taylor, who served in the Union Army and represented Albemarle County in Virginia's 1867 state constitutional convention. James is buried nearby in Oakwood Cemetery which opened in 1860 to handle the overflow from Maplewood and a portion of which served the burial needs of many of the city's newly freed Black families.

Walking through the cemetery one comes across a variety of ways that families are dealing with the emotional tenor of death. Many

Fig. 04-06 - Photographs from Maplewood Cemetery.

take on a stoic attitude, claiming that the loved one is simply gone from this life and on to the next or is sitting with god. see it as a kind of pruning—plucked from this life to bloom, plucked from this life too soon but now in heaven. A particularly moving stele uses its four sides to mourn the death of daughters Maggie and Jennie, who perhaps passed from an illness that swept through the family. "How desolate our home, bereft of our loved ones... Gone but still loved and remembered... Gone from our home but not from our hearts... Sweet flowers transplanted to a clime where never comes the blight of time." This final stanza imagines death as an eternal ecosystem, a lonely Eden lost in time. A space for lovely transplants from our precarious realm. Another headstone, Little Roberta, who died just shy of her 5th birthday: "She was too sweet a bud For Heaven to lose the bloom." Another metaphor of transplantation, of transformation, however here interpreted to mean that we are all cultivated in heaven and our bloom on earth is but a brief showing until we return to our eternal garden.

Maplewood suffers from a state of mild disrepair. While at City Hall the lack of housing opportunities and the rise of congestion are frequent topics, over on Maple Street the tenants also suffer from population growth and lack of sufficient infrastructure—gravestones propped up on other gravestones, cracked and crumbling marble, encroaching lichens, text rendered illegible, fallen magnolia branches covering entire family plots. "Perpetual Care" is written on several

OF ALICE FLEMING SAUNDERS
AND JAMES M M DAVIS

metal stakes—a promise in perpetuity—whether or not this promise is kept is unclear (Fig. 07). An NBC 29 news article from March 2021 shows that some concerned, living citizens blame the dog owners for worsening conditions in the cemetery, reporting that people are, "walking their dogs through the land and not picking up after them, allowing their dogs to rip up the turf, and even knock over tombstones."[3] On a later visit to the cemetery, I noticed that lawn signs addressed dog owners, asking that their dogs play in another section of the lot to allow the lawn to recover from overuse. The sign warns that non-compliance could lead to a loss of the privilege of using the cemetery, which points to a tenuous truce between the dogs of downtown Charlottesville and the volunteers who tend to Maplewood.

Fig. 07 (above) - Grave marked with "perpetual care" sign.

The grave of Brigadier General John M. Jones shows a case of careful intervention. A fresh piece of marble, clean and free from erosion, sits next to a decrepit stone where the name John M. Jones is barely discernible. His grave bears a carved southern cross of honor, a symbol conferred to confederate soldiers, whose deaths en masse demanded a reimagining of the American burial system due to the sheer volume and great distances. The word "RACIST" is also carved on Jones's grave, seemingly with a pin or thin blade (Fig. 08). It's unclear if the guerrilla gravecarver knew of any particular violence this man had committed or if the newness of his grave stood out amongst his fellow veterans. Did this carver feel that the repair and

Fig. 08 - Defaced grave.

care of a confederate soldier's grave constitute a memorialization of the confederacy?

Fig. 09 - Photograph from Maplewood Cemetery.

Nearby the patch of Confederate soldiers, two headstones in particular merit our attention. They read "Linie Winston" and "Hagar," respectively, and each short gravestone bears the simple but telling phrase, "a faithful servant," a gloss over the horrible fact of enslavement. As the historians and designers of Charlottesville's new Memorial to Enslaved Laborers are well familiar, identifying enslaved individuals by name requires great effort, and it's unclear whether Maplewood is the final resting home for other "faithful servants." Identifying where many enslaved people are buried has proven to be a challenging endeavor, and the discovery of these sites throughout the country underscores the discomforting knowledge that many of our cities and institutions were constructed on the basis of violence and forced servitude. In 2012, the University Cemetery, located on the University of Virginia's grounds, uncovered a mass grave site beneath a former plant nursery.[4] Sixty-seven grave shafts were found in total, the final resting place of many enslaved people who resided on grounds as support staff for the University families and students, who were taught enlightenment principles such as liberty and free will. At the Univeresity of Virgnina, this is a contradiction that each of us must grapple with.

On a chilly spring day I brought my dog, Louie, with me on a site visit. He was quickly approached by a big friendly greyhound wearing a balaclava and a brave toy terrier and I let him run off to play among the rows. The greyhound's owner welcomed me and we chatted about the play group. She said that a group of dog-owners congregate daily, using a group text chain to coordinate timing and making sure that someone brings water in the warmer months. She showed me pictures from a doggy birthday party from the previous weekend and we looked towards Louie and her greyhound, who had formed an alliance and alternated between sniffing the headstones and chasing the terrier. Downhill from the group are a set of slightly newer plots. Despite nearly filling to capacity in the mid-nineteenth century, Maplewood has continued to take in new tenants. The cemetery is a survey in southern funereal markers from the last two centuries, and a few of the more recent graves display the advances that have been made in stonework and engravings. One caught my eye, a polished marble bench with the family name "WEBER" cut into the side. On one of the two base blocks is a marker for Susan Carrick who died in 2018. Hers is one of the few graves that includes a portrait, laser-etched onto the stone. She holds her dog, a hound, close to her chest and smiles at her visitor. I like to think that Susan is one Maplewood resident who would enjoy her plot being visited by the city's dogs.

Notes

1. *"Opinion Share: People Using Cemeteries As Dog Parks : Charlottesville."*
2. *Check Citation http://weblink.charlottesville.org/Public/0/edoc/793461/Maplewood%20Cemetery%20History_HP.pdf*
3. *Grimes, "Residents near Maplewood Cemetery Say Some Visitors Are Disrespecting the Grounds, Leads to Community Cleanup."*
4. *Wolfe, "Unearthing Slavery at the University of Virginia."*

SEE CHANGE

Pick a very small spot and draw everything you see, at the size it appears.

Fig. 03

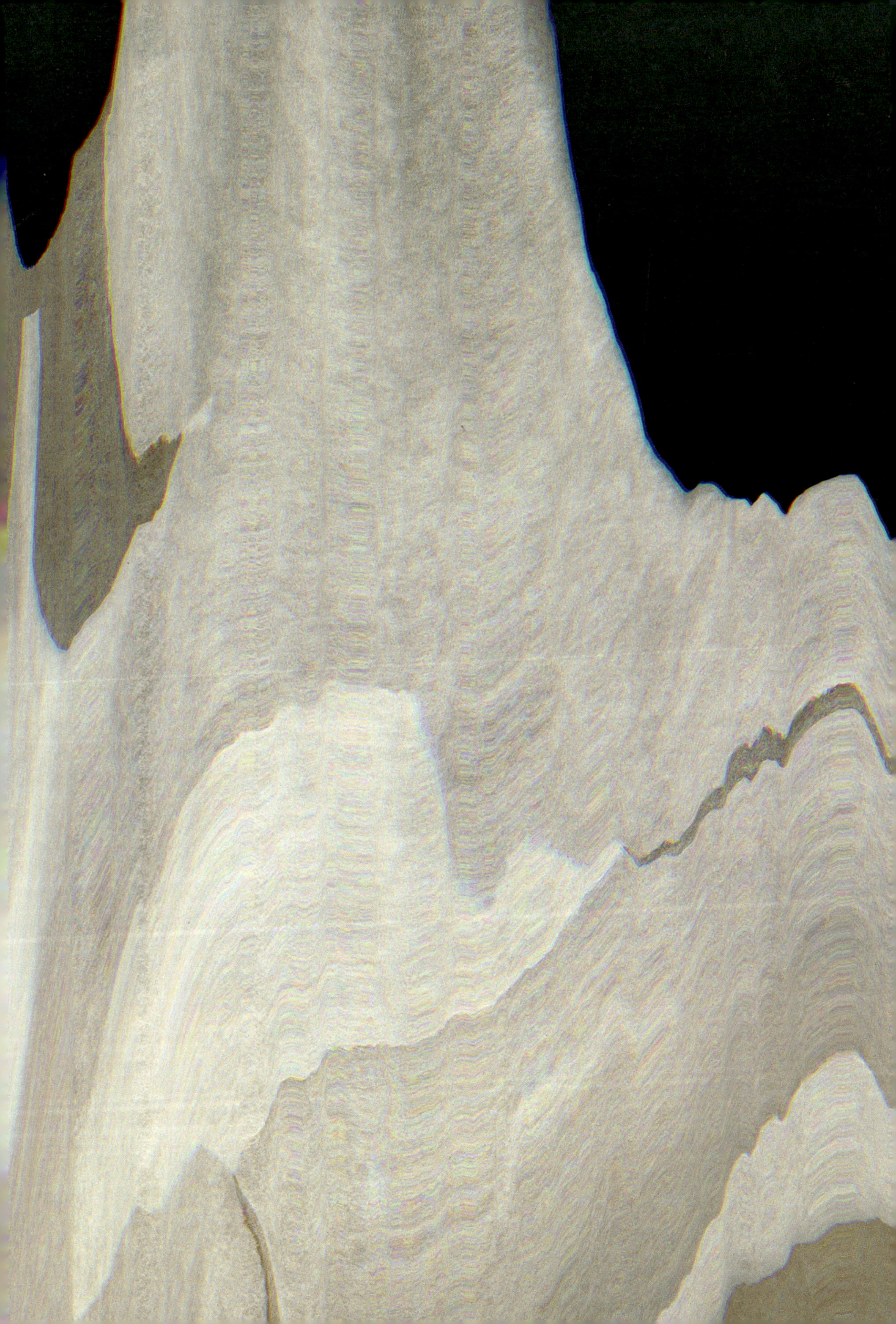

Does deeper knowledge enhance experience?

Is physicality the ultimate mediator of reality, what we understand and perceive as fact?

Does deeper knowledge enhance experience?

Is physicality the ultimate mediator of reality, what we understand and perceive as fact?

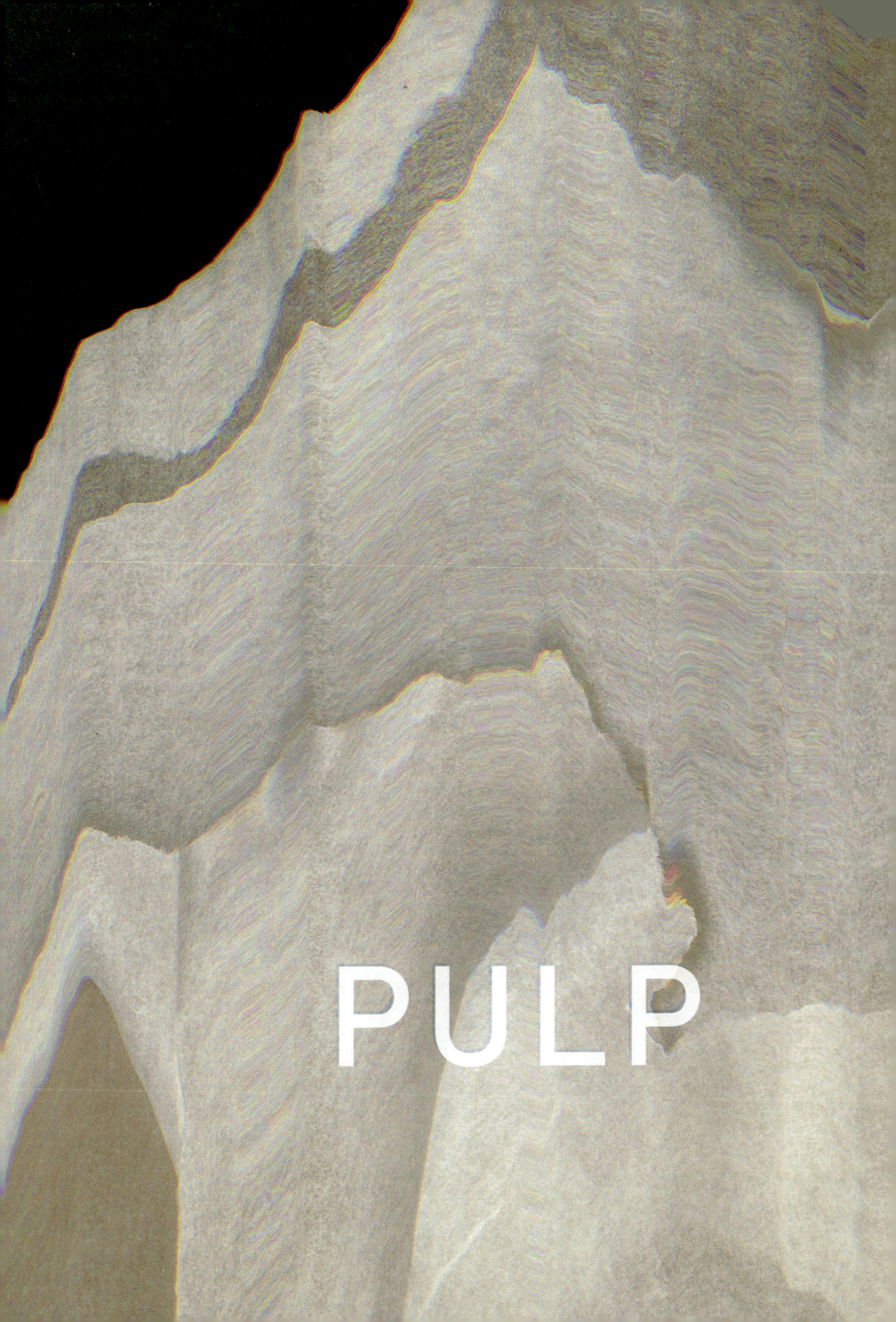
PULP

Fig. 01 - City of the Mind, Sanda Iliescu.

THE COLOR OF CRAFT

Sanda Iliescu, Ailsa Thai, and Nita Wareechatchai

EMPTINESS

When ground and figure become one,
    We sense an emptiness that is also a fullness.
When the ego of the maker becomes one with the making,
    We sense an emptiness that is also a fullness.
When signs and symbols fade,
    Color and craft remain.
Color
    Is a vibrating yet still emptiness.
Craft
    Is a patient stillness: an intensity of making that radiates outwards.
As the pencil touches the paper,
    Adding grains of color—
    Grain after grain after grain—
    We see a landscape of microscopic ridges and valleys,
A city,
A place,
A garden,
    Where emptiness becomes fully itself.

Fig. 02 - Two Litte Suns, Ailsa Thai.

OPENESS

Craft is open.
        It cannot be reduced to methods and formulas.
Color is open.
        Fields of color invite your gaze to see in many ways.
One moment,
        A violet plane advances.
The next,
        That same plane recedes,
                Suggesting deep space.
Yet this depth does not last.
The moment you question it,
        A beautiful shallowness asserts itself.
Parallel planes with only narrow intervals
        Between invite and intimate—
                Layered space vibrates, becoming
                        At once shallow and deep.
As you gaze, space mutates.
        In a perpetual state of becoming,
                The field opens and new possibilities arise.

Fig. 03 - Quadratic Color Wheel, Nita Wareechatchai.

TIME

The leaves are turning
Orange, rust, and gold,
Beginning to peak through clouds of green....
I turn to the white paper.
Adding orange and green.
Then, slowly, building up more color.
Time unfolds gently,
Green turns russet,
Then brown,
Then gray,
Then black.
Each color nearby this mutating green turns too,
For days and days,
turning and turning from one into the other...
But the colors were never quite right.
They refused to settle.
I start to erase—
Adding layers upon layers of erasure...
I begin again,
Adding oranges and greens,
And a host of unnamable hues.
In this slow process,
Measured not in seconds or minutes or days,
Color marks time.

Sanda Iliescu, CITY OF THE MIND

I worked very slowly, creating multiple color layers overlapping each other and forming a sense of transparency. I balanced this transparency by a simultaneous sense of opacity, as color block adjoins color block, each displaying its own uniquely vibrant hue. I hoped to create a sense of openness: to invite the viewer's gaze to see not in one way, but in many. One moment a rosy plane comes forward, locating itself in front of neighboring color planes; at the next, that same rosy plane recedes, giving way and suggesting deep space. This ambiguity renders the composition open and fluid—at once vibrating and standing still.

Ailsa Thai, TWO LITTLE SUNS

I composed this piece with the intention of creating two concentrated moments of brightness - one saturated with red-orange, and one glowing from the exposed white of the paper. These figures, one positive and one negative, depended on their surroundings to aid in their intended perception. Around the little orange square was the lightest and, in some cases, almost imperceptible layers of pigment, while the "empty" square was formed by the most concentrated swathes of color (second only to the orange). Working free hand resulted in blurred edges where the colors were especially delicate, which created a sense of luminosity.

Nita Wareechatchai, QUADRATIC COLOR WHEEL

My process began with the application of color in layers to form a desaturated milieu. Moving across the page, filling opposite corners in shades of green and red, then filling between in shades of blue and purple. Late in this process came the realization that I was making a color wheel. Add yellow and orange. In perceiving the composition, one may first see depth and darkness of the desaturated colors or the pure and bright forms of the saturated. Perception moves between these poles.

INTERCONNECTEDNESS
a view from here
BEYOND
the Magnitude of it
DISAPPEARING
HERE
the TERRAIN of MYstical
TERRITORY
of memories
the mystical journey
BEFORE
Another sky
old STAR LIGHT
region of the Spirit
cosmic Light
stardust
WHOLE
SURFACE

BETWEEN PLACE AND THOUGHT

Karey Kessler

Fig. 01 - Source material by Karey Kessler, image altered by LUNCH editors.

I use art-craft, inspired by map-craft, to explore spaces between: between place and thought, between space and time, between the external world around me and the internal worlds within.

We live in a world that is digitally mapped from outer space right down to our front doors. We can look at 3D cities, 360-degree views of most locations, and even a photo of the cosmic viewpoint of planet Earth, yet we still have no idea why we are here, or what here really means.

Working with traditional fine art materials such as watercolor, archival ink, stencils, stamps, and freehand writing, I create map-paintings that contain ideas about physical places, but also spiritual, internal, and temporal spaces as well. They explore the entangled ways in which our minds, time, and place are deeply interconnected.

A geographer once asked me, "Does a map show reality or does it create the reality"? Geographers don't always realize that they too create worlds when they label their maps. There are real world political and ecological weight to their labels—who gets to name the land, the rivers, and the streets? Who decides the boundaries and protected lands? These labels affect everything: ownership, accessibility, paradigms. In 1966, the painter Jean Dubuffet perfectly described my struggle to make visual my "mental space." He said,

> "Mental space does not resemble three-dimensional optical space and has no use for notions such as above and below, in front or behind, close or distant."

He goes on to say,

> "...it presents itself as flowing water, whirling, meandering and therefore its transcription requires entirely different devices from those deemed appropriate for transcribing the observable world."

My map-paintings are void of specific geographic locations; the "places" don't exist in the real world. By labeling abstract marks (dots, lines, and areas of color) I create a complex network of "worlds" and "locations" that exist only in my mind. The "symbols" purposefully mean more than one thing: dots can be birds, rocks, or stars; lines can be roads, rivers, or the passage of time; pools of color can be clouds or lakes or a mysterious presence.

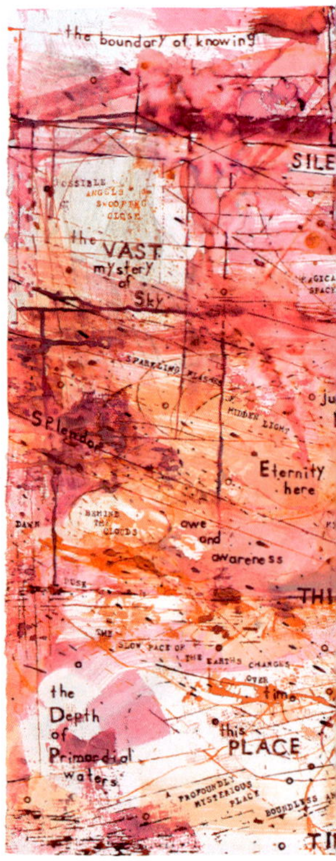

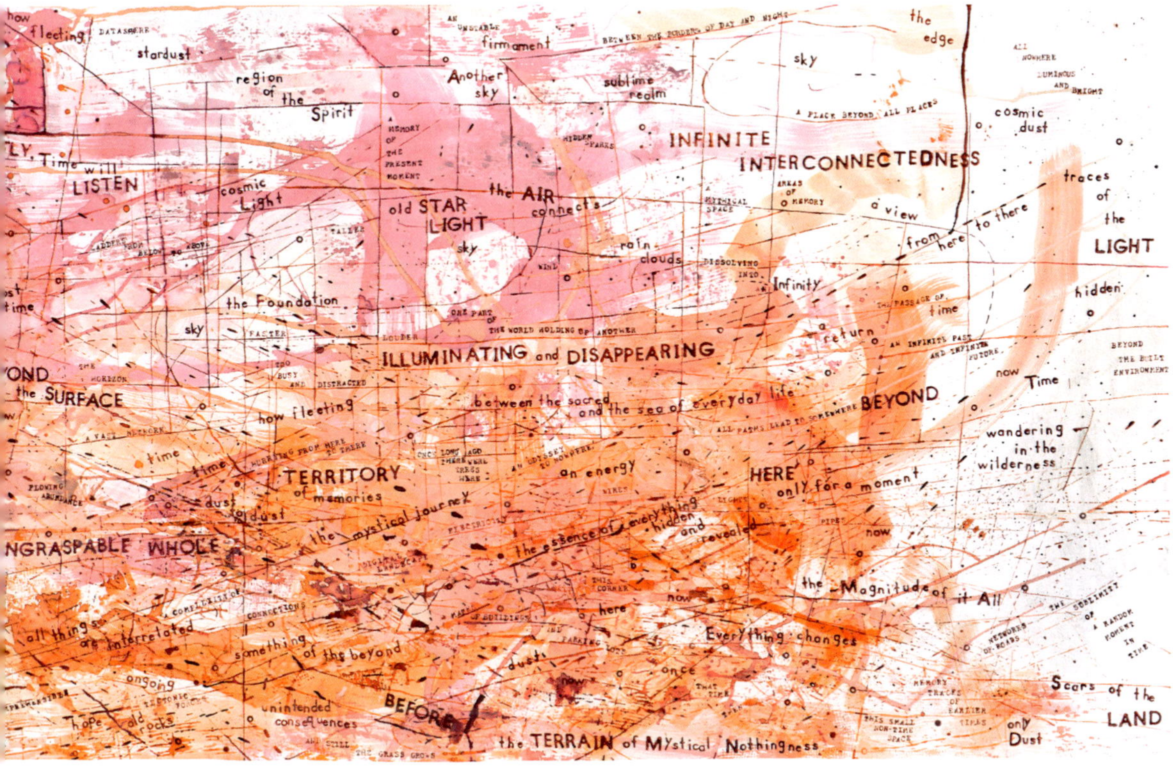

Fig. 02 - This Ungraspable Whole, Karey Kessler, ink on paper.

SHAPE HUNTING

Take a leisurely walk outside. Look for and record shapes that catch your eye and interest.

Fig. 04

LOLLYGAGGER

Eli Sobel

Fig. 01 - Hamtramck, Eli Sobel, Woodcut, 21" x 31", 2019.

I use drawings and prints to synthesize the most important features of buildings. For me, sketching gives a physical body to an idea, since it provides a framework or guide that can be iterated or riffed upon. Drawings are a quick way to draw a subject from multiple perspectives, with a range of linework and to see what core ideas or traits are consistent throughout. These observational iterations act as points of reference for the prints. Sometimes the scale of the drawings needs to be blown up or the linework needs to be simplified, however, the core gesture remains relatively untouched.

From the end of 2018 to the start of 2020, I ping-ponged between living on the East Coast and the Midwest. For a two-month period, I landed in Hamtramck, Michigan, a small city that is surrounded by Detroit. In the early twentieth century, Hamtramck supplied housing to many of the workers at the large Detroit car manufacturers, such as Ford and General Motors. Many of the residences had the same fundamental structure: a rectangular one-level, balloon-frame house. The initial residents were of Polish descent but as demographics changed, the population shifted to mostly that of Bangladeshi, Pakistani, Arab, Lebanese, and Macedonian origin. What drew me to the area were the methods by which the buildings were converted over the last hundred years.

A Baptist church on a side street that caught my eye was clearly once a house. The building was brick, one level and had wooden framing. The front face had three boarded up windows: two that protruded from either side of the door and one above the entrance. Although the windows were covered with bricks, the materials were split in a way to make the shape of the holy trinity. Providing further emphasis that the building was a site of worship, a spire had been erected on top. When crafting the print of the church, I immediately felt as if it was meant to be a single-tone print. Because of when it was sketched, the building was backlit and the front face of the building was reduced

Fig. 02 - Gyre, Eli Sobel, Drypoint and woodcut, 11" x 20", 2019.

Fig. 03 - Headgear,
Eli Sobel, Drypoint
and woodcut,
9" x 16", 2019.

Fig. 04 - *Inside, Out*
Etching, 3.75" x 10", 2019.

to an immense shadow. Despite this shade, reflected light from the ground illuminated the edges of the building's brickwork, glass and wooden planks. Finding a balance between the simplicity of the silhouette and delicacy of the light played into the construction of the print. Recreating this reductive quality entailed stripping away the background to show the paper.

Hamtramck has two main streets, one that serves as the *de facto* entry to the city and one as the exit. The entry disconcertingly resembles a boulevard because of the double-wide lanes for traffic and the phalanx of flags from countries of the world on either side of the road. A highway that borders Hamtramck provides a clear sightline to the structures in the city. At their base, the structures are rectangular and homogenous but their personalities feature heavily in the articulation of their roofs. Some of the roofs are triangular, a couple are square and several are rounded. Presumably this is

because many of the houses have extended their footprint upwards rather than outwards, so that the newest additions are vertical rather than horizontal. Many of these alterations read as coded punctuation since they cover the spectrum of roofing, and recycle and reuse the same form. The layering of reductive, codified shapes influenced the layering and repetition in the three prints Pilcrow, Head Gear, and Inside, Out. Injecting color was a method to further draw out and reveal their presence. Figuring out how the layers fit together is almost like trying to make a puzzle out of found objects—most pieces do not match and must be whittled down in order to fit.

Printing often is a study of boredom since a considerable amount of the time is spent proofing. Hours can pass unnoticed while chiseling wood and then, only after putting on some ink, it becomes apparent that some lines need to be expanded. This first inking is akin to being jolted awake. Linework of an image can be washed out from too

much ink or too shallow cuts into a plate, which requires revisiting the sketches. While I might have a clear idea of how the print will appear, the body of the material has yet to catch up with that idea. Flitting from the carving and rendering to the revealed image is to chase the boundary of mindlessness and focus.

Fig. 05 - Pilcrow, Eli Sobel, Drypoint and woodcut, 11.5" x 3.75", 2019.

What does it take to fashion a church or a nightclub? A couple of crosses? Some neon lights? An underlying assumption about craft is that it requires refinement and mastery. As demonstrated by the homes and workplaces of Hamtramck, a building's identity can be modified intuitively and transformed with materials at hand. What cannot be truly captured with pen or pencil drawings is that the buildings are living. Finding the appropriate animating substance for a print is as simple as looking at construction materials. Wood

boards, such as birch, oak and maple that are used for cabinet sidings or flooring, work well for relief printmaking. Each kind of wood has a specific grain pattern that provides various types of texture and depth. Similarly, copper plates that are used for the siding of houses can also be run through a printing press. With either a metal stylus or acid, the metal can be etched to provide tone and atmosphere. Printing acts as a vehicle to animate the buildings in a way that pen and pencil fall short of fully communicating.

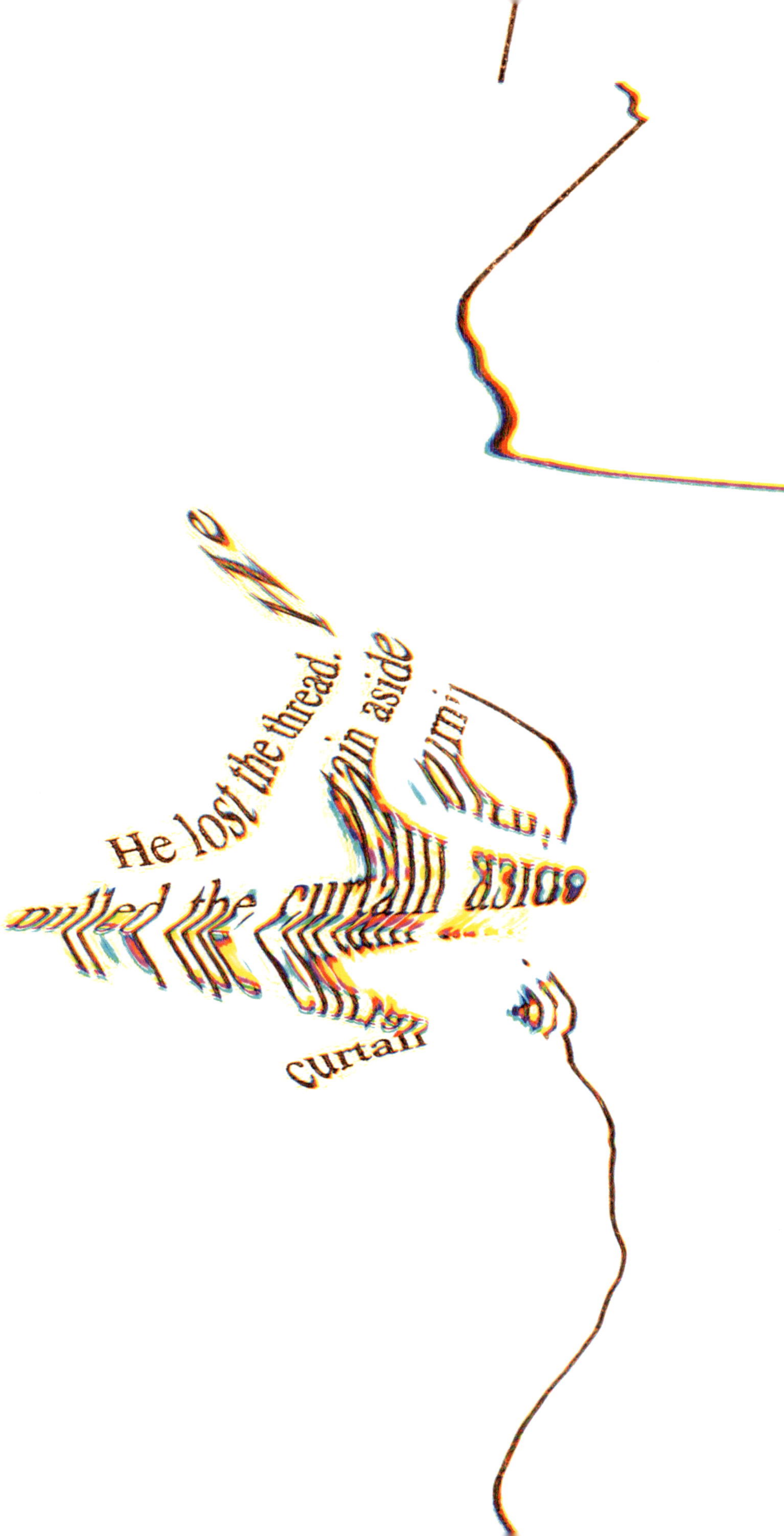
He lost the thread.
He
in aside
curtain

DOG EAR

Erica Baum

Fig. 01 - Source material by Erica Baum, image altered by LUNCH editors.

The Dog Ear photographs are begun with a simple operation: folding the page of a book; colloquially referred to as “dog ear-ing” it. A typical routine to save one’s place in a book, I use this exercise to create a square of diagonally bisected text, in turn resulting in a found poem from the mix of sentences. More than just chance juxtapositions of bifurcated text, these works can—and should—be read. This work uses an economy of means to create a richly poetic language on the page.

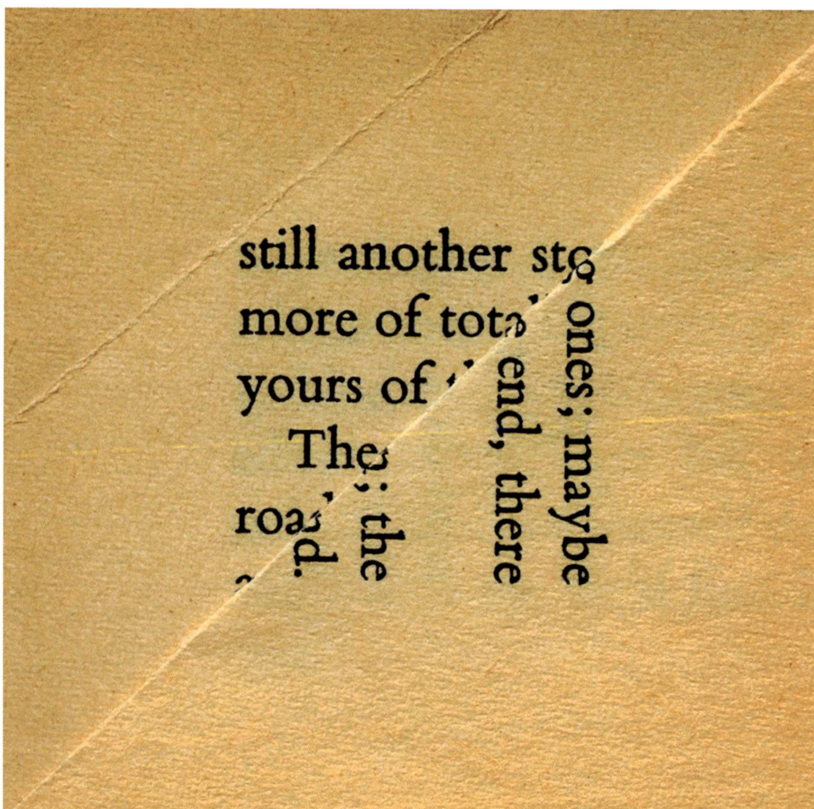

Fig. 02 - End There,
Erica Baum,
Archival pigment
print, 9" x 9", 2009.

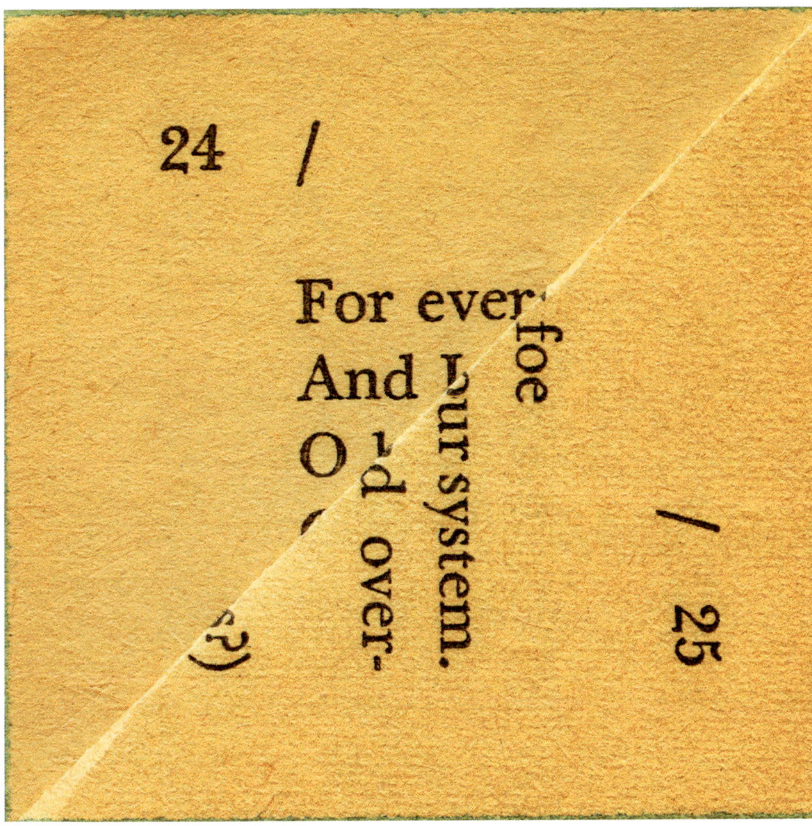

Fig. 03 - Forever Foe, Erica Baum, Archival pigment print, 9" x 9", 2018.

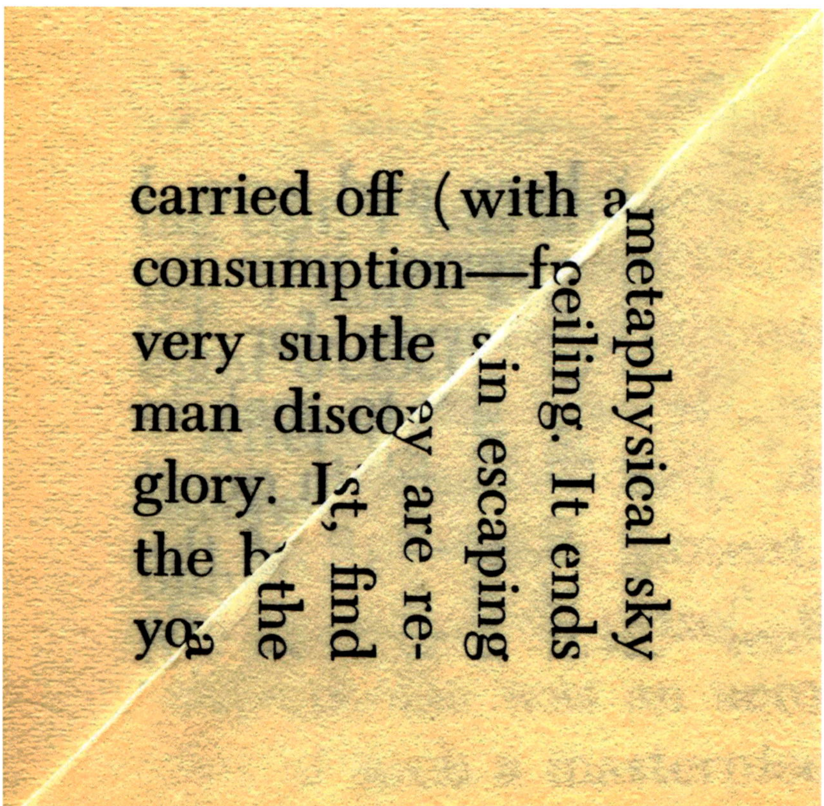

Fig. 04 - Metaphysical Sky, Erica Baum, Archival pigment print, 9" x 9", 2010.

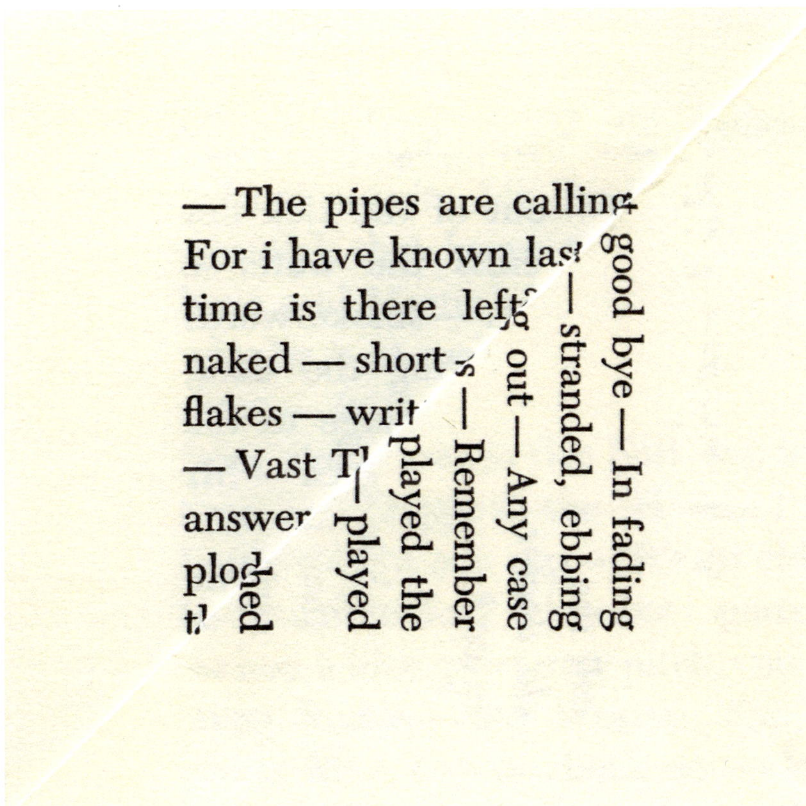

Fig. 05 - Played,
Erica Baum,
Archival pigment
print, 9" x 9", 2016.

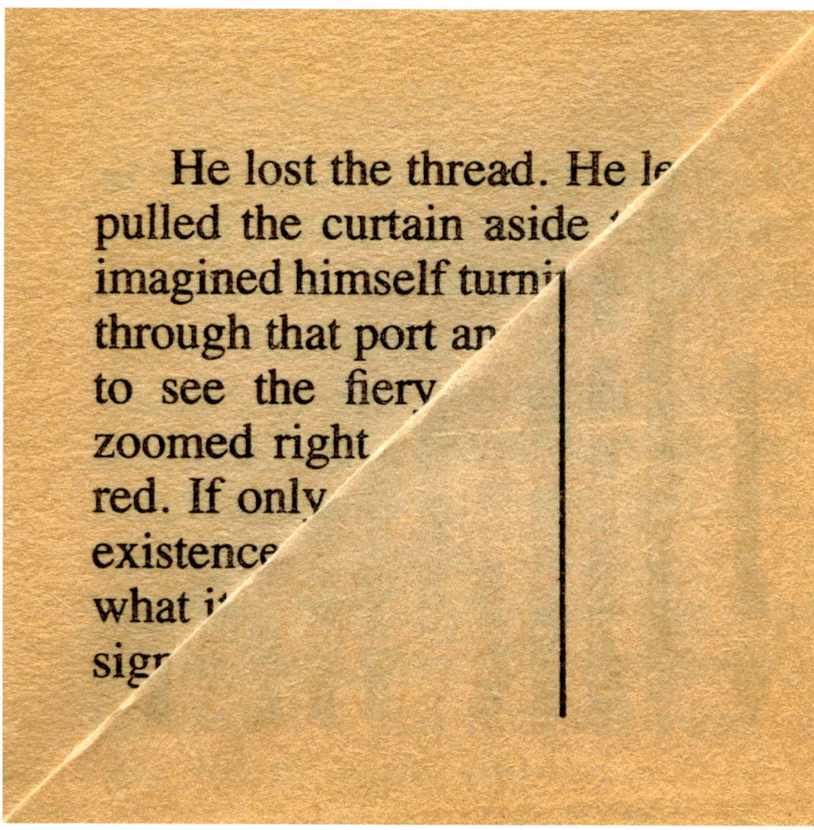

Fig. 06 - Thread, Erica Baum, Archival pigment print, 9" x 9", 2020.

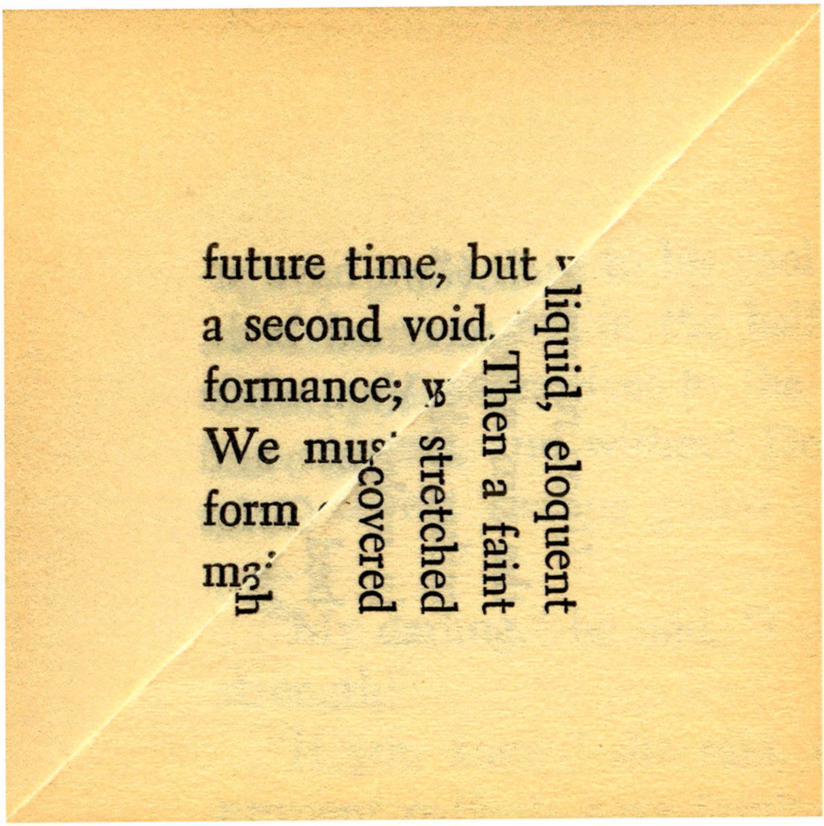

*Fig. 07 - Void,
Erica Baum,
Archival pigment
print, 9" x 9", 2013.*

Is technique always replicable?

When is doing or making distinct from knowing?

TECHNE

HISTORY OF DRILL.

FOR EXPLANATION OF PLATE SEE PAGE 17.

HISTORY OF DRILL.

FOR EXPLANATION OF PLATE SEE PAGE 17.

TOOLING TOOLS & DIGITAL DIGITS

Kyle Schumann

Fig. 01 - Source material by the Smithsonian U.S. National Museum, image altered by LUNCH editors.

Craft is a laden term, conjuring thoughts of skilled work, patience, love, and artisanship, more often than not steeped in nostalgia. It is easy to associate craft with bygone days in which one had the time to whittle and partake in other such leisurely acts of making.

For example, scrimshaw (the art of engraving or carving bone) was borne of unoccupied time on whaling ships that could be filled with leisurely activity. The basic material of scrimshaw—whale bone—was essentially a byproduct or waste stream of the whaling industry, whose main output was oil. This material was made more precious, desirable, or valuable through the application of human labor and skill in crafting it. In scrimshaw, a variety of factors are evident that together we can consider to constitute craft: the use of tools and application of labor to transform material into a more desirable state.

Desirable, in the case of scrimshaw, refers to aesthetics or beauty, but in other crafts such as woodworking, ceramics, or weaving might refer to the utility or function of an object which increases its inherent value to humans. Material relative to craft has been discussed at length by Juhani Pallasmaa, Adolf Loos, Alvar Aalto, Ray and Charles Eames, and many others, so will will not be the focus of this essay. This shifts our attention to labor and tools.

It is easy to get caught up in reminiscing about scrimshaw and thinking of an age when people spent their leisure time crafting, as

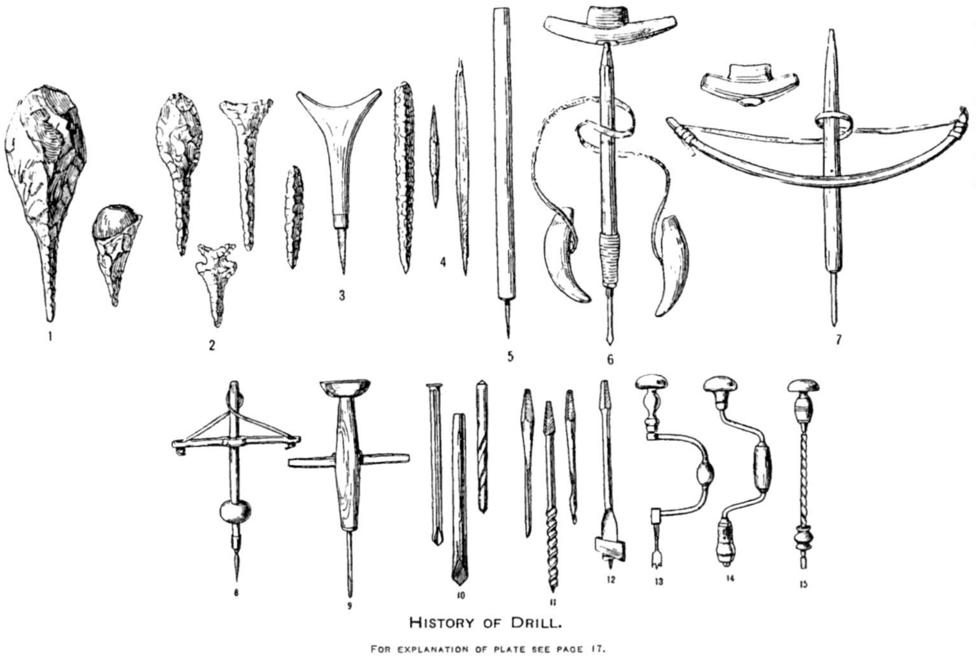

Fig. 02 - Proceedings of the U.S. National Museum. "History of Drill," Vol. 60, Art. 9, Plate 18. Produced for the Trans-Mississippi Exposition, Omaha, Nebraska (1898).

opposed to scouring the depths of the internet on tiny screens. But today is a fundamentally different time in terms of our relationship to both leisure and labor. The Industrial Revolution brought machines and tools that could automate certain processes, removing or reducing human labor from many steps in the production of goods. Later, the Information Age brought access to nearly infinite media for us to consume. The average American now spends over five hours a day online, nearly three-quarters of the eight-hour workday. Manual and industrial production has been shifted largely out of public consciousness, often across borders and oceans.

But despite—or perhaps because of—these many detachments from transforming matter with our hands, craft seems to be having a contemporary renaissance. Championed by platforms such as Kinfolk and likely accelerated by a reaction to two years of isolated, virtual lives, the renewed interest in craft fosters a love for the bespoke, laborious, and exquisite.[1] In many ways, this moment parallels the birth of the Arts and Craft Movement in England, which was a rebuttal of both the perceived inferior quality of industrially produced goods and their ingenuine ornamentation. Once again the cultural pendulum is swinging toward the fetishization of certain handcrafted aesthetics, in which the more hours of human labor and skill applied produce a more valuable object. Conversely, this preference for the analog shuns all things digital, for how can human labor bestow value if this labor is performed by a machine?

Questions of the value and role of labor confront issues of both access and equity. Having the time to devote to learn and master a craft is a luxury not available to all, nor is the time or ability to access training to use advanced tools. Emerging technologies have the potential to become increasingly democratized. Technologies are simultaneously becoming more complex and more user friendly—a side benefit, perhaps, of capitalism. It would be impossible to sell over two hundred million iPhones a year if everyone buying one also needed a degree in computer science and the ability to write code to use it. This ongoing shift in the intelligence of our tools, from the skill and knowledge required to create and use them, to the design and programming of the tool itself, demands that we rethink our relationship to craft and human authorship.

DEVELOPMENT OF TOOLS

In his book "Cræft: An Inquiry Into the Origins and True Meaning of Traditional Crafts," archaeologist Alexander Langlands uses the crafting of hedges to illustrate the development of associated technology over time:

"The craft of trimming hedges can be broken down into three physical functions. Number one is the application of power. Number two is the kinaesthetic sensibility that enables us to shape our body, arms and hands into a position that allows us to achieve number three, the act of cutting....Perhaps harshly, I would not consider a topiarist who uses electric hedge trimmers a true craftsman on the simple grounds that the tool mutes their level of engagement with the material properties of the entity they are working."[2]

Langland traces the development of the topiarist's tools from the hand shear to the electric hedge trimmer. He argues that because the electric hedge trimmer does not require the artisan to provide the physical power to trim the hedge, it results in a fundamentally altered and distilled form of craft. This argument overlooks the fact that there exists a huge gap between someone skilled with an electric hedge trimmer who precisely shapes form, and someone who has never used such an implement. The argument is anti-technological, disregarding the fact that the hand shear is also a deceptively clever piece of technology, albeit one that does not make use of electrical power or computing ability.

In 1898, a collection of plates documenting the ethnographic collections of the Smithsonian Institution were produced for the

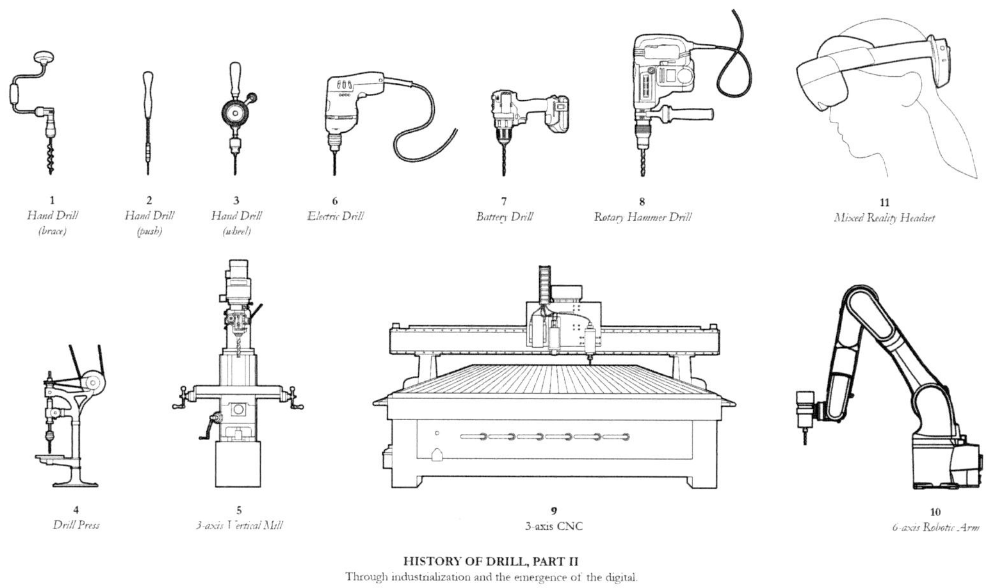

Fig. 03 - "History of Drill, part II". Kyle Schumann (2002).

Trans-Mississippi Exposition in Omaha, Nebraska. Within these illustrations, "The specimens are arranged in the order of their grade of development irrespective of race, place, or time. The series therefore do not always represent a direct genesis of invention. They suggest rather the genesis and indicate how the mind of man has arrived at certain datum points which mark epochs in progress."[3] The documentation of the "History of Drill" describes the drill's beginnings as "a natural object with a hard point... Stone drill points are followed by those of metal, which are pointed, chisel-edged, tubular, screw-shaped, or bladed, as in the latest forms. The manual part of the drill is at first a mere adaptation to the hand of a portion of the tool. This is followed by crude handles, spindle shafts, strap drills, pump drills, and so on, up to the machine drills of our factories."[4]

Similarly, when Sigfried Giedion lays out his explanation of mechanization, he begins with describing the human hand as "a prehensile tool, a grasping instrument. It can seize, hold, press, pull, mold with ease. It can search and feel. Flexibility and articulation are its key words. The triple-articulated fingers, the wrist, the elbow, the shoulders, and, on occasion, the trunk and legs heighten the flexibility and adaptability of the hand. Muscles and tendons determine how it will seize and hold the object."[5]

Giedion's understanding of the hand (and body) as a highly articulated machine for using tools shapes his understanding of mechanized tools.

The progress of the "History of Drill" illustrates this contentious relationship. Upon reaching industrialization, the drill becomes removed from the human hand and, having been produced over a century ago, the record does not describe subsequent developments in this lineage. Today's "History of Drill" might continue to include electric and battery powered hand drills, followed by CNC routers and robotic arms. These digital tools seemingly operate at the most removed distance from the hand, but reframing our relationship to material might amend this assumption.

TOOLS AND FEEDBACK

Giedion gives us a description of the hand and body as several components constituting a kind of machine but continues to elaborate on other components of the system: "[The hand's] sensitive skin feels and recognizes materials. The eye steers its movement. But vital to all this integrated work is the mind that governs and the feelings that lend it life."[6] This elaboration expands upon the body as a machine to include the visual and tactile sensors and software that drive it.

A central split among those who favor hand crafts and those who welcome the digital exists around an argument of feedback. A skilled woodworker might feel the way a chisel moves along or across the grain or the resistance given at a dense knot. This real-time tactile feedback from the material is translated through the tool and into the hand. If we accept that contemporary tools of crafting common to the architecture industry—3D printers, laser cutter, CNC mills, industrial robotic arms, etc.—are simply more advanced digital options than traditional counterparts, then we might find analogs in how the tools are used. A digital woodworker operating a CNC router may not have a hand on the cutting implement, but likewise receives real-time feedback, this time aural, with the whining and chattering of the bit providing instructions for how to fine tune feed rate and spindle speed.

Physical removal from a tool does not preclude real-time feedback from it. Likewise, control systems and software can be authored (one might even say designed or crafted) to respond to feedback much in the way that the hand might. Robotic fabrication systems can now incorporate visual, pressure, and other sensors, essentially transferring a tactile bodily response into the tool itself.

TOOLS AND ACCESS

As succinctly put by Mario Carpo: "Digital tools no longer need to separate the thinker and the making; on the contrary, if pertinently put to use, digital technologies may reunite most of what mechanical technologies had alienated—including the various communities that in the preindustrial world were associated with, and dignified, all Things handmade."[7] The entry of these devices into the DIY space enables this merger of digital tools and craft. Greater access than ever before is provided to non-disciplinary users, increasing access and reducing the time needed to learn and implement new skills and tools.

This is not an argument against analog hand craft—an intricate work of handmade scrimshaw will always carry a degree of allure and admiration generated by the skill and many hours put into its creation. Nor is this an argument that more technology will always improve any given product or process—certain things are more easily accomplished by hand—but an acknowledgement that the production needs of contemporary society require automated and digital processes. A shift in the embodied intelligence of the tool—now capable of moving, sensing, and perhaps even thinking in an ever-closer analog to the human hand—means that we might not see this reliance on the digital as a burden or a loss, but an opportunity to author or craft in new ways. Processes might be authored that program certain responsive sensibilities of the hand into the new tools we create; tools which can become accessible to an ever-broader portion of the world's population, welcoming the intelligence of other modes of craft to enter a shared discourse.

Notes

1. *John Clifford Burns et.al., eds., Kinfolk, 2011-present. https://www.kinfolk.com/*

2. *Alexander Langlands, Cræft: An Inquiry Into the Origins and True Meaning of Traditional Crafts (New York: W.W. Norton & Company, 2017), 36.*

3. *Walter Hough, "Synoptic Series of Objects in the United States National Museum Illustrating the History of Inventions," in Proceedings of the U.S. National Museum, Vol. 60, Art. 9 (Washington: Governments Printing Office, 1922), 1.*

4. *Walter Hough, "Synoptic Series of Objects in the United States National Museum Illustrating the History of Inventions," 17-18.*

5. *Sigfried Giedion, Mechanization Takes Command: a contribution to anonymous history (Minneapolis: University of Minneapolis Press, 2013), 46.*

6. *Sigfried Giedion, Mechanization Takes Command: a contribution to anonymous history*

7. *Mario Carpo, The Alphabet and the Algorithm (Cambridge: The MIT Press, 2011), 119.*

RECIPROCAL ECOLOGY

A Digitally Fabricated Reciprocal Frame Prototype with Invasive Wood Material

Ehsan Barlou, Junhong Fu, Lizzie Needham, Evelyn Saunders

Fig. 01 - Reciprocal ecology prototype. Authors.

Advanced computation and digital fabrication technologies have facilitated a more direct connection between design and build. These tools enable greater designer involvement within the entirety of a design process from ideation to fabrication. Although this can lead to a more responsive form-finding design process, a lack of care towards dynamic material characteristics still encourages designers to operate in a top-down fashion. A design methodology focused on what Tim Ingold refers to as the "textility of making approach" encourages form-making derived from material flows and characteristics as opposed to a predefined outcome.[1] Through this methodology, material agency determines the form and expands socio-ecological design possibilities within the realm of digital fabrication.

Neri Oxman's research demonstrates that working between the digital and the physical allows for environmentally sensitive and smart fabrication methods that facilitate material expression.[2] Acute understanding about how materials fit into the ecological surroundings encourages designers to think more holistically about built objects as part of a broader ecological system. Multidisciplinary design processes and cyber-physical technologies lead to "novel spatial, structural, social and ecological potentials to form their

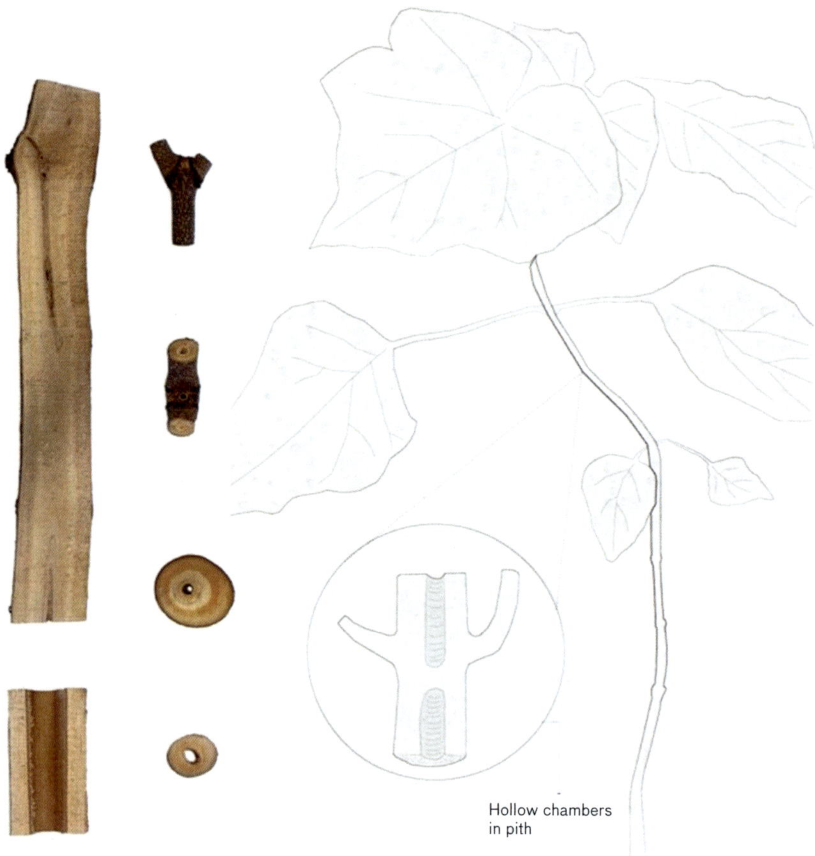

Fig. 02 - Analysis of Paulownia tomentosa. Authors.

own unique material culture."[3] This gives agency to the materials themselves and pushes architects to think beyond their own visions and ideations. Emphasizing material ecology in the digital realm not only allows for a more precise use of irregular, organic, and unprocessed materials, but also generates novel form finding and evolvement over time.

Reciprocal Ecology (Fig. 01) combines careful analysis of plant attributes, advanced digital technologies, and landscape maintenance practices to build upon these theories of material agency. Our process began with harvesting and processing prominent invasive tree species in central Virginia's Piedmont region that are typically cleared through city public-works projects. The material experiments suggested that *Paulownia tomentosa* offered the most interesting possibilities for material expression through its naturally occurring stem void in juvenile species (Fig. 02). This characteristic inspired the use of a reciprocal form (RF) prototype as the holes enabled a unique edge-to-edge connection system. Reciprocal Ecology's RF prototype consisted of an additive 3D-printed joinery system within the stem void and a subtractive 6-axis milled edge-to-edge connection strategy.

The RF structure has a long history in human culture due to its flexibility with material use and ease of construction. Expressive forms can be achieved through simple and repetitive construction techniques out of almost any linear material. RF structures allow for the use of materials typically overlooked in the field of architecture including byproducts of restoration ecology maintenance. This opens opportunities for democratized and inclusive fabrication.

Merging digital technologies with material agencies has driven exciting innovations for RF structures. Lamella Flock, by Martin Tamke et al.,[4,5] used a generative design strategy based on the relationship between interdependent linear units to develop its form. Their computation method included a Finite Element analysis that checked for structural behavior, which enabled them to assess the feasibility of construction as they moved through design iterations. Complex Timber Structure 2 by Gramazio & Kohler at ETH Zurich utilized a computational model that determined exact cut placement and connection angles within RF units for the robotic fabrication process.[6] Ashiawa Ryuichi laboratory and Toki Hirokazu's Ryuboku Hut used recycled driftwood and fishing line as the components for an RF structure.[7] The structural integrity of mutually reliant beams in RF construction warranted the novel use of driftwood, which spoke to the landscape's cultural history.

The logic of RF structures is defined by three categories of connection types between reciprocating pieces: edge-to-edge, edge-to-end, and end-to-end. All of them can be abstracted into the aggregation of basic units that in each unit, pieces rely on each other in the form of a polygon. According to Olga Popovic Larsen's book, *Reciprocal Frame Architecture*,[8] a basic polygon reciprocal unit ("n" for the number of pieces in each unit) can be demonstrated with corresponding equations (Fig. 03). Pertaining to the basic reciprocal unit, this study showed the changes in increasing height in the collided pieces have a positive correlation with the radius of the wood and negative correlation with the ratio of where pieces are connected.

Our prototype (Fig. 04) combines modernized RF construction methods with material-led design. We reversed the traditional western architectural practice of manifesting an idea through material construction in favor of letting the material drive creative interventions.

ADDITIVE MANUFACTURING METHODS: A RESPONSE TO THE MATERIAL AGENCY

Traditionally, the simplest method for building RFs is derived from a structure of mutually supporting linear flat or inclined elements

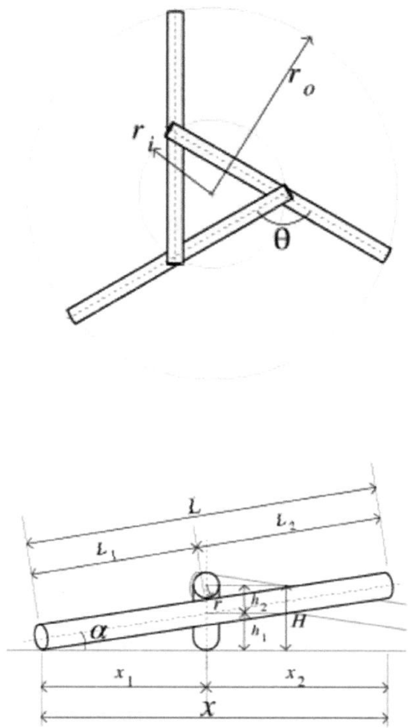

$$\theta = \frac{360}{n}$$

$$x_2 = 2r_i \sin\frac{\theta}{2}$$

$$x_1 = \sqrt{r_o^{\,2} - \left(r_i \cos\frac{\theta}{2}\right)^2} - \frac{x_2}{2}$$

$$x = x_1 + x_2$$

$$\frac{x_1}{x} = \frac{h_1}{H}$$

$$L = \sqrt{x^2 + H^2}$$

$$\frac{H}{L} = \sin\alpha$$

$$\frac{2r}{h_2} = \cos\alpha$$

$$\frac{h_1}{x_1} = \tan\alpha$$

$$\frac{L_1}{L_2} = \frac{x_1}{x_2}$$

Fig. 03 - (left) Geometrical parameters of a reciprocal unit. (right) Equations corresponding to the basic unit. Source: Redraw of Geometrical parameters for RF structures (Larsen, 2008, pp. 37–38)

that are arranged to form a closed unit.[9] This method uses friction and pre-cut notches to stack material at precise connecting points. With precise notches, the pieces can interlock with each other firmly. However, the entire structure may not fit as expected should the notches not be cut precisely enough.[10] Paulownia tomentosa is regarded as a fast-grow species with hollow pith in its saplings; and therefore, is unable to perform like mature lumber products when it undergoes large amounts of subtraction. Thus, this species called for an additive manufacturing joinery system to connect the pieces. Simultaneously, an additive system also eliminated the need for extremely precise subtractive cutting to accommodate the unique characteristics of each wooden piece.

The additive joinery system consisted of a digitally generated family of standardized joints that took advantage of the stem void trait. Each joint responded to the material within its RF unit including the angle between pieces and the pith thickness between stem void and the peripheral surface. Our physical model prototypes demonstrated that an edge-to-edge connection joinery system could withstand the highest levels of force and most accurately account for stem void inconsistencies. The joinery system (Fig. 06) defines connections, adapts with the material, and determines assembly guidelines. In addition, the digital generation of the joint family corresponds with reciprocal form finding, milling, and assembly plans.

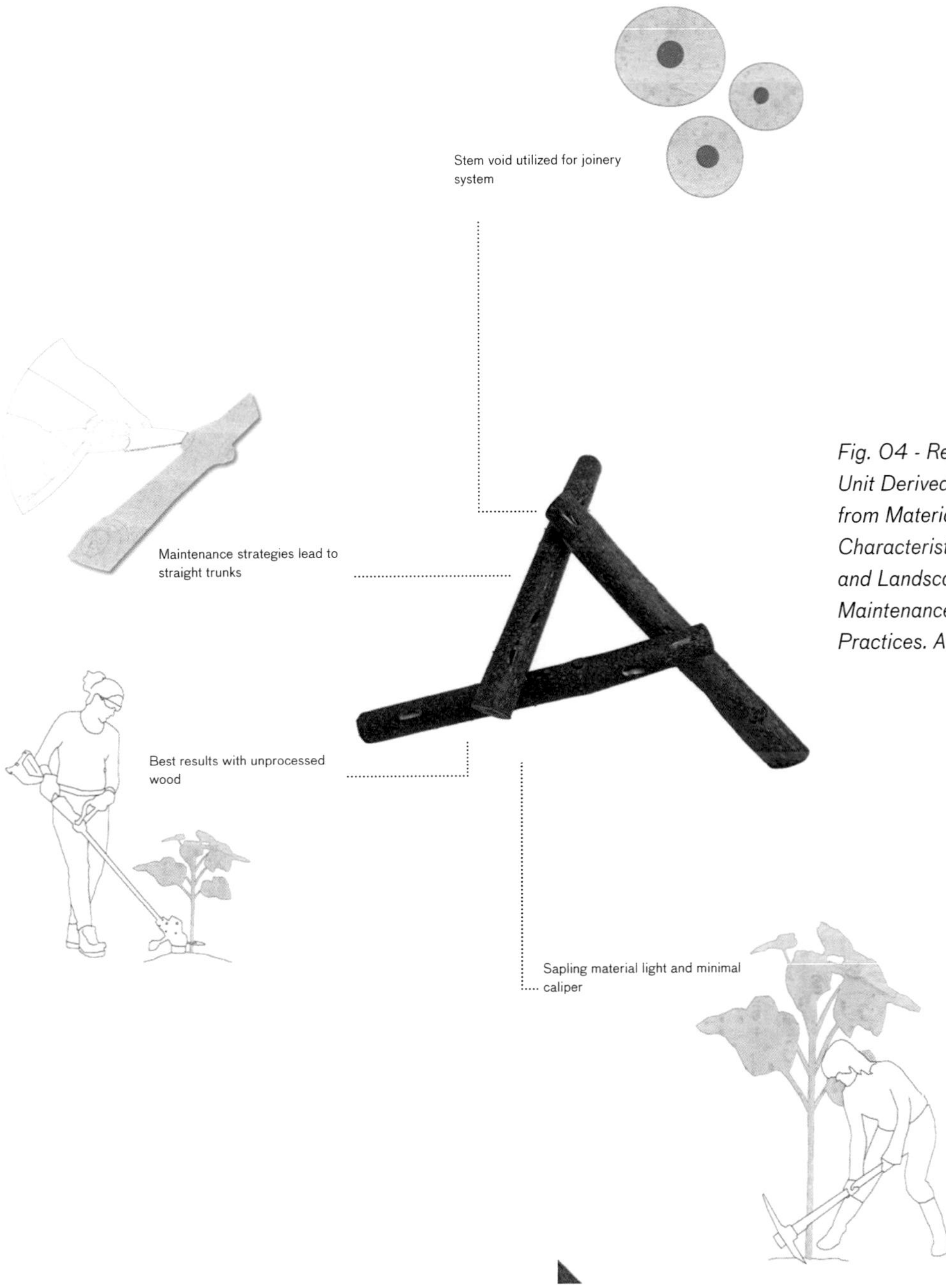

Fig. 04 - Reciprocal Unit Derived from Material Characteristics and Landscape Maintenance Practices. Authors.

Fig. 05 - (above) Subtractive Milling Using 6-axis KUKA Robotic Arm. Authors.

Fig. 06 - (below) Individual Joint and Reciprocal Connection in Joinery System. Authors.

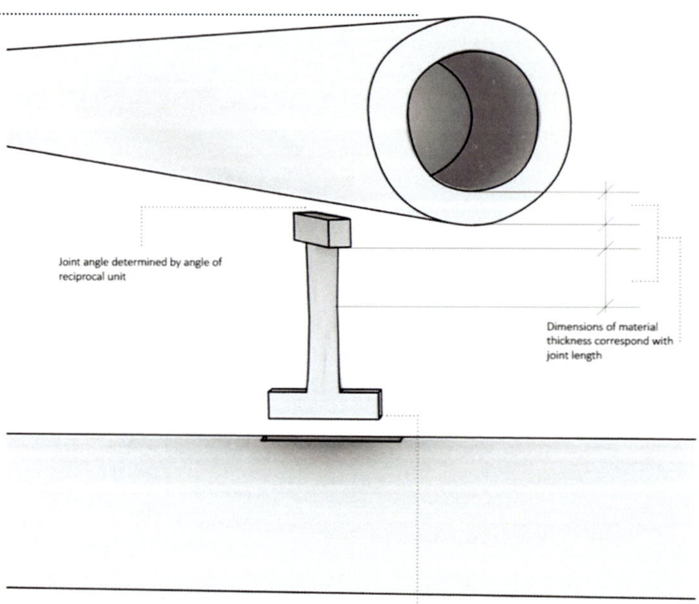

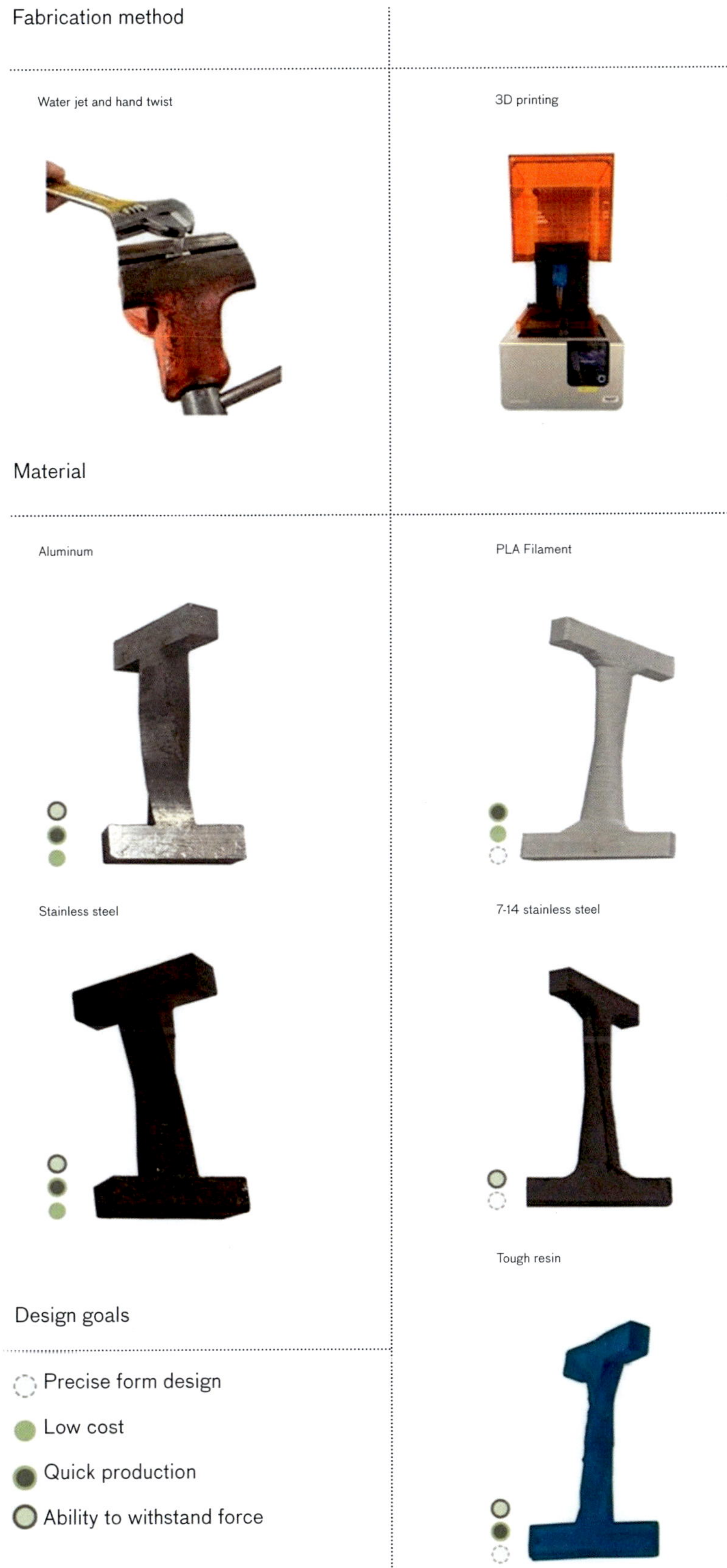

Fig. 07 - Material tests. Authors.

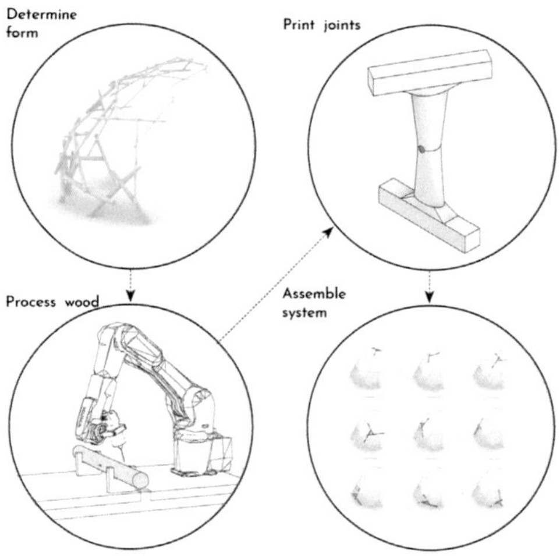

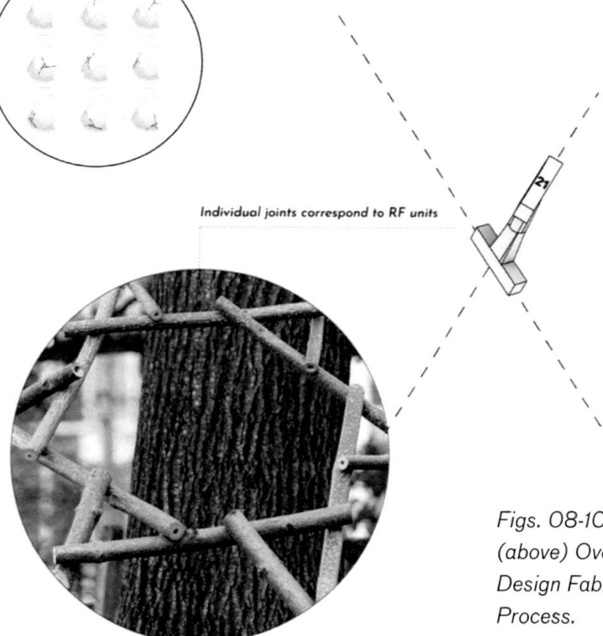

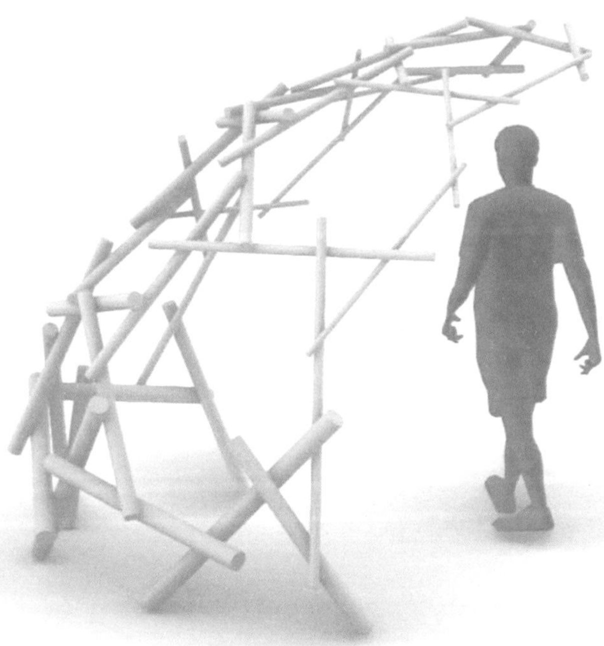

Figs. 08-10 - (above) Overview of Design Fabrication Process. (middle) Additive Joinery System Results and Process. (below) Final Form Digital Model. Authors.

A series of material tests of 3D printed joints were conducted using a variety of 3D printers and cut on a water jet (Fig. 07). Out of these options, the engineering-grade tough resin on the Formlabs Form 3D printer offered the highest levels of precision and material strength within the fastest time frame.

We developed a computational framework to specify the correct location of each joint within the RF unit that adapts with the respective edges. This customized joinery system aligned with the individual qualities of the material and ensured a standardized system with precise connecting pieces (Fig. 08).

SUBTRACTIVE FABRICATION APPROACHES

A subtractive milling strategy that matched each individual joint partnered with the additive joinery system. Custom slots were milled using the KUKA robotic arms (Fig. 05) at connecting points of collided pieces to give the 3D printed joints access to the stem voids. The location of the milling slots together with the printed joints defined the angle of connection between each piece. This ensured the accuracy of the spatial relationship between slots on two sides with simple control and allowed some degrees of tolerance for the ease of assembly.

The method of structural form-finding was highly integrated with the amount of the material in hand. When aggregating the prototypes, the structural form is made up to be a dome-like shell, and our final structural form took one of the iterations from all the transformations and analyzed its structural stability. We developed a digital catalog for harvested material by categorizing pith thickness and centerlines of each piece. These dimensions were regularly assessed to build tolerances for the irregularity in the material, while changes were made to the design and the wood was cut to the specified length for its unique placement within the overall structure.

Assembly of the structure (Fig. 09) with mass customization relied on detailed labeling to connect individual pieces and joints. Basic modular units derived from the Computer Aided Design model (developed using Rhinoceros CAD software) made up of three pieces of wood and three connection joints were prefabricated before taking them into the field to build the final structure. During assembly, clamps were used as an aid to stabilize the structure, accounting for shear force and movement. Once all the connections were established, the structure became stable, and the clamps were removed to allow pieces to simply reciprocate within the complex structure.

CONCLUSION: ECOLOGY, MATERIAL AGENCY AND MULTI-DISCIPLINARY OPPORTUNITIES

Reciprocal Ecology's wood materials expanded the rationale behind the design of the form. This logic deemphasized the importance of a linear design-build process and gave material exploration and design iteration the same hierarchical position. Material ecology encourages the emergence of opportunities for contemporary computational-aid design methodology, leading towards a more reciprocal practice of form making that speaks to a relationship between materials and designer. Based on the traditional reciprocal intellect, the prototype revitalized this ancient oriental building practice with the aid of advanced computational technologies and generated a novel jointing system through a deep investigation of materials. This working process offers potential futures for a range of architectural fields, with more open-ended design outcomes. In addition, a more in-depth understanding with materials enables designers to be more aware of the sustainable site and build stronger partnerships with associated fields such as restoration ecology.

Notes

1. *Daniel Baerlecken and Katherine Blair Wright, "Nominalized Matter: Agency of Material," International Journal of Architectural Computing 12, no. 3 (September 1, 2014): 339–56, https://doi.org/10.1260/1478-0771.12.3.339.*

2. *Neri Oxman, "Towards a Material Ecology." In ACADIA 2012: Synthetic Digital Ecologies: Proceedings of the 32nd Annual Conference of the Association for Computer Aided Design in Architecture (ACADIA), (New York, NY, 2012). Jason Kelly Johnson et al., eds.,*

3. *Achim Menges, "Fusing the Computational and the Physical: Towards a Novel Material Culture," Architectural Design 85, no. 5 (2015): 8–15, https://doi.org/10.1002/ad.1947.*

4. *Martin Tamke, Jacob Riiber, and Hauke Jungjohann, "Generated Lamella" (ACADIA 2010: LIFE in:formation, New York, USA, 2010), 340–47, https://doi.org/10.52842/conf.acadia.2010.340.*

5. *Martin Tamke et al., "Lamella Flock," in Advances in Architectural Geometry 2010 (Ambra Verlag, 2016), 37–48, https://doi.org/10.1515/9783990433713-004.*

6. *Jan Willmann et al., "Robotic Timber Construction — Expanding Additive Fabrication to New Dimensions," Automation in Construction 61 (January 1, 2016): 16–23, https://doi.org/10.1016/j.autcon.2015.09.011.*

7. *"Ryuboku Hut (Okishima Island, Japan) – Design Spectrum | 設計光譜," accessed March 29, 2023, https://www.designspectrum.hk/project/ryuboku-hut-okishima-island-japan/.*

8. *Olga Popovic Larsen, Reciprocal Frame Architecture (London: Routledge, 2007), https://doi.org/10.4324/9780080556000.*

9. Olga Popovic Larsen, "Reciprocal Frame (RF) Structures: Real and Exploratory," *Nexus Network Journal* 16, no. 1 (April 1, 2014): 119–34, https://doi.org/10.1007/s00004-014-0181-0.

10. Larsen, *Reciprocal Frame Architecture*. 146.

11. National Wildlife Federation. "Invasive species." Accessed March 7, 2021. https://www.nwf.org/Home/Educational-Resources/Wildlife-Guide/Threats-to-Wildlife/Invasive-Species

12. Rodrigo Olave et al., "Survival, Early Growth and Chemical Characteristics of Paulownia Trees for Potential Biomass Production in a Cool Temperate Climate.," *Irish Forestry* 72 (November 1, 2015): 42–57.

COOK A MEAL FOR SOMEONE YOU LOVE

Make a meal with yours hands that sustains yourself and your relationships. Make something delicious.

Choose a forgiving recipe, or assemble a plate of delights.

Fig. 06

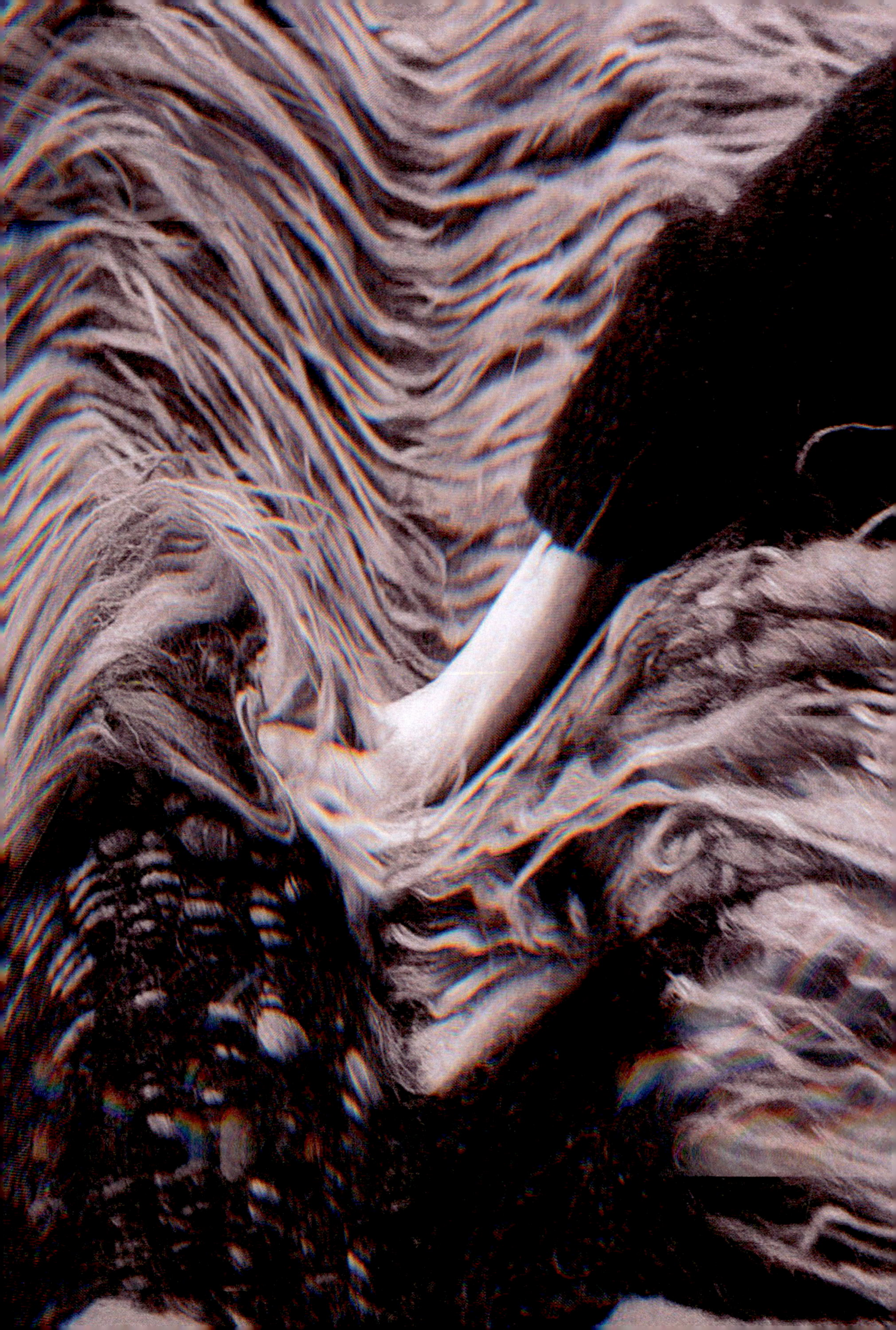

SHEEPCRAFT

Theodore Teichman

All images courtesy of Theodore Teichman

Fig. 01 - Source material by Theodore Teichman, image altered by LUNCH editors.

Every year in June, Iceland's sheep are released from the lowlands to roam for the summer in the highland grazing pastures. Then in September, local residents–both former and current–of each district join to ride on horseback through the highlands and bring the sheep back home. Iceland is a "taskscape" of sheep farming.[1] This taskscape has not only been crucial for survival in this intense landscape, but has been a way to make sense of the environment there, a focal practice. Albert Borgmann extends Martin Heidigger's concept of focal things to develop an argument for the role of focal practices as activities which connect people to a deeper sense of reality through an intimate and repetitive engagement with the environment for the sheer sake of enjoyment in that engagement.[2] His argument is increasingly important today as people are further alienated from aspects of their experience in the world.

Before settlement (894 CE), there is no evidence of humans having lived in Iceland. At the time of settlement, somewhere between 15-40% of Iceland was covered by shrubs of birch and willows and two-thirds of the land was vegetated. However, by the beginning of the 20th century the forest coverage was down to 1%, and the vegetation below 15%.[3] The settlers not only brought their sheep companions with them from Norway, but they also brought their familiar land use practices. While Iceland's unique soils (Andosols and Vitrisols) and fluctuating climate exacerbate these processes, the landscape we see today is a product of cultural and social paradigms

of land use. This degradation began with the cutting of trees for charcoal, and intensified during the mid-19th century, when there was a simultaneous cooling period and the institutionalization of capitalist trade by Danish colonial merchants. This marked the shift of sheep bred for export rather than merely subsistence and, as a result, became overstocked. With many more sheep on the land–now not being used for their milk–they were allowed to roam unsupervised and graze the highlands and lowlands year-round.[4] These practices, especially the winter grazing, came with consequences of soil erosion and intense dust storms which led to the abandonment of farms and threatened the end of inhabitation throughout the south and northeast portions of Iceland.[5] However, the winter grazing ceased at the beginning of the 20th century with the introduction of cultivated lowland pasture, sheep numbers have dropped by half in the last 20 years, and very little of the sheep production is for the export market.

For approximately 40 years, satellites have detected an increase in the productivity of tundra vegetation which has been described as, "the greening of the Arctic."[6] This means profound changes to the socio-ecological system (nature-culture) in places like Iceland. As mitigation efforts appear an increasingly dimming hope, we instead turn our attention to the question of adaptation. Sheep farming in Iceland is full of contradictions; it is a practice that has both scarred the land and sustained life on the island. This is not unique to Iceland, but an acute reification of the practice of living and shaping land with animals everywhere. Perhaps we would benefit from looking again with concerned engagement at our companionship with mediator species–a non-human other through which we read our environment differently. How might these serve as focal practices for making sense of our damaged worlds? What lessons can we learn from seeing the world through sheepcraft? How might we translate traditional land practices to the new natures we will have to connect with? How do we craft a resilient future with our companion species?

LEARNING FROM OLAFUR, RAGNHILDUR, AND EYJOLFUR: ICELAND'S SHEEP FARMING HISTORY

For over 1000 years, sheep were a staple for life in Iceland, producing milk, meat, wool, and skins. Until the 1890s, a typical farm was small, isolated, and self-sufficient, just the family and workers, a cultivated infield, an uncultivated outfield (for grazing and hay harvesting), 1-3 cows, 15-40 sheep, and 2-4 horses. The Icelandic sheep is an old breed, and the largest representative breed from the Northern European Short Tailed species. The breed originated in Norway or the Scottish Isles and was brought to Iceland at the time of settlement. Since then, it has remained relatively unchanged. Before Iceland was settled in 894 CE there were no land mammals in Iceland save for the arctic fox. The Norwegian settlers brought sheep with them. Grazing allowed for agile land use, making nutrients without intensive cultivation, which became necessary to cope with the frequent changes in climate and adapt to an entirely different landscape.[7]

Until the 20th century, farms in Iceland were often dependent on winter grazing for sheep and horses, a practice particularly at risk for overgrazing on fragile plants and soil. In the 20th century, this practice began to be discouraged due to the efforts to halt massive scale soil erosion. During the 1950s, to supplement the feed in the winter, wetlands were drained (on a massive scale) for infield grazing in spring and autumn and hay feed production for winter feeding.[8]

The Hestur Sheep Experimental Farm, located in the Andakill Area of the Borgarfjordur District, was established as a research institution in 1944. It is now part of the Agricultural University of Iceland, raising sheep for agricultural research and educational purposes. Of Hestur Sheep Experimental Farm's 1200 hectares, today, 90 hectares are cultivated hayfields and over 900 hectares are vegetated. Sheep graze freely in the highlands during summer, but are housed in the

barn from November until May. Feed is collected in June-August and stored in round bales for the winter. At present, while one-fifth of land area in Iceland is suitable for agriculture or grazing, only 6% of this area is cultivated.[9]

LEARNING FROM HULDA AND MAJA: WOOL CULTIVATION AND CAREFUL LABOR

Hulda Brynjólfsdóttir co-founded Uppspuni in 2017 with Tyrfingur Sveinsson in Lækjartún, near Hella in Southern Iceland. She described the motivation for starting the 'mini-mill' as multifaceted, wanting to make better use of all products of the sheep, and to increase the respect for the multicolored Icelandic sheep. Since 2020, they have been focusing on adopting regenerative grazing practices, mainly on cultivated lowland pastures, to better care for the soil in the long term and to reduce the use of short term artificial fertilizers. Hulda has already seen positive changes to the vegetation in her fields. Last year they bought only half the fertilizer they normally do, and this year only a quarter; Hulda would like to see that number get to zero.

Hulda models the tog fiber to show its length. Wool is composed of two fibers. The tog fiber is the longer, outer layer of wool that is waterproof, strong, and itchy. The þel fiber is the shorter, inner layer, next to the sheep's skin which provides insulation. Hulda relates that the first step of processing really begins in the barn, deciding which ewe goes with which ram. She explains that compared to the same machines at ÍSTEX (the largest wool mill in Iceland), these are the dollhouse size. At Uppspuni, Hulda is doing all the jobs. After

shearing in the fall, the wool is sorted, washed, and sorted again, refining the classification at each step of handling. Next, the wool goes through the picker which fluffs the wool. Then, unless it is being used for socks, the wool goes through the fiber separator which calibrates the ratio of tog and þel depending on the purpose for the yarn. The wool is then straightened out on the carder which aligns the fibers in the same direction. It is refined and evened out on the drawframe, making it easier to spin. The processed wool is passed onto the spinner and then the plier, which takes two strands together and winds them into yarn. Finally, the yarn is passed through the steamer, which relaxes the wool, and onto the skein binder.

Maja Siska, a freelance architect, shows off her installation, "Helix," commissioned for an exhibition in "Að bjarga heiminum - To save the world" at Verksmiðjuna á Hjalteyri, Iceland (June 2015). She emphasizes how her approach connects the textural quality of the wool to the rawness of the highlands where the sheep graze in the summers. She speaks to the connection one feels with nature when witnessing the sheep running wild in the natural landscapes. Hulda relates that the wool of the sheep is fluffier and the meat is more aromatic when sheep are grazed in highlands compared to the lowland homefields. The sheep farmers can trace where their sheep have been through their senses, inspecting the health and materiality of the sheep's bodies. By developing these sensory practices, the sheep farmers also develop ways of looking at the health and structure of the landscape their sheep encounter.

Maja describes her long infatuation with woolworking and the tactile experience of the material. To her, working with wool is about the intimate bond between herself and the sheep, the tangible and pleasurable connection through the hands. She attests that even the act of slaughter is a form of craft, and, for her, an important means to connect and respect the gifts of the sheep. To her, it is an important part of this respect that the gifts of the sheep are reciprocated by careful labor.

Maja shows the wool she has dyed herself using gathered lichens. These lichens are known in Icelandic as dye moss due to their long standing use in dying techniques. Maja describes that there is an element of stewardship for the woodworkers who forage natural dyes. They keep the locations secret to avoid overexploitation and are always cognizant of the growth rates of lichens to determine what they can extract.

These wools were dyed with the leaves of the Nootka Lupin Lupinus nootkatensis), which renders a yellow color on the white wool and a rich green color on the grey wool of the Feldfé ram, a unique strain within the Icelandic breed of sheep with which Maja and her local hand spinning group, the Spunasystir, have worked to preserve. The Nootka Lupin is widespread in the plains of Iceland. It was introduced to halt soil erosion through aerial seeding and large industrial activities over huge desertified regions and is now generally considered invasive.[10] This material is a "new nature" as fibercraft: it embodies the story of landscape change in Iceland, combining two introduced species (sheep and Nootka lupin), from different moments in the definition of dwelling in this land.[11, 12]

FIELD NOTES: THE RÉTTIR

Families look onto the sheep as they run into the rétt. The rétt in Fljotstunga is constructed in the old style, with walls made of volcanic rock, gathered and stacked by hand, often using existing lava formations to form as many walls as possible.[13] The rétts are located in a liminal zone between the improved lands (homefields) and the unimproved lands (the highland grazing commons). The rétt is a focal point in the landscape, often situated with respect to natural sorting features, such as canyons or rivers.[14] Usually situated in the highland foothills, the rétt takes the form of a circle nested in another circle, with wedges between. Each wedge belongs to a particular farm, while the inner circle, the sorting-pen, is common for the district. This design is optimized for the sorting of sheep, a microcosm of the larger spatial and social structure of the island itself.

Icelandic sheep are characterized by the unique strain, called the Leadersheep, classified as a special breed since 2017, with its heritable behavioral attribute. These sheep function as herders, working with the farmers to take the other sheep on their own to their familiar grazing areas in the spring, and then helping to lead the herd back down from the highlands during the fall. The sheep provide a way for the farmers to see the landscape, the soil, and the ecosystems, narrated through experience across years and generations.

The gathering of the sheep, known as the réttir, is an important social affair much like a festival for the whole community. On the second day of the réttir, comes the sorting. The sheep are all herded into the sorting pen of the rétt. In the sea of sheep, the people dash to catch a sheep by the horns or head if polled, read its ear-tag and ear-mark, and drag the sheep over to the gate for the wedge of the farm to which the sheep belongs. Many who have left for the city come

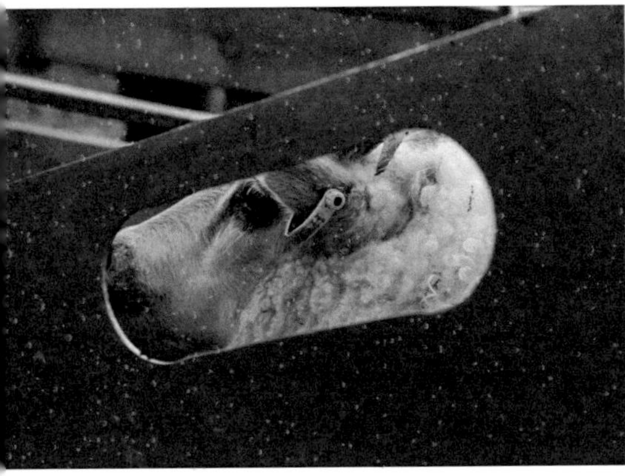

back to participate in the réttir where their parents or grandparents once had farms. This process takes extensive organization from all stakeholders and is usually coordinated by the district's two "Kings of the Mountain" elected by the farmers in each distinct, where one coordinates the ride into the highlands and the other coordinates the sorting activities and the logistics of returning the sheep to the right farms when they are brought back down.

A lamb looks out at the rétt from the truck ramp that will take the sheep back to the farm. Most of the lambs, save 15-20% for breeding replacements, will be sent to the slaughter almost immediately after the réttir. All slaughter is required to happen at one of the six slaughterhouses in the country. Eyjólfur Kristinn Örnólfsson, director of research at the Hestur Sheep Experimental Farm, relates that Hestur is given a dispensation to slaughter sheep for educational purposes, but the meat cannot be removed from the farm. As agriculture has become increasingly centralized it has ceased to be an option for the farmers to be with the sheep through the whole process of life and death in the land.

Farmers have a deep knowledge of their lowland district and the highland districts they frequent; a knowledge that has been passed down intergenerationally. However, as fewer and fewer of the current generations are opting to continue farming in the same way, this deep knowledge of the land is at risk of being lost. Fundamental to this knowledge are the planning procedures of when, where, and how to graze, the routes to ride into the highlands, and the ways to herd the sheep. The structure of this practice is characterized by a need for a certain critical mass of population for the réttir. At present, Iceland is facing increasing rural depopulation as more and more people move to the cities, and families grow smaller, there are fewer children to take over the farms. However, it is these same structures that are being utilized for the new adaptive management program, GróLind, which commenced its monitoring activities in 2019. The goal is to develop a cohesive inventory of annual vegetation and soil resources, integrating remote sensing with measurements taken by farmers in the field and during the réttir.

Sheep farming is one of Iceland's oldest ways of connecting to nature. It has been implicated in the desertification and land degradation of the island. Yet it has also sustained life on the island by providing sustenance, and strengthening the social infrastructures that have enabled communities to persevere.

Notes

1. *Tim Ingold, "Taking taskscape to task," In Forms of dwelling, ed. Ulla Rajala and Philip Mills (Oxford: Oxbow Books, 2017), 16-27.*
2. *Albert Borgmann, "Focal things and practices," In Readings in the Philosophy of Technology, ed. David Kaplan (Rowman & Littlefield Publishers, 2004), 115-136.*
3. *A. Arnalds, "Approaches to landcare—a century of soil conservation in Iceland," Land Degradation & Development 16, no. 2, (March/April 2005) 113-125, https://doi.org/10.1002/ldr.665.*
4. *Anna Guðrun Þórhallsdóttir, Árni Daníel Júlíusson, and Helga Ögmundardóttir, "The Sheep, the Market, and the Soil: Environmental Destruction in the Icelandic Highlands, 1880-1910." In Northscapes: History, Technology, and the Making of Northern Environments, ed. Dolly Jørgensen and Sverker Sörlin (UBC Press, 2013), 155-173.*
5. *Ian A. Simpson, Garðar Guðmundsson, Amanda M. Thomson, and Jonathan Cluett. "Assessing the role of winter grazing in historic land degradation, Mývatnssveit, northeast Iceland," Geoarchaeology: An International Journal 19, no. 5, (June 2004) 471-502, https://doi.org/10.1002/gea.20006.*

6. *Michon Scott and Rebecca Lindsey, "2021 Arctic Report Card: Strong greening trend continues across Arctic tundra," National Oceanic and Atmospheric Administration, December 14, 2021.*

7. *Ólafur R. Dýrmundsson, Interview with the author, January 20, 2022.*

8. *Ragnhildur Helga Jónsdóttir, Interview with the author, April 19, 2022.*

9. *Eyjólfur Kristinn Örnólfsson, Interview with the author, February 8, 2022.*

10. *A. Arnalds and S. Runolfsson. "The role of Nootka lupin (Lupinus nootkatensis) for revegetation in Iceland." In Wild and cultivated lupins from the Tropics to the Poles: Proceedings of the 10th International Lupin Conference, Laugarvatn, Iceland, June 19-24, 2002, (Canterbury, New Zealand: International Lupin Association, 2004), 94-96.*

11. *Hulda Brynjólfsdóttir, Interview with the author, January 30, 2022 and February 3, 2022.*

12. *Maja Siska, Interview with the author, January 30, 2022.*

13. *Ragnhildur Helga Jónsdóttir, Interview with the author, September 19, 2021.*

14. *Oscar Aldred, "Réttir in the landscape. A study on the context of focal points," In Dynamics of Northern Societies: Proceedings of the SILA/NABO Conference on Arctic and North Atlantic Archaeology, Copenhagen, vol. 10 (2004) 353-63.*

Additional References

Olafur Arnalds, The soils of Iceland (Dordt, Netherlands: Springer, 2015).

"Hestur Farm," NAT. Nordic Adventure Travel, December 20, 2021, https://nat.is/hestur/.

"GróLind – Sustainable Land Use Based on Ecological Knowledge," International Grassland Congress Proceedings (2021), https://uknowledge.uky.edu/cgi/viewcontent.cgi?article=4177&context=igc.

PREPPERCRAFT: SPECULATIVE FICTION FROM THE USABLE PAST

The Story of the Backwoods Bugout

Kira Clingen

Fig. 01 - North East Retreater's Survey, Kira Clingen.

Preparers, commonly known as preppers, perform acts of landscape-making in anticipation of their particular visions of TEOTWAWKI, or "the end of the world as we know it." These visions are motivated by some apocalyptic vision of the future.

Mainstream media discourse puts preppers "out there," separated from society. This speculative fiction project, "Preppercraft: Speculative Fiction from the Usable Past", argues that they are not out there. They're around here: on television, in cities, suburbs, and next door. They doom-scroll through the same supply chain issues, climatic uncertainties and inflation rates that we're all worried about, and they take action.

To build their bugouts and hideaways, end-of-the-world bunkers and getaway gardens, preppers rely on crafting through *bricolage*, a process of construction using the materials that are on site and on hand. Bricolage depends on an intimate knowledge of materials and ingenuity to piece different parts together to create new landscapes and structures for the unknowns at the end times. Preparing, therefore, is an act of world building and creative design, made through repetitive experiences and encounters in the landscape.

By looking at prepping as acts of bricolage, we can situate the material and technological practices that preppers use in the landscape itself. Each material, from old tires and cinderblocks to live willow and mushroom plugs, has a long historical provenance. These techniques, materials and ideas are unpacked and elaborated within Preppercraft, arguing that design crafted for an unknown future relies heavily on the known, usable past.

By using techniques developed before the advent of cheap electricity and convenient supermarkets, preparation challenges our contemporary societal reliance on just-in-time production and market security. Preparing rejects ornamental garden culture and decorative landscape architecture in favor of productive practices, like planting companion food crops, retaining water, growing building materials, and attracting fauna. These practices build self-reliance in the landscape. This also clarifies that Americans have been preparing for hundreds of years, long before the movement came to be associated with the conservative right wing.

To unfold this story, this speculative visual essay tells the story of an American family who have prepared 100 acres on some tract of non-disclosed land in the New England backwoods. The drawings trace the evolution of an American family alongside their homestead as they plant a black locust barn for their livestock in the event of inclement weather, harvest and boil sap in an old shipping container, erect solar panels, and disguise a gap garden in the woods. They refashion materials and refuse found on site, giving new form to waste materials as they craft a resilient future in the present.

As we stare down an uncertain future, don't be scared, be prepared.

Fig. 02 - North East Retreater's Survey, Kira Clingen.

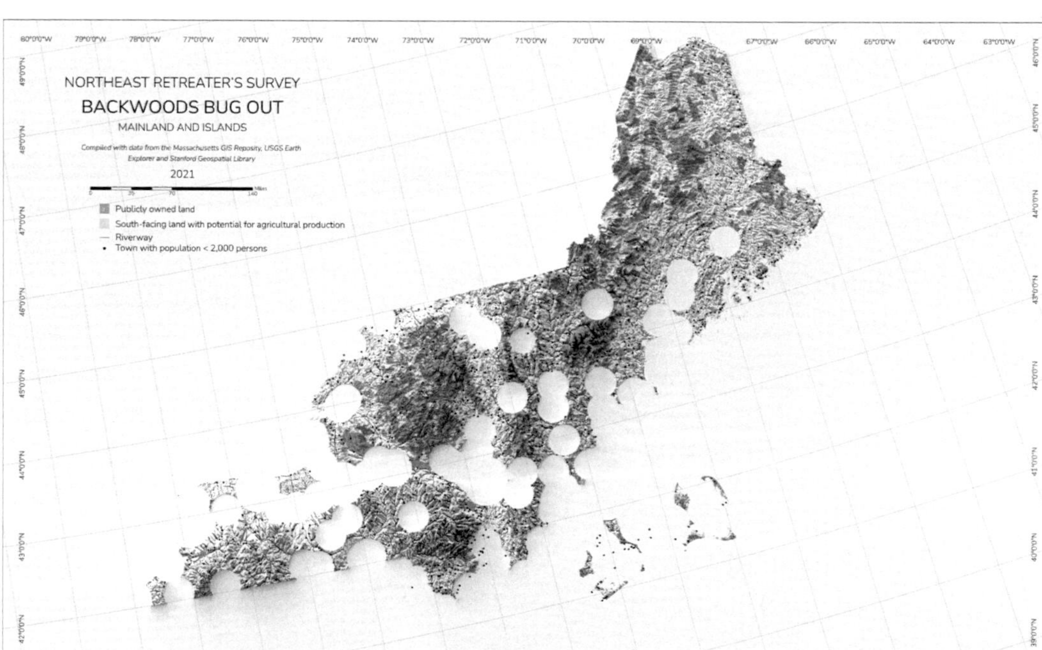

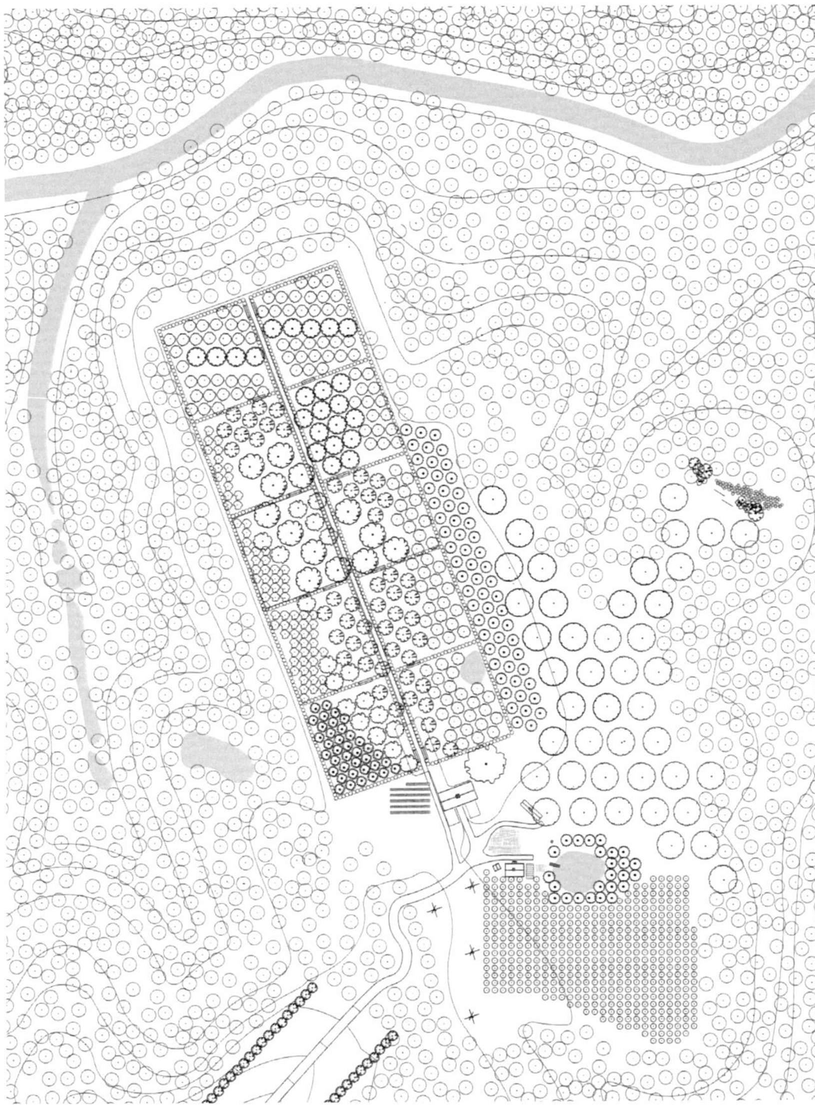

Fig. 03 - The Surroundings, Kira Clingen.

Joe, Ruth, Cal, Owen and the family pointer, Buster, live in the hills, surrounded by water on three sides. Ruth grew up in the Intermountain West, went back to the land in the 1970s, came back from the land in the 1980s, met Joe in the city, and finally abandoned her office job on the eve of Y2K to live outside of the northeast mega-corridor somewhere the sugar maples grow tall and the light pollution is low.

Today, she sells handwoven willow baskets from their coppice, and handles the books for the property. Joe's trade translated from the the city to the country. He's the only plumber in their county, and when he's not on call, he leads their two major cash crop operations: maple sugaring in the spring and logging their silvipasture in the fall. Their sons, Cal and Owen, spend their summers roaming the federal forest adjacent to their property and practicing their shooting skills on the hidden family range.

They chose the 100-acre property for the existing geography, with steep slopes leading down to a meandering river that secludes their property. There are very few visitors to the federal forest land, except loggers who haul their machinery down the unpaved roads once every few years to harvest timber.

On the only side of the property that isn't naturally cut off by a waterway, they've carved a bottleneck into the driveway to funnel all visitors into a trench through a series of observable checkpoints. They continued the trench down the driveway, adapting the military tradition of the abatis, where soldiers put out dead trees heeled into the soil as an obstacle, and instead planted the slope with live willow cuttings that have started to grow into a tangled mat, stabilizing the soil and making it difficult for anyone to approach unless they go up the driveway.

Behind the quick-growing eastern red cedars at the top of the hill, Ruth inoculated matsuke mushrooms into oak logs they cut down elsewhere on their property. They stay shaded under a covering of ostrich ferns, which they harvest for ramps, and damp, surrounded by native wild ginger.

They also rolled larger logs over to the site and positioned them behind the red cedars on angled blocks. If they need to quickly seal the perimeter they can chop down the cedars and roll the logs down the hill. Otherwise, they'll eventually log them for timber and replant on a fifteen year cycle.

Fig. 04 - The Long Road, Kira Clingen.

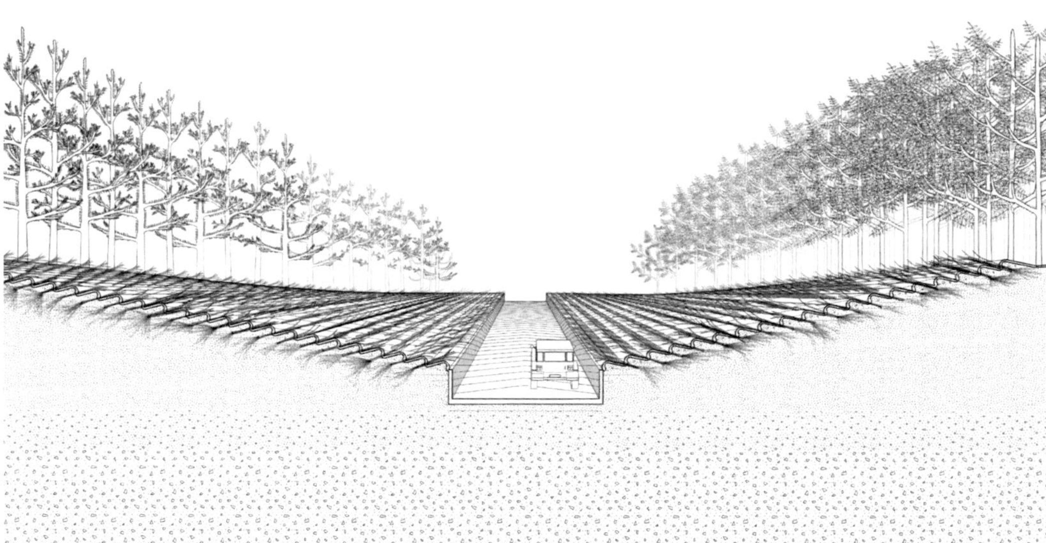

Fig. 05 - Rollway Road, Kira Clingen.

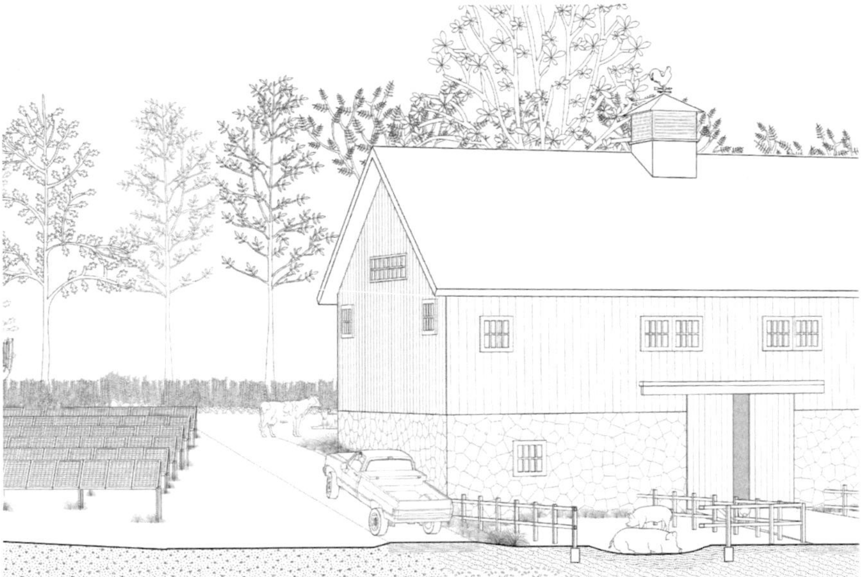

Fig. 06 - (Cattle) Run on the Bank (Barn), Kira Clingen.

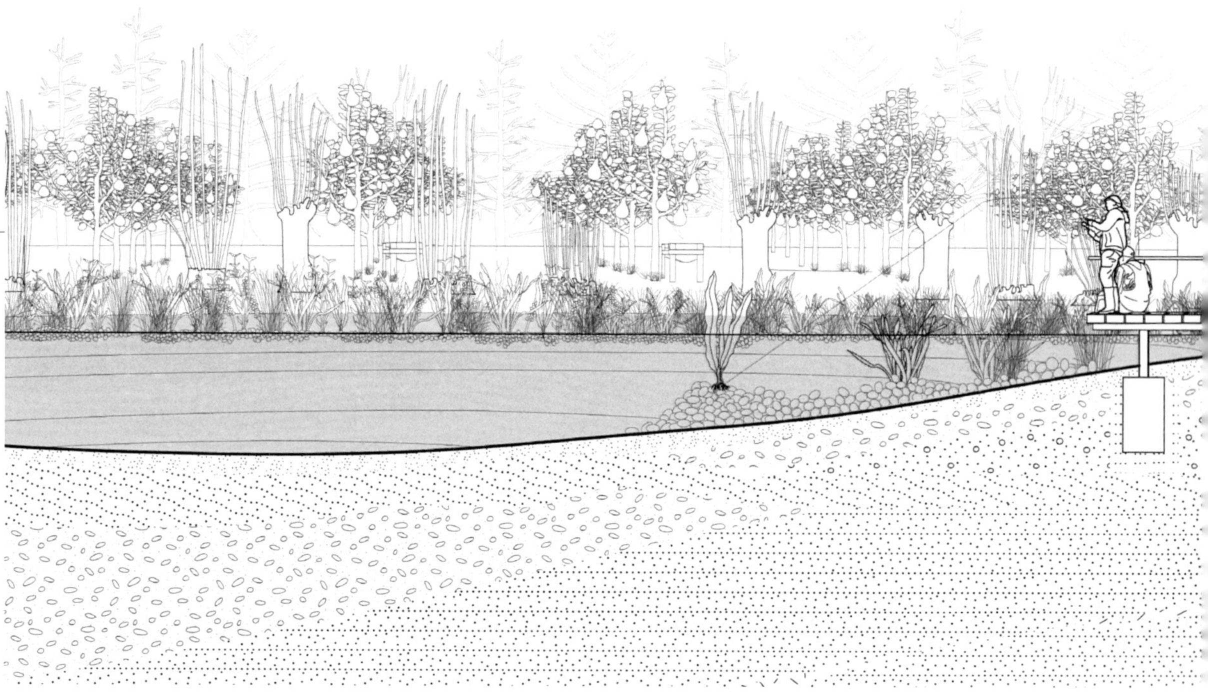

Above the driveway, up on the homestead, the boys fish from the pond they've stocked with crabbies and perch. Joe plans to excavate it to hold bass, but they catch enough protein that they salt and store for the winter months. They kick the extra fruit from the pears, plums and apples in the orchard into the pond to supplement the feed. To keep the orchard prolific, Ruth built top bar bee hives that she's arranged to pollinate the orchard. She also stewards the willow coppices and pollards that she weaves and sells for a premium online.

They grow most of their own vegetables in a large garden bed by the house, which they start in the plastic hoophouse they built with found parts. The family spends most of their time outdoors, though they've added an additional layer of protection to their house with spiky plants under the windows, and an off-grid power system including wind and solar to ensure the security system stays on.

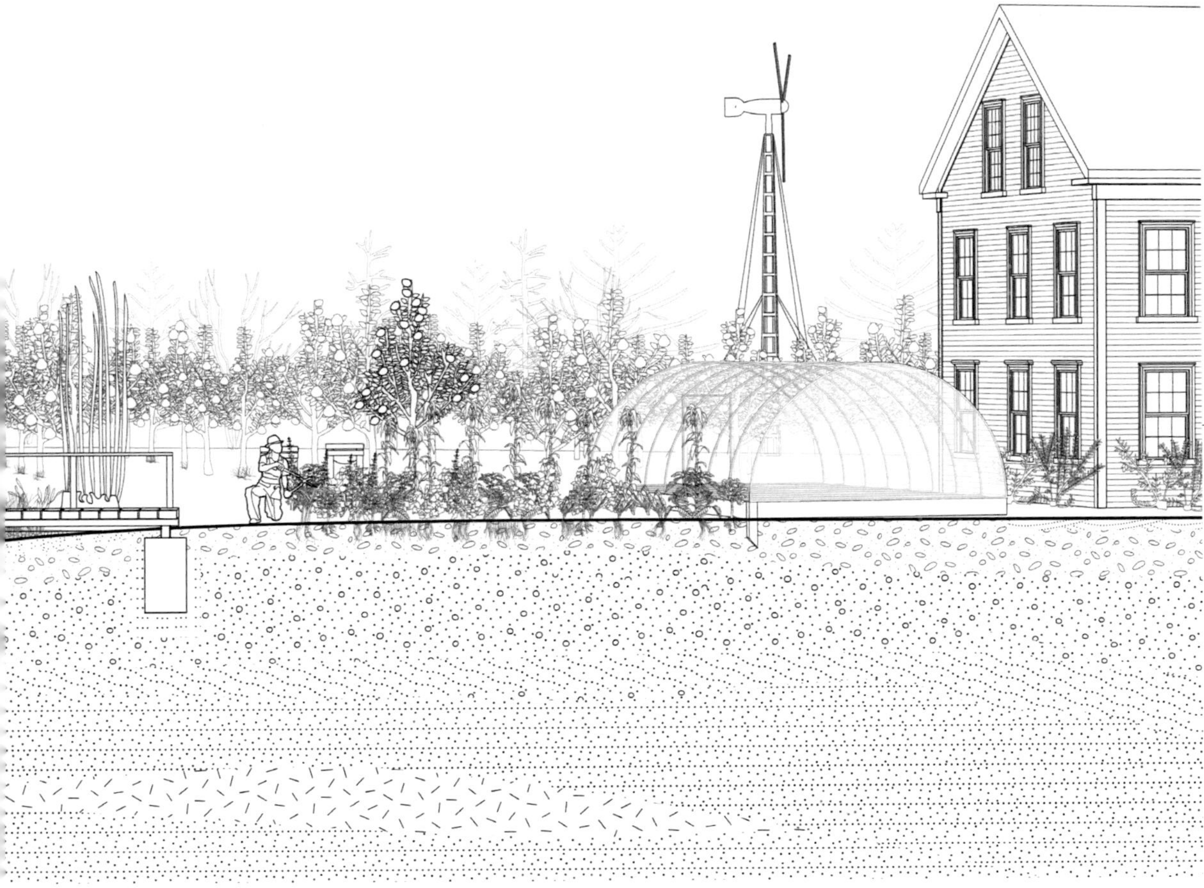

Fig. 07 - Homestead, Kira Clingen.

The solar array is installed on the south-facing slope next to the bank barn. They keep the cows and goats that graze rotationally through the paddocks on the second floor of the barn. The pigs are too destructive to move through the paddocks, tearing up roots and decimating the forage, so they are kept in a pen outside the first floor. They use the manure as compost, and sell anything they don't use to local farmers and nearby homesteaders, who they keep in contact with on Facebook.

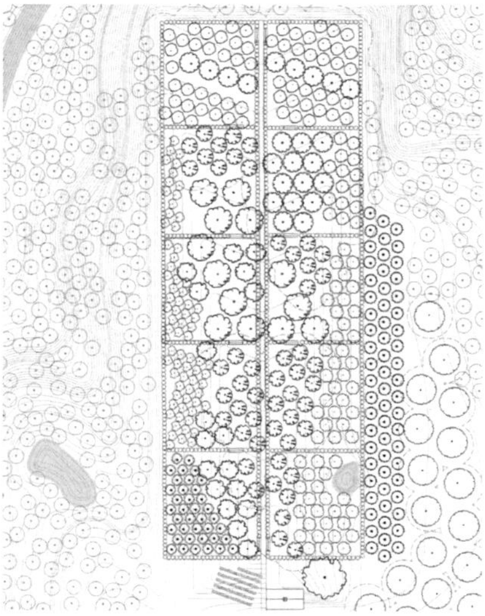

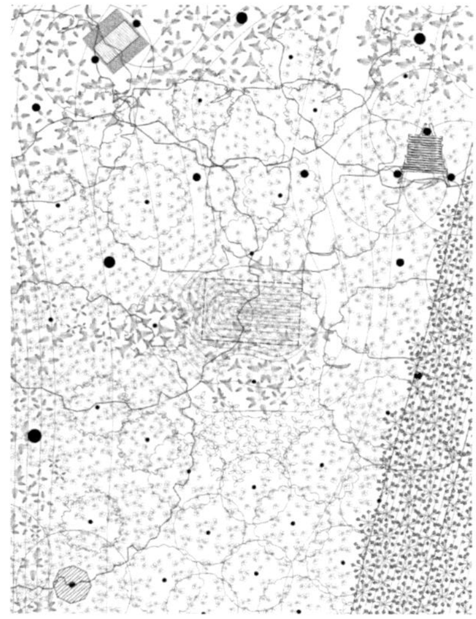

Fig. 08 (Left) - Nutty Silvopasture, Kira Clingen.

Fig. 09 (Right) - The Long Road, Kira Clingen.

Fig. 10 (Next Page) - Rotational Grazing Through the Living Edge, Kira Clingen.

When they're not in the barn for the coldest winter months, their cows graze rotationally through twelve one-acre paddocks, spending five days in each, grazing under the shade cast from various timber species, planted by slope. At the very back of the paddocks is the living barn, a tight cluster of black locust and black walnut where the cattle are moved in the event of a quick-moving summer thunderstorm. The paddocks are bound by a massive osage orange living hedge.

The garden began as a tight cluster of oak , maple and hickory trees. They selected the hickory and sugar maple trees to keep as canopy cover, and logged the rest, plugging mushrooms into oak stumps, and selling timber that they didn't need to build the treehouses. They built a dugout shelter from cheap cinderblocks and piled soil on top of the tin roof to provide insulation and disguise the shelter from prying eyes. They've planted edible species like paw paw, ramps and blackberries over time.

The trees are kept well fertilized by the quadrupeds, who pack the soil with their heels as they move through the trees of the silvipasture, drop manure, and carry seeds from paddock to paddock. Ruth and Joe started the silvipasture with a careful mix of low and tall grasses, borage and herbs, but they've relinquished control and let different species pop up.

They've also relaxed their schedule to rotate the flock through the pasture, and now they go out to pasture each morning and observe the height of the grasses, and move the animals when the grasses are grazed above the soil.

They let the flock into the sugar bush for three days each autumn to mow down the bush and chew down any large shrubs.

Otherwise, the sugar maple stand is empty until early February, when Ruth and Joe load up the sugar shack with wood from their north slope woodlot and fire up the boiler. They sell the syrup they can't use at a farmer's market and an online market-place throughout the year.

They built the sugar shack from an old shipping container, which they sited near their well, which they hope will come in handy in the event of a fire. The willow around the well help to filter away ash and any other contaminants that wash down from the paddocks.

Tucked away in the back southeast corner of their property, Joe went to work putting up a tire berm, which was inspired by "Mike Reynolds Earthships". He carefully followed the NRA's shooting range regulations to make his boys a shooting range where they take out old Pabst Blue Ribbon cans.

The tires are stabilized by staghorn sumac that suckers through the tire bodies and helps to disguise the massive earthwork installation. In the future they'd like to continue experimenting with tire construction, though Ruth is hesitant to bring anything that's been contaminated with road salts into their living areas.

Fig. 11 (Left) - Shipping Container Sugar Shack, Kira Clingen.

Fig. 12 (Right) - The Berm Shooting Range, Kira Clingen.

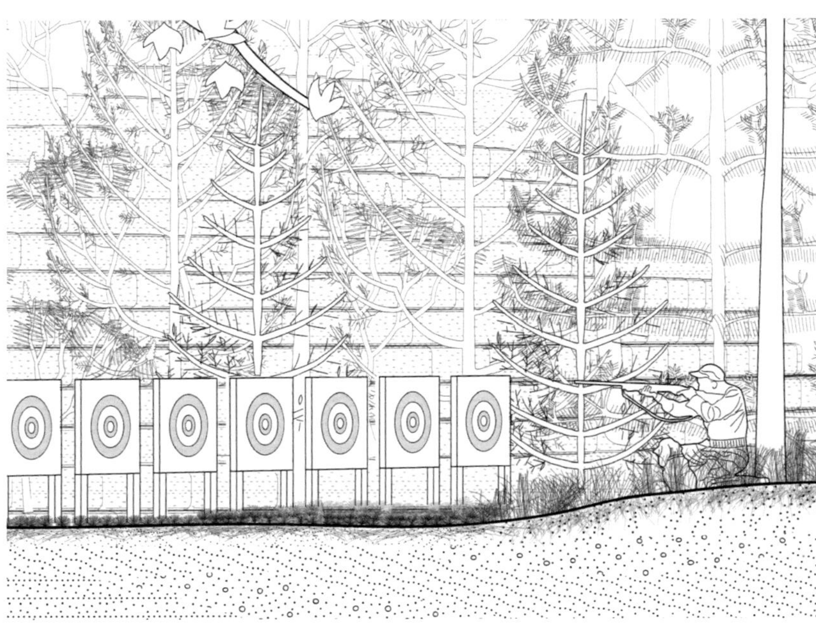

Across the property, Ruth worked for twenty years to establish a gap garden. She and Joe cut down the existing deciduous canopy cover and began to plant an edible understory with ostrich ferns, ramps and berries, shaded by fruit and nut species that camouflage into the existing forest.

Fig. 13 - Bugout Dugout, Kira Clingen.

The family thinks of the space as an outpost on their property—a bugout for their rural home that they can escape to in the event of an emergency. They put up three treehouses in the canopy above their buried shelter, which they modeled after old Cold War fallout building manuals.

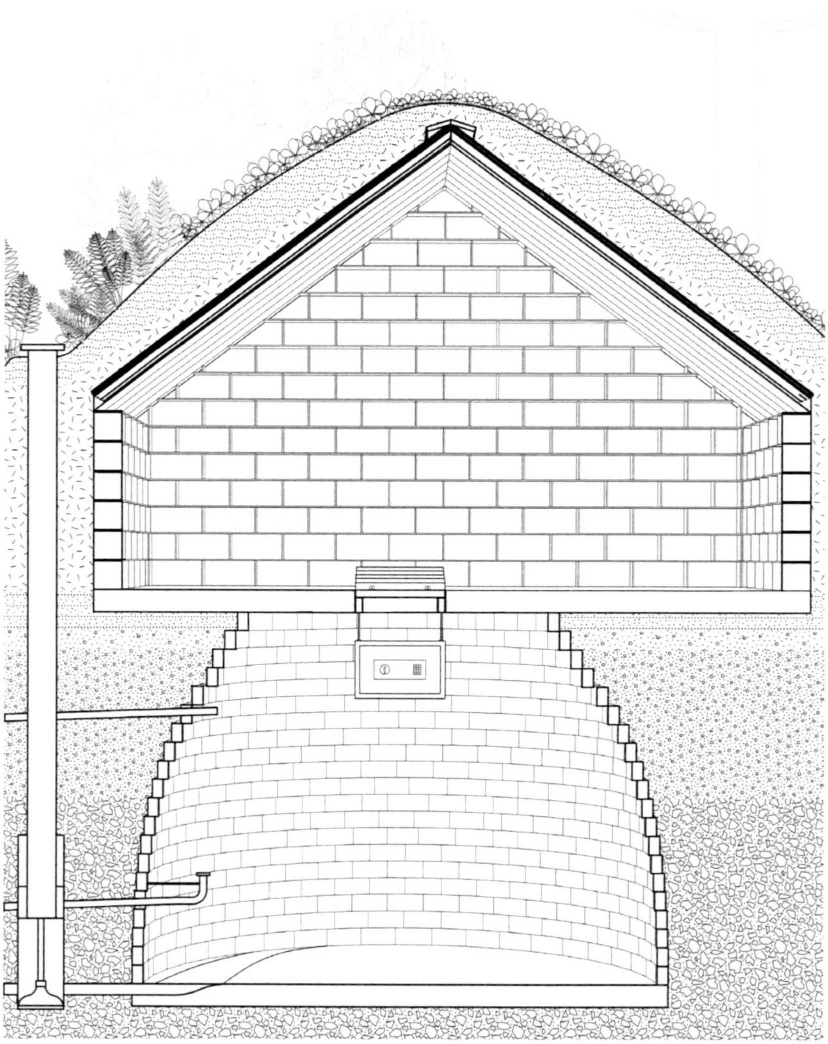

Fig. 14 - Safe House, Kira Clingen.

Even though the garden was originally built as an emergency measure, it's one of the most used areas of the property, where Ruth enjoys a book in the canopy, and Cal and Owen hang out with friends.

While they were digging they also carved out a cistern with a hidden safe buried in case of emergency. For the meantime, they're more than happy watching the stars from their retreat, waiting for the world as we know it to end, and happy that good fences make good neighbors.

References

1. *Crandell, John Stanley. "Constructing the Drive." Country Life 41, 1941.*
2. *Kohlstedt, Kurt. "Hostile Terrain: Tank Traps, Fake Towns and Secret Tunnels of the Korean Borderlands." 99% Invisible. August 14, 2017. www.99percentinvisible.org/article/hostile-terrain-tank-traps-fake-towns-secret-tunnels-korean-borderlands/*

3. Gordon, W.J. "Our Timber and Our Trees." The Leisure Hour, April 1886.

4. Jacke, Dave with Eric Toensmeier. "Edible Forest Gardens: Ecological Design and Practice for Temperate Climate Permaculture Volume II". White River Junction, VT: Chelsea Green Publishing, 2005.

5. Rezvani Motors. "2021 Models." www.rezvanimotors. com/rezvani-models

6. Russell, Stephen. The Essential Guide to Cultivating Mushrooms: Simple and Advanced Techniques for Growing Shiitake, Oyster, Lion's Mane and Maitake Mushrooms at Home. North Adams: Storey Publishing, 2014.

7. Blomgren, Ted and Tracy Frisch. Using Low-Cost Technology to Increase Yields, Improve Quality and Extend the Season. Burlington: University of Vermont Center for Sustainable Agriculture, 2007.

8. Stephens, Don and Barbie. The Survivor's Primer and Up-dated Retreater's Bibliography. Glendale: Stephens Publishing Company, 1976.

9. Wang, Dan et al. "A physiological and biophysical model of coppice willow (Salix spp.) production yields for the contiguous USA in current and future climate scenarios." Plant, Cell and Environment 38, no. 9 (2015): 1850-1856.

10. Ensminger, Robert. The Pennsylvania Barn: Its Origin, Evolution and Distribution in America. Baltimore: John Hopkins University Press, 2003.

11. Birdseye Architects. Bank Barn. Woodstock, New York, 2019.

12. Radford, William A. Radford's Practical Barn Plans Chicago, IL: The Radford Architectural Co., 1909.

13. Gali-Izard, Teresa. "PRODUCTIVE RESURGENCES: The Garden of the XXI Century." Cambridge: Harvard University Graduate School of Design, 2019.

14. Hawken, Paul. "Silvopasture." Drawdown: The Most Comprehensive Plan Ever Proposed to Reverse Global Warming. New York: Penguin Books, 2017, p. 50.

15. Sundqvist, Anneli Carter. "Small Scale Forestry for the Homestead." Mother Earth News. March 12, 2013.

16. Pliny the Elder. "Chapter 77 - Walnuts: Twenty-Four Remedies." The Natural History Book XXIII. 77 AD.

17. Undersander, Dan, Beth Albert, Dennis Cosgrove, Dennis Johnson, Paul Peterson. Pastures for Profit: A Guide to Rotational Grazing. Madison: Cooperative Extension Publishing, 2002, p. 2.

18. United States Department of Agriculture. "Osage Hedges." In Report of the Commissioner of Agriculture: for the Year 1869. Washington, D.C.: Government Print Office, 1869, p. 246.

19. Dirr, Michael. Dirr's Encyclopedia of Trees and Shrubs. Portland, O.R.: Timberland Press, 2008, p. 53.

20. Lancaster, Kenneth F., Russell S. Walters, Frederick M. Laing, Raymond T. Foulds. "A Silvicultural Guide for Developing a Sugarbush." Res Paper NE-286. Upper Darby, P.A.: US Department of Agriculture, Forest Service, Northeastern Forest Experiment Station, 1974.

21. Richard G. Mitchell, Jr. Dancing at Armageddon: Survivalism and Chaos in Modern Times. Chicago: The University of Chicago Press, 2002, 85.

22. United States Department of Defense. Family Shelter Designs. Washington, D.C.: United States Department of Defense, 1962.

23. Loomis, Alfred F. "Homely Experiments in Iceless Refrigeration." Country Life 33 (1918): 74.

What fills up the space of spaced repetition?

Does one have to be aware of a ritual to take part in it?

How does a practice transcend space or time?

What fills up the space of spaced repetition?

Does one have to be aware of a ritual to take part in it?

How does a practice transcend space or time?

RITUAL

TEST PLOT

Jenny Jones

Figs. 01-07 - Documentation of Test Plot's installation and maintenance, by Jenny Jones.

Test Plot is an ongoing experiment in community land care. The test is straightforward: what are the simplest inputs required for the re-establishment of native ecologies in neglected public spaces? And what is our community capacity for ground-up land stewardship?

Test Plot operates with a repair and care mindset. Before we spend money and time on high-gloss park designs, we ought to take care of the public and open space we already have. Vacant lots, blacktop schoolyards, roadside planting strips, outdated parks. Before we go to Mars, maybe we ought to figure out this Earth thing?
Test Plot grew out of frustration with the state of Elysian Park, the oldest public park in Los Angeles, a city where the lack of municipal investment in land care is glaring. Elysian Park, which has been called a 'zombie forest'[1], has swaths of formerly fashionable Eucalyptus trees that are dead or dying, and a ground plane of aggressive invasive annuals that like to catch fire.
We wondered if we might just start our own garden in the park. Would the city let us? Yes...as it turns out, they are desperate for help. So long as we are doing right by the site and the people involved, they approve. We sort out conditions and logistics, design it all around available working infrastructure, and consult with as many people as we can. We promise to care and to communicate.
Our first Test Plot was installed around the perimeter of Marian Harlow Grove, an established community garden centered on a lone public hose bibb. This water source is sacred in a summer-dry city

arcing towards desertification. We honor the existing garden of aloes, jade, cypress, and palms, and skirt around to the dry edges of the grove. Here we plant black sage, oaks, lemonade berry, and grasses. The gophers promptly eat every single grass, and we kick ourselves for deciding to forgo gopher cages.

But we accept our failings and are happy to be learning. We rethink, replant. We document and collect data, but we also call our volunteer days 'Plant Church' and leave room for improvisation and intuition. Test Plot lies somewhere between ecological restoration and gardening, and we are happy to be in that grey area.

The original vision was for Little Test Plots Everywhere, and we are on our way. With USC's with department of Landscape Architecture, we have installed two more plots--at Rio de Los Angeles State Park and Baldwin Hills Scenic Overlook. And a fourth is on the way in Debs Park, in partnership with the local Audubon Center.

Each site has its own geographic and ecological parameters , and its own particularities of community engagement. We are both agile and slow in our work, and we meet sites and people where they are, using who/what is available in ways that are efficient.

We hope to keep growing, and to connect with more members of the land care community to honor the art of maintenance and the value of caretaking.

(Test Plot was founded by Terremoto and Saturate, in collaboration with the Citizen's Committee to Save Elysian Park)

Figs.02-03 (opposite page)

Notes

(1) Los Angeles Times. "Recovery Plan Lies Dormant as Elysian Park's Exotic Trees Die Off," December 21, 2015. https://www.latimes.com/local/california/la-me-elysian-park-dieoff-20151221-story.html.

Figs. 04-05

Figs. 06-07

ECOLOGICAL
RESTORATION IN
PROGRESS —
Feel free to use spigot, but
Please replace hose and make
Sure water is ON when finished
Thanks!

TOWARDS THE CORE

working (worming) underneath landscape architecture

Larissa Belcic, writing for Nocturnal Medicine

Fig. 01 - Source material by Nocturnal Medicine, image altered by LUNCH editors.

The techniques of landscape architecture as we were instructed in them include distance as a starting condition. During our education, not once did someone ask us—how does land live in you, and you in it? Our identities and ancestral legacies were subsumed into a milky monogamous slush poured into the molds of our tools; the instruments we were instructed to wield in order to, ever so surgically, operate on the environmental-cultural body.

Within the idea of distance is interwoven the notion of Separate. I am over here, and you are over there. Mind separate from body, human separate from nature, woman separate from man, etc. But ideas of distance are now an absurd pantomime, and those who cling to them increasingly play the fool as insect populations face extinction, wildfires rage on, extreme storms grow more rampant, and crude oil spills out across the ocean. As designers reckoning with these realities, we look at the tools that we were given, and find them, on their own, pretty inadequate to the task. Technologically, the tools of the trade advance consistently, but their ontological evolution is much slower, and the technological advancements tend to reproduce stances of distance that have been foundational for so long in Western perspectives.

And so in our practice, Nocturnal Medicine, we've been asking ourselves—How can we crawl underneath, into a new way of working? How can we get sticky with it, dirty with it? And by "asking," we mean more like—we've just been trying to do it: to get underneath, to get inside, to swallow, to intertwine.

Timothy Morton has a great phrase to describe this—the "zero landscape."[1] That there is no more first, or second, or third person perspective in relation to "landscape" (me and landscape, you and landscape, them and landscape), but a total collapse wherein us-and-landscape are just all mashed up together.

In our work right now, we've moved away from designing the landscape to attempting to operate on the cultural body itself. Ecocide has emerged from cultural dynamics, and therefore to address it, we need cultural change. We do this through a few ways: creating sacred spaces and rituals that guide people to face and connect with the implications of our changing planet, and creating transformative experiences that allow for deep learning at the level of the unconscious with the potential to shift worldview. Research in climate psychology and sociology shows that these methods are key tentpoles to constructing healthier relationships with the environment.

What do we ourselves need to do, and be, in order to do this work? What kind of techniques does the work itself require? What follows is a dive into this—a partially-illuminated journey into the caverns of our unlearning and relearning craft. Partially-illuminated by necessity, because there is so much we don't know and are still working to understand, so much knowledge held by others that we stand humble before, and so much to discover within ourselves.

INTUITION	TRANSMUTATION	TRUTH TELLING
TRANCE	RESEARCH	EMBODIMENT
PRACTICE	ANCESTRY	UNCERTAINTY

INTUITION

"Setting my life free from the head's agenda...to unfold where intuition is leading me."[2]

Fig. 02 - (above) Chaos Blossoms, Nocturnal Medicine.

We move from intuition. Intuition is the opposite of detachment from the subject; it is embodying the sensing body and moving with other forms. It is "the journey from our conscious mind to the unconscious level."[3] When we are caught up in confusion, constructs and restraints, intuition allows us a way out through going down—through submersion into the unconscious seas. It is the sinking below the thinking body into the feeling self.

TRANCE

Trance is discussed within meditation, religion, collective dance, magic, art-making (as in a flow state). It is often understood as a kind of altered consciousness—a liminal state of suspension between wakefulness and deep sleep. Trance can be a pathway through which intuition moves from within to the without, a channel through which it is accessed and flows into material form. There are known gateways to trance states (i.e. dance, hypnosis, meditation, chemical substances), and through practice they may be achieved at will. In trance states, we may discover truths and connections that otherwise elude us; we may touch into the underneath of ourselves, and journey through the flow of ourselves, through our collectivity with others, through time-space, and intertwine with the dynamic forces at play.

In the tradition of mediumship, working from trance states allows us to bring forth emanations from the void that may be beyond our conscious mind.

Fig. 03 (previous spread) - Under the Tongue, Nocturnal Medicine.

PRACTICE

I cannot speak on what I have not known; I cannot lead to where I have no understanding. Thus the necessity of practice. Practice within the design disciplines often refers to a professional vehicle—"my practice." The structure of technical and organizational authority through which I exercise my expertise. This is different from "practice" as in to keep trying without finality on the immediate horizon—to grow a set of skills through the definitively unfinal doing of the thing.

The exploration and transformation of the self is the practice. Practice is the continuous return to the attempt: to unlearn what must be unlearned, to understand what has been beyond understanding, to surrender in the face of what can never be known, controlled, or changed, to "unfold where intuition is leading me."[4]

Practice is the nights spent on the dance floor. In the words of choreographer Michele Rizzo, dancing is "the practice that compensate[s] for the fact that we can never be each other."[5] Practice is the daily living with grief and joy, the constant calling of attention to my relationships, my context, and my responsibilities. Practice is the time spent in reverence to and communication with the sacred, wherever you find it. Such as—"For me the clubs are kind of the new temples," says musician Aisha Devi.[6] Clubs are sites of deep play—places that offer the potential for altered states of liberation, for touching into "the sacred and the holy" and in so doing sinking into "who we are and all we wish to be."[7]

TRANSMUTATION & MOVING BETWEEN REALMS

> How [to] represent on a two-dimensional surface a three-dimensional form, or in a three-dimensional image a multi-dimensional meaning?...As dreams that were momentous by night may seem simply silly in the light of day, so the poet and the prophet can discover themselves playing the idiot before a jury of sober eyes. But...the work of representing eternity in time, and perceiving in time eternity, cannot be avoided.[8]

It doesn't seem to be enough to voyage the intuitive realms, to sail the blissful seas of sensuality on the creative journey. What has been learned must be brought back and shared with the world-at-large. In a recent conversation with Mahtab Max Moinian, we discussed the phrase "as within, so without;" that while the interior journey and the development of the self are necessary (as within), there is a responsibility to communicate learning and enact change (so without). It is the responsibility discussed by Joseph Campbell in *The Hero with a Thousand Faces*—that the true task is not the journey, but the conveying of what was seen and learned.

Here, the rigors of architectural technique have their place. These tools have been developed over millennia in order to structure our perceptions of the polyphony of entities that churn, squirm and gyrate themselves to form "the world." Through these tools, we may create the grounds for clarity of intention and intervention. The movement between modes of perceiving and articulation is iterative and non-linear—from intuition, trance, practice and play to the plan and diagram, translating multi-dimensional understandings into precise forms with a specificity of dimension, scale and material.

RESEARCH

Reference to and reverence for what has come before. Research is a conversation with what is outside myself—across space and time—and through research my body of understanding can grow beyond the limitations of my own locality. Research allows us to receive that which has been metabolized and understood by others. Through research, we map the ground on which we stand; we uncover its caverns and byways, the texture of its soils, and we receive support in envisioning what is possible.

ANCESTRY

> "We carry the energetic suffering of our ancestry."[9]

Designing for a world shaped by violences demands that you know who you are. What worlds do you contain? What is yours to mend, to reckon with, to heal from, to release, to reclaim? On what grounds do you step into the realm of intervention?

Within our practice, we work as a hybrid body with multiple parts. We are not one legacy, we are many. Persian, Istrian, Italian-American, Jewish, Catholic, Los Angeles, New Jersey, brown, white, immigrant: 1st-generation, 2nd-generation, 4th-generation. And we are designing for communities that are like this—complex agglomerations of ancestral pasts who've all shown up in the same space at a particular moment.

And so it is like this—being the thing that you are, being grounded in your own identity and your own ancestral legacy and its pain and joy, knowing your own place in the story and your own set of responsibilities, and from there feeling out when to follow, when to speak, when to nod your head and shake your hips from the edge of the circle, and when to guard space fiercely without stepping into it.

TRUTH TELLING

> "Commitment to truth telling lays the groundwork for the openness and honesty that is the heartbeat of love."[10]

bell hooks teaches that honesty is the foundation of a loving society. In this way, commitment to truth telling is at the heart of the work. When we talk about climate change, when we talk about environmental degradation, we need to be as clear as possible about the truths on the table. How did we get here? For the first time, this year the Intergovernmental Panel on Climate Change (IPCC) put out a report that named "colonialism" as a cause and perpetuator of climate change. In the words of Brazilian Indigenous activist Taily Terena, "Colonialism caused climate change. Our rights and traditional knowledge are the solution."[11]

Fig. 04 - (below) Sun Stone Abyss, Nocturnal Medicine.

The United States of America is built out of ideologies that call for massive-scale acts of genocide and enslavement of peoples and war-fueled, wealth-oriented domination of land. Those ideologies continue to govern the country, its actions towards those not protected under its patriarchal white supremacist model, and its attitude towards the global community. Let's be honest about that.

Being honest is not about guilting or shaming; really, it has nothing to do with them. Listen to Layli Long-Soldier citing Faith Spotted Eagle, saying "for non-Native people, hearing and listening to these narratives, these histories, and engaging in a conversation, it is not about guilt, and it's not about shame. It is about...'freedom from denial.' It allows a liberation."[12]

Truth telling is liberation. Sociologist Kari Norgaard identified that at the heart of climate change inaction in wealthy Western countries is a form of denial that is orchestrated at the social-cultural level—a system of relational protocols that help people avoid acknowledging the realities of climate change with their deepest selves; that keep the truth outside so that the illusion of existential safety can be preserved.[13] Deep transformational shifts are not only necessary, but they are coming, denial or not. Through truth telling, we can rise to the occasion of our own evolution.

EMBODIMENT

We are trying to make work as an instance, an occurrence, of a regenerated world. We do not make models or prototypes—no, it IS the thing, temporarily formed. The work takes seriously the idea that things could be different, and it embodies that world, often only for a night before the sun rises and things are as they are. "The apocalypse is always easier to imagine," writes Rebecca Solnit, "than the strange, circuitous routes to what comes next."[12] In the face of harm and destruction, we aim to walk, crawl, slither the path to what comes next.

This is not just true of the work itself, but of the way it's done. Can we embody, in our relationship with each other as partners, in our relationships with networks of allies, collaborators, conspirators, in our relationship with money and resources, a world that is the one we dream of? We fail often, and even more often we don't know the path, but it is a constant, active practice of refusal to succumb to the terrors of what is.

The work itself is an invitation to embodiment. To let our collective pain and pleasure flow within us, to invite it to entangle and swirl with the visceral sensations of mud in our fingers, smoke in our lungs, to grow our vitality from and with the muck.

Through the touch of bodies, we open to the beauty and power of others. We allow ourselves to be changed through the touch of another, and for that touch to remind us what is sacred in them, and in us. Embodiment can pierce avoidance and the illusion of tidiness and separateness, and bring us into the stew of "everything everywhere all at once."

UNCERTAINTY

> "Darkness might be a medium of vision, and descent may be a movement toward revelation."[15]

The welcoming of uncertainty as the inescapable state—in the design process, in the construction and enacting of work, and in living. The ability to thrive in uncertainty, and to be resilient and flow with the unpredictable, is essential as we continue our roll into an era marked by shifts in longstanding patterns (i.e., in seasonal cycles).

In our work, we often work in the format of the event and experience—formats in which the participants are invited agents in the tenor and lifespan of the work. Its "success" rides on them. As designers, we feel the way this tempts anxiety—the knot of fear in our bellies birthed from knowing we cannot control the outcome and failure is possible. Again and again, we bring ourselves to face the uncertainty inherent in relational work (which all landscape architecture is, whether it acknowledges it or not), and to face the fear it provokes. A design that attempts to edit out the possibility of the unexpected is grasping at the illusion of complete power in the face of the truth that we can't know, we can't control; living is an act of risk.

We hope to find the strength that comes from embracing the unknown—that paradoxically this may be the only way to be safe, or at least, to be at ease. And that through this stance, we can ride with the changes that are to come our way. We want to make work that can be a lantern—that walks you down the darkening path, the light slowly diminishing as you go, until you are left in the void to discover in yourself your own capacity for swimming in nothing. We want to make work that celebrates you once you find yourself there, and through that celebration, births a community resilient, loving, and ready.

Notes

1. *Timothy Morton, "Zero Landscapes in the Time of Hyperobjects," Graz Architectural Magazine, Spring 2011, 78–87.*

2. *M.A. Beat feat. Laraaji, "Brain Off," Track 1 on Sans soleil, BMM Records, 2017.*

3. *Erkka Laininen, "Transforming Our Worldview Towards a Sustainable Future," in Sustainability, Human Well-Being, and the Future of Education, ed. Justin W. Cook (Cham: Palgrave Macmillan, 2018), 178.*

4. *M.A. Beat feat. Laraaji, Brain Off.*

5. *Isabel Parkes, "Michele Rizzo Stages Acts of 'Communal Becoming'," Frieze, November 24, 2021, https://www.frieze.com/article/michele-rizzo-stages-acts-communal-becoming.*

6. *"The Ritualistic Live Celebration of Aïsha Devi: MUTEK 2016." Youtube video. Posted by FACTmagazine, August 4, 2016, https://www.youtube.com/watch?v=e_HiQJSoH4A.*

7. *Maria Popova, "Diane Ackerman on the Evolutionary and Existential Purpose of Deep Play," The Marginalian, August 4, 2016, https://www.themarginalian.org/2016/08/04/diane-ackerman-deep-play/.*

8. *Joseph Campbell, The Hero with a Thousand Faces (Princeton: Princeton University Press, 1968).*

9. *Lama Rod Owens (@lamarodofficial), Liberation of Ancestors, May 4 2022, https://www.instagram.com/p/CdJY7Q3jz9W/.*

10. *bell hooks, all about love: new visions. (New York: Harper Perennial, 2001), 53.*

11. *Yessenia Funes, "Yes, Colonialism Caused Climate Change, IPCC Reports." Atmos: The Frontline, April 4 2022, https://atmos.earth/ipcc-report-colonialism-climate-change/.*

12. *Layli Long Soldier (Layli Long Soldier: The Freedom of Real Apologies), interview with Krista Tippett, On Being, podcast audio, March 30, 2017, https://onbeing.org/programs/layli-long-soldier-the-freedom-of-real-apologies/*

13. *Kari Norgaard, Living in Denial: Climate Change, Emotions, and Everyday Life. (Cambridge: MIT Press, 2011).*

14. *Rebecca Solnit. Hope in the Dark: Untold Histories, Wild Possibilities. (Chicago: Nation Books, 2006).*

15. *Roberb Macfarlane (Robert Macfarlane: The Worlds Beneath Our Feet), interviewed by Krista Tippet, On Being, podcast audio, November 14, 2019, https://onbeing.org/programs/robert-macfarlane-the-worlds-beneath-our-feet/.*

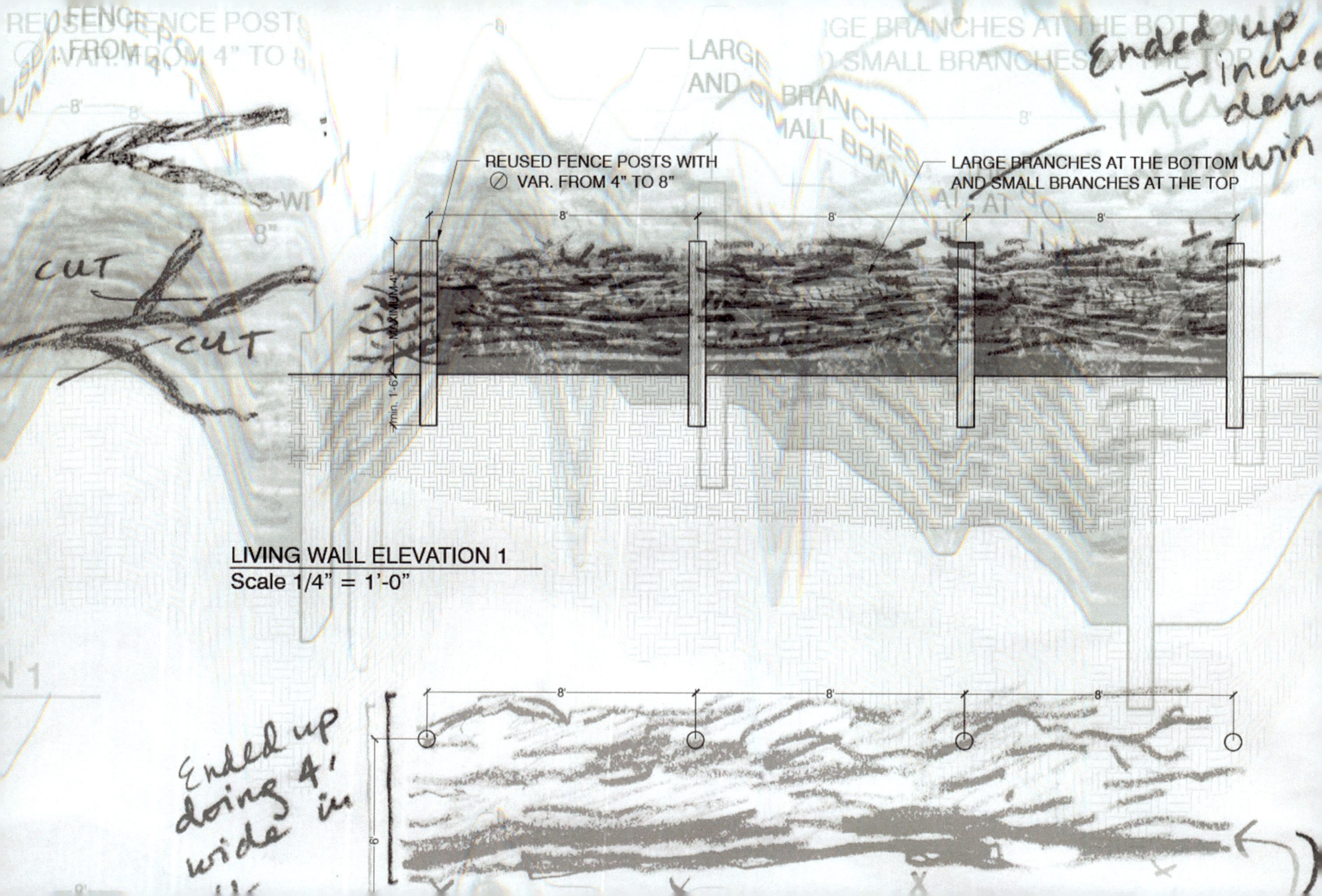
REUSED FENCE POSTS WITH
∅ VAR. FROM 4" TO 8"
LARGE BRANCHES AT THE BOTTOM
AND SMALL BRANCHES AT THE TOP
8'
8'
8'
MAXIMUM 4'
min. 1'-6"
CUT
CUT
LIVING WALL ELEVATION 1
Scale 1/4" = 1'-0"
8'
8'
8'
6'
Ended up doing 4' wide in

GROW CLOSER:
PRUNE, CHIP, AND STACK

Practice Landscape (Sarah Diamond, Rosetta S. Elkin, Emily Hicks, and Joanna Lombard)

All images courtesy of Practice Landscape

Fig. 01 - Source material by Practice Landscape, image altered by LUNCH editors

To embrace the ubiquity of land-based practices is to acknowledge two facets of the human condition: First, the depth and diversity of human-plant relationships and second, the restraints of life on the land. The relationship humans cultivate are land-based because we are terrestrial species. This essayette (thank you, Ross Gay)[1] draws on the paradoxical situation that despite the increasing attention to human identity, landscape connectivity is diminishing.

The paradox becomes our most pressing opportunity to link seemingly disparate earthly relations. Which is why we turn to practice; simple acts of repetition, common refrains of everyday reprise, asserted over time and across place, establish the character of this connection. Quotidien rituals that require us to work together reveal these relationships through commonplace acts, and it is through these acts that landscape extends beyond form and instigates process. Processes, events, and systems deepen human-plant relationships, fostering closer bonds with the land.

Robin Wall Kimmerer uses the phrase "becoming indigenous,"[2] in reference to an Ojibwe origin story that describes how humankind grew closer to the newly formed lands of Turtle Island. To grow closer is to change or adapt such that becoming "indigenous to place" becomes a matter of survival that originates in relation to the soils, plants, and waters of a regional environment. But Kimmerer goes beyond the mythology and suggests that familiarity between people and place is cultivated through everyday practices—practices of respect for the plants that sustain humans and other creatures and reciprocity for the relationships between all breathing organisms.

Practices are found in listening, observing, learning, and contributing. The term "contributing" appears often in Kimmerer's prose,[3] extending the meaning of practice to include that which brings together. The Oxford dictionary proposes that a contribution must be made and received; it indicates common purpose and shares the spirit of gift giving. Contributions are codependent. Marijke van der Veen explores contribution in the context of mutual processes;[4] for instance, the ways in which people are changed by the properties of plants, and plants are changed by their interactions with humankind. This is more than chemical exchange, it is a radical form of collaboration, a mutual contribution.

The question this essayette asks is how can contribution—a bringing together—be synchronized with the temporal scales of landscape architecture? Can design defend the abundance of existing biotic materials to deepen the relationship between people and place? Contributions between humans are familiar and reappear in the kindness of emotional support, the generosity of mentorship and the selfless acts of care found in medicinal and therapeutic traditions, for instance. We suggest that the urge to grow closer is an act of design that requires attention to what is at hand, and under foot, and we highlight three practices that represent this attentiveness to illustrate human-plant contributions.

Fig. 02 - photos of prune, chip, and stack technics

SAWDUST ... HELLEBORE ... ON PATH

COFFEE CHAFF

doubled posts (4' o.c.) ... to prevent collapse

...mella foliacea?

Amanita flavoconia
OR Mycena leaiana

PRUNE

Woody plants respond to damage. As trees and shrubs break, bend, snap or split, their cambium—the layer of actively dividing cells below the bark—makes secondary growth possible. Careful pruning can take advantage of this vigorous response to disturbance. Pruning is a practice between human and plant life that has persisted for centuries as seen in the methods of coppicing and pollarding trees for fuel, food, and settlement.[5] The most abundant species are those best adapted to disturbance. When a large storm rolls in, the forces that prune woody plants are akin to a vast army of massive and indiscriminate clippers. Consider the episodic disturbances in South Florida, as waves crash, salination creeps and hurricanes smash into woody plants (Fig. 03).

Fig. 03 - Prune. Captiva, Florida.

On Captiva, a barrier island formation on Florida's Gulf coast, a large Australian pine (*Casuarina equisetifolia*) falls, suddenly introducing sunlight to a patch of soil and subsequently transforming the ground into a dense stand of sprouting Royal poinciana (*Delonix regia*).[6] Sea grape (*Coccoloba uvifera*) along a footpath's edge topples and uproots in a storm, sprouting new growth up and down its horizontal trunk. The remnant of a Gumbo limbo (*Bursera simaruba*), long-ago cut down and forgotten in an overgrown thicket, is found with three vigorous new shoots growing vertically from the stump. Young trees, from old stumps.

Ecologists and botanists frame disturbance in the context of ecological succession. More colloquially, horticulturalist and botanist Peter Del Tredici calls stump sprouters "deeply disturbed."[7] For designers, disturbance lays the foundation of adaptive management practices aligned with care for individual plants. Prune too often or incorrectly and you kill the plant. But, with careful study and in response to plant behavior, pruning is not only a means to bring in sunlight, increase air circulation and make an area safer for humans, but a long-term management strategy for an increasingly extreme climate.

> To prune is to design with disturbance.

Humans manipulate plants, and in response, plants change people. Humans can make choices, have intentions, while plants respond reflexively to stimuli, to disturbance. If we allow ourselves to slow down and work with the time scales of other species, novel management practices emerge. Root suckers become chip mulch, vigorous branching is cut and stacked as material for screens, and live cuttings are planted to grow a living fence.

1. Cabbage palms are "de-bearded," (dead, brown fronds removed)
2. Leaf sheaths are removed from fronds before storage
3. Frond storage in "frond rows" with all stems aligned.

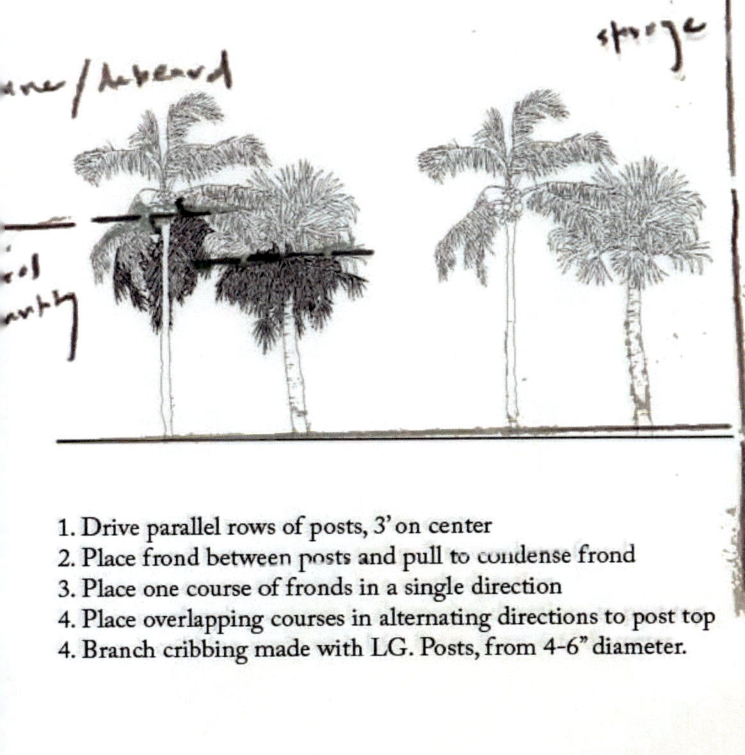

1. Drive parallel rows of posts, 3' on center
2. Place frond between posts and pull to condense frond
3. Place one course of fronds in a single direction
4. Place overlapping courses in alternating directions to post top
4. Branch cribbing made with LG. Posts, from 4-6" diameter.

CHIP

Mulch is not a noun; it is a biology.

Mulching not only reduces waste, it fosters and encourages the growth of microorganisms. Thinking about mulch as a process rather than a product is a critical distinction to engendering landscape practices. To mulch is to work with a biology of microorganisms by converting plant materials for different design consequences. Mulching, much like composting, requires a consideration of the multitude and variety of plants that support our terrestrial species. Designing with mulch is an offshoot of designing with plant life because mulch itself is alive. Consider wood chips, the biproduct of brush sites, woodworking efforts, and municipal chipping programs. Any size or scale of wood chip refers to the shredded, chipped, and ground up waste from woody plants. There are as many kinds of wood chips as there are trees and shrubs, and thousands more in the mixing and mingling of species.

Fig. 04 - Chip. Southern Vermont.

Wood chips work to suppress spontaneous plants because the micro-organisms that decompose wood chips require nitrogen in amounts greater than are available in the wood chips alone. The myriad micro-organisms will seek the nitrogen they need to survive from the soil, which means that they compete with plant roots for the available nitrogen. And they usually win, or at least if the mulch is deep enough, the microorganisms will forage more successfully than the plants.

When brought to scale, mulching enables practices to connect with other local laborers since it is a byproduct of so many industries: forestry, municipal maintenance, farming, roasting, and fishing. Chip is readily available in southern Vermont, where design not only considers where to place woody mulch, but necessarily includes where to source mulch. When a designer works with process, they activate a network of local and regional businesses. When designers consider where to order mulch, they activate a sector of the economy based on consumer demand. Buying mulch begins to look like a malpractice if mulch itself can be seen as design. Typically, mulch is purchased in a plastic bag, dyed various tonal colors, and delivered to a site by the cubic foot.

The substantial scale of this industry is quickly confirmed by the number of mulch calculators and mulch competitors vying for attention and business. Landscape architects who specify mulch are essentially shopping, rather than designing. Pick up some chip instead, and if it cannot be sourced—make some.

SAWDUST AROUND HELLEBORES + H... ON PATH

COFFEE CHAFF

OR HOPS?

NO TRUCKS PAST THIS POINT

LEAF MOULD FOR INSULATION

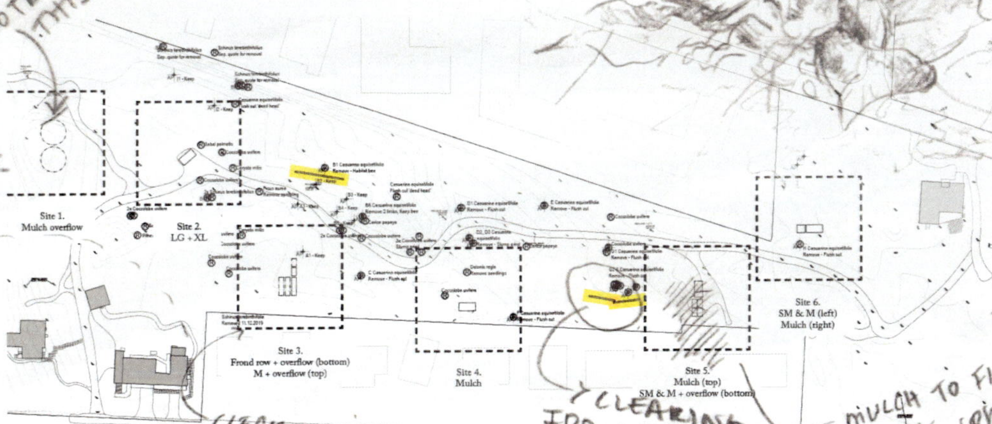

CLEARING FROM 11/19

ACCESS FROM NORTH, NOT WEST (TO AVOID COMPACTION)

CLEARING FROM CASUARINA REMOVALS

→ GOOD CHIP MATERIAL

MULCH TO FILL + HEAL TRUCK COMPACTION

NO MORE DRIVING HERE!

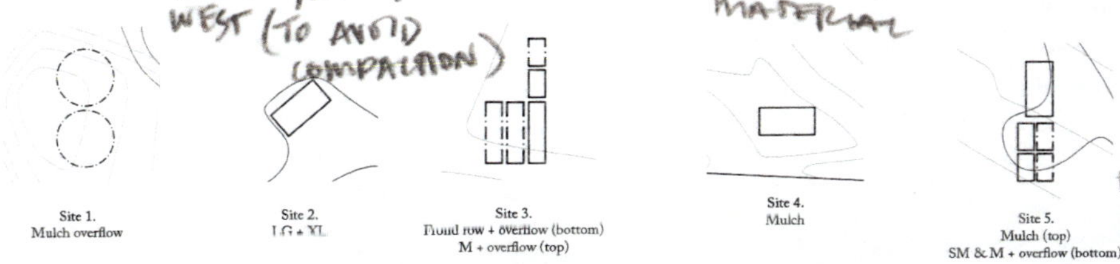

LARGE STORAGE AREA — USED TO BE CUT THROUGH

hipped

ralian pine branches

edlings >> Make space for Coccoloba spread

STACK

The arrangement and displacement of material, whether by chance or agent is an ever-present stage in any landscape process. Organizing material, defining areas of order or cultivation from areas of chance or chaos, while not uniquely human, fulfills an essential human desire. Stacks of fallen, pruned, or decayed organic material satisfies this need and keeps "waste" on site where it belongs. Stacking blocks and encloses views, creates topography, hosts organisms, and composts over time, slowly sinking back into the ground, nourishing concealed organisms, and feeding chemical cycles. Stacking has visual and ecologic impact: it is a multispecies practice in measuring time.

Across acres of farmland in Illinois, pruned deadwood was stacked from an adjacent Silver maple (*Acer saccharinum*) grove, layering large branches and twigs between an existing wire fence and recycled posts from a dismantled animal enclosure.

Small debris falls between the cracks of the larger pieces, filling in the stack and strengthening it for another layer of branches. The cracks, the interstitial spaces between, are part of the process, attracting a number of fungi that thrive, settle and fill these pockets. Molds, mushrooms, and yeasts are already finding a home in the wall and as they break down the material, it will slowly sink, making way for anything and anyone who wishes to call it home, including a human eager for another round of pruning. As with chips, there are as many ways of stacking as there are forms of plant; stacks reflect the morphology of the plant communities from which they are derived (Fig. 05). Narrow branches from coppiced trees or densely packed saplings can be stacked in tight weaves between poles, creating screens and providing enticing surfaces for vines and creepers. Large, straight branches from mature hardwoods can be used as posts or added as ballast to weigh down a stack of twigs and vines. Twisting, knotty branches, like those from old farmstead yews (*Taxus sp.*) have a rougher, more irregular form and the pockets between their sinews become havens for insects and field mice, and secret storage space for nuts and seeds.

Fig. 05 - Stack. Lake County, Illinois.

Stack is a verb and an outcome

Stack is a verb and an outcome a lost and found material that emerges from an established community. Stack is a scalable human effort, a way of collaborating with place. The design emerges over time, in the accumulation and break down of material and the fostering of new life. As described in the actions to prune and chip, to stack is to engage in an ongoing human-plant collaboration that rises to meet Marijke van der Veen's definition of contribution.[8]

We doubled posts (4' o.c.) to prevent collapse

Tremella foliacea?

Amanita flavoconia OR Mycena leaiana

XS
Extra Small
Use: Mulch
<1/2" dia.

SM
Small
Use: Fill
½" to 2 ½" dia.

M
Medium
Use: Posts
2 ½" to 4" dia.

LG
Large
Use: Light Edge
4" to 10" dia.

XL
Extra Large
Use: Heavy Edge
10" to 18" dia.

XXL
Extra Extra Large
Use: Mulch / Other
18" dia.+

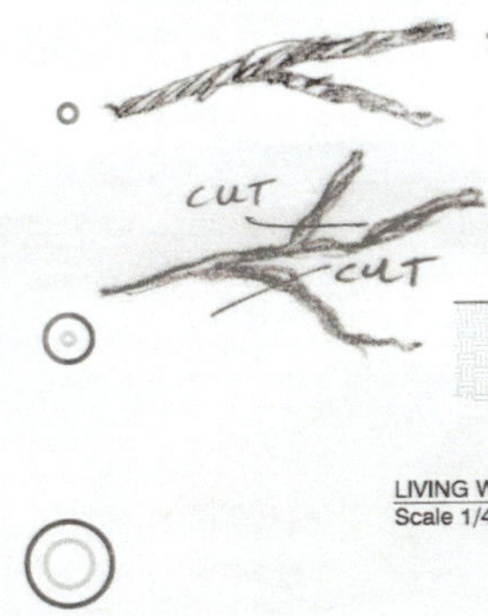

Ended up layering → increases density + wind-resistance

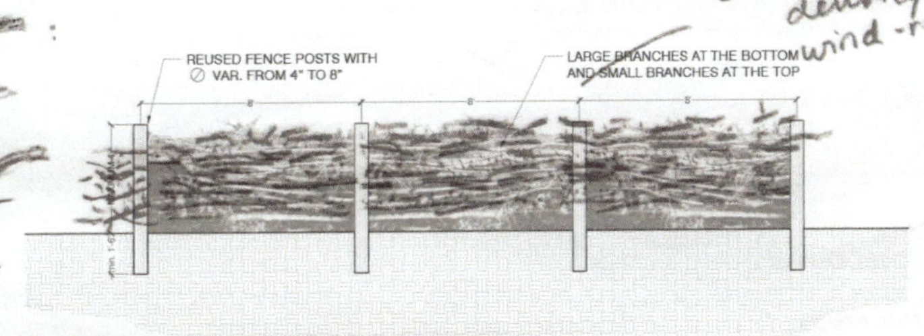

LIVING WALL ELEVATION 1
Scale 1/4" = 1'-0"

Ended up doing 4' wide in 1L

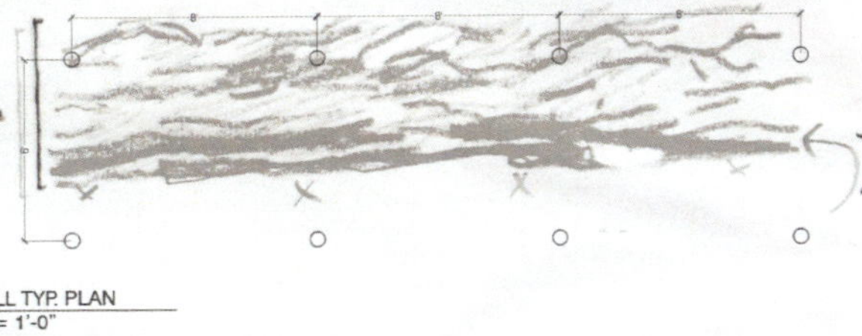

LIVING WALL TYP. PLAN
Scale 1/4" = 1'-0"

Brace between posts with longer branches

- Dump twigs over larger branches
- Tuck branch ends under next row of branches
- Weave together large branches for density

These three practices provide a ground on which humans and plants have consistently interacted to mutually enhance life. The lessons of these commonplace acts, performed with the attentiveness and humility achieved through awareness of the brevity of human existence and deference to the time scale of plant and land, link the quotidian to the profound and transform the transactional into the relational, which is where human aspirations for landscape have long sought to reside.

Fig. 06 - Source material by Practice Landscape, image altered by LUNCH editors

Notes

1. *Ross Gay, The Book of Delights: Essays (Algonquin Books, 2019).*
2. *Robin Kimmerer, Braiding Sweetgrass: Indigenous Wisdom, Scientific Knowledge and the Teachings of Plants (Milkweed editions, 2013).*
3. *Kimmerer, Braiding Sweetgrass: Indigenous Wisdom, Scientific Knowledge and the Teachings of Plants.*
4. *Marijke Van der Veen, "The Materiality of Plants: Plant–People Entanglements," World Archaeology 46, no. 5 (2014): 799–812.*
5. *Lisa Höpfl et al., "Initiating Research into Adapting Rural Hedging Techniques, Hedge Types, and Hedgerow Networks as Novel Urban Green Systems," Land 10, no. 5 (2021): 529.*
6. *R.S. Elkin and J. Lombard, Tabula Rasa: Designing South Florida," OASE #110 / Journal for Architecture, Tijdschrift voor architectuur, Part 3: Soil as an Urban Design Challenge (153-165), 2022.*
7. *"Lectures," Peter Del Tredici, accessed March 11, 2023, https://www.peterdeltredici.com/lectures.*
8. *Van der Veen, "The Materiality of Plants: Plant–People Entanglements."*

Additional References

Farrand Beatrix and McGuire Diane Kostial, "Beatrix Farrand's Plant Book for Dumbarton Oaks [District of Columbia].," 1980.

Henk Gerritsen, Mark Speer, and Dagmar Speer, Essay on Gardening (Architectura & Natura Press, 2010).

Julian Raxworthy, Overgrown: Practices between Landscape Architecture and Gardening (MIT Press, 2019).

Leanne Betasamosake Simpson, As We Have Always Done: Indigenous Freedom through Radical Resistance (U of Minnesota Press, 2017).

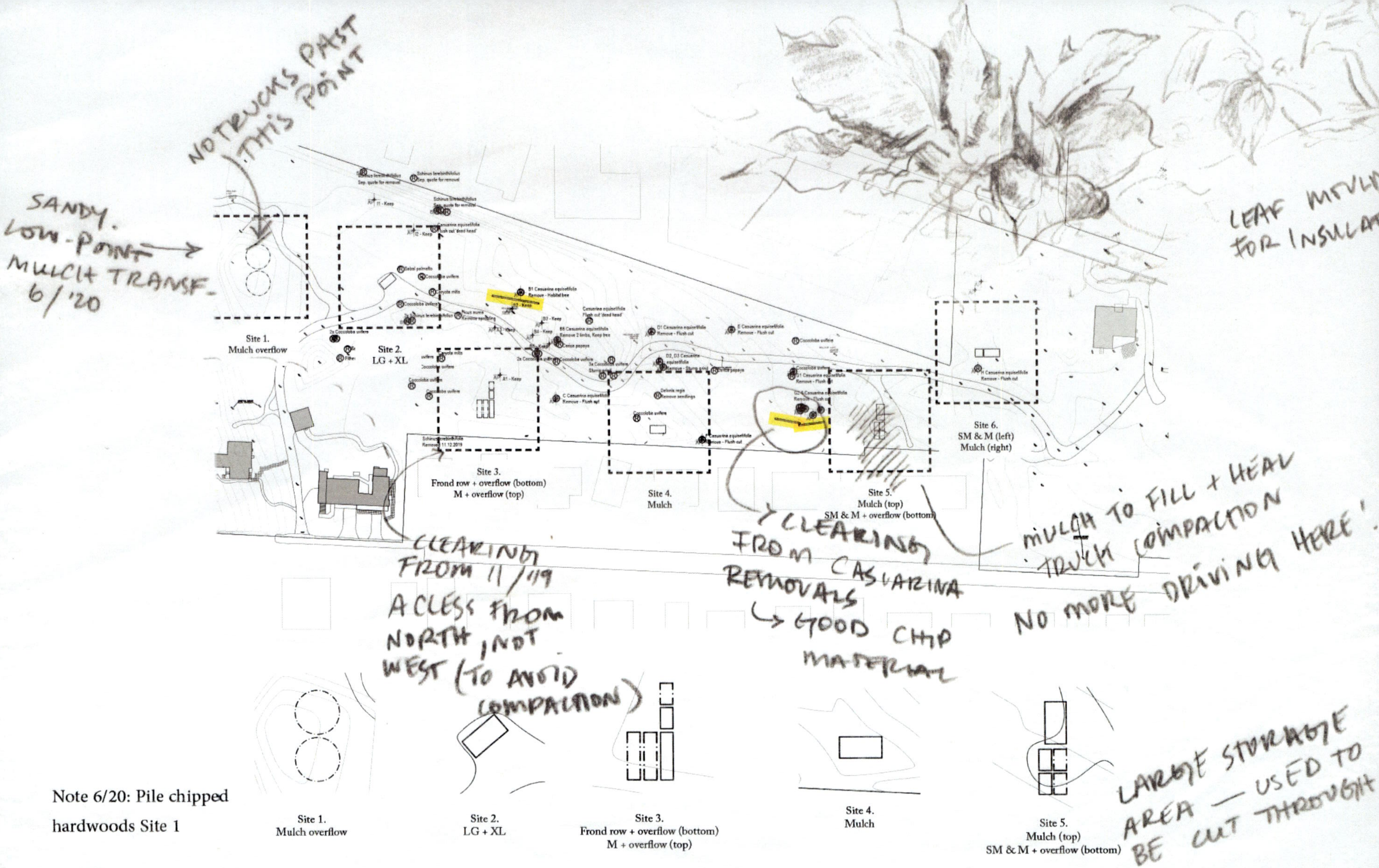

Note 6/20: Pile chipped hardwoods Site 1

Storage for Australian pine branches

Chip Delonix seedlings >> Make space for Coccoloba spread

CONTRIBUTORS

Anthony Averbeck

Anthony Averbeck is an architect, urbanist, author, and educator. His teaching and research with the UVA and the Harvard Graduate School of Design have accompanied collaborations on numerous international design projects. He has recently developed and taught design studios and seminars focusing on both collective housing and architectural representation. His present research at Harvard, Small Town Matters, is advised by Peter Rowe and Eve Blau and examines the growth and development of the American small town.

Ehsan Baharlou

Dr. Ehsan Baharlou is an Assistant Professor at the School of Architecture, UVA. His work focuses on computational design and robotics construction. Before joining the UVA, he was part of the MIT Composite Architecture Group as a postdoctoral researcher. He earned his PhD at the University of Stuttgart, Germany.

Erica Baum

Erica Baum is an artist based in New York. She is well known for her varied photographic series capturing text and image in found printed material, from paperback books to library indexes. She received her MFA from Yale University in 1994 and her BA in Anthropology from Barnard in 1984. Her work is held in the collections of the Whitney Museum of American Art, Solomon R. Guggenheim Museum, The Metropolitan Museum of Art, San Francisco Museum of Modern Art, MAMCO, Albright-Knox Art Gallery, Centre National des Arts Plastiques, FRAC Ile de France, and Yale University Art Gallery.

Larissa Belcic

The work of Nocturnal Medicine is dedicated to healing & regenerating individual and culturalconnections to "nature." While addressing climate change certainly demands many solutions that exist in the realm of the material, the political, the technical, it also demands examination of the cultural soul. At its core, the work of reforging connection is spiritual work, implicating each person's sense of the sacred and the values and meanings through which they understand their own existence and relationality.

Bailey Briggs
is a Master of Landscape Architecture candidate at the UVA. After completing her Bachelor of Arts in Art History and Spanish at Villanova University in 2018, she worked in New York City at landscape architecture firm Hollander Design, where she deepened her knowledge and enthusiasm for the profession. Her work at UVA has varied from infrastructural applications of landscape architecture, such as dredging and power line corridors, to theoretical and historical practices of anti-colonial landscapes and garden traditions.

Kira Clingen
Kira Clingen works at The Office for Urbanization with Charles Waldheim and Mohsen Mostafavi on the Future of the American City Initiative. She graduated from the GSD with a Masters in Landscape Architecture and Masters in Design Studies in Risk and Resilience programs, following a B.S. in Ecology and Evolutionary Biology and B.A. in Environmental Policy from Rice University, where her effort focused on big data and climate adaptation.

Marantha Dawkins
Marantha Dawkins is a landscape architect and scholar whose work is interested in wet ecologies at the end of the world. She is currently a PhD student at the UVA School of Architecture specializing in urban resilience through lenses of ecology, hydrology, computation, and infrastructure. Her current research investigates issues of ecological emergence, climatic uncertainty, and terra formation as they relate to coastal adaptation.

Junhong Fu
Junhong Fu currently works as a Landscape designer at Design Workshop, mainly on residential gardens and planning projects. She is always inspired by nature and technology, and her other researches are focused on environmental justice and sustainability.

Chloe Hawkins
Chloe Hawkins is the Founder and Director of Cohort, a landscape architecture practice that aims to deepen the reciprocal relationships between people and their surrounding environments. Chloe is also a Lecturer at and alum of the UVA's School of Architecture (MLA 2010), and a practicing visual artist. As a designer and teacher, she draws on her background in visual arts and sculpture to use drawings

and full-scale mock-ups as essential tools for sparking connection, imagination and collaborative space-making.

Jennifer Jones

Jennifer Jones is a Partner at Terremoto, a landscape design firm based in Los Angeles and San Francisco. Terremoto approaches landscape and garden-making with an experimental, hands-on approach, with projects spanning residential, institutional, commercial, private, and public. Through their Test Plot projects and Land and Labor working group, Terremoto seeks to celebrate stewardship and labor on the land and to elevate the importance of land care in our society. Jenny received her MLA and MUEP from UVA in 2010.

Sanda Iliescu

Sanda Iliescu currently teaches as an associate professor of architecture at UVA. Born in Romania, Iliescu received her BSE in Civil Engineering and M.Arch in Architecture, both from Princeton University. Her professional awards include The Rome Prize, a McDowell fellowship in painting and The Distinguished Artist Award of the New Jersey State Council of the Arts. Scholarly writing on Iliescu's artwork include essays by Carmen Bambach, Curator of Drawings and Prints at the Metropolitan Museum of Art in New York, and Paul Barolsky, Commonwealth Professor of Art History at the University of Virginia.

Nita Wareechatchai

Nita Wareechatchai is a dual degree student pursuing a Master of Landscape Architecture and Architecture at the UVA. She holds an B. Arch from UVA with a double major in Philosophy. Her interest is in computation and making, through which she try to capture process, temporality, and movements.

Ailsa Thai

Ailsa Thai is a landscape designer in training. She spent four years having fun with form in architecture school, but realized that her true calling was prying into the making of public space. Upon completion of her MLA at the University of Virginia, she is currently based in Los Angeles at Studio MLA, on a quest to learn about the place she calls home.

Karey Kessler

Karey Kessler is a Seattle based artist. Kessler earned her BA in Anthropology and Fine Arts from the University of Pennsylvania and her MFA from the Pennsylvania Academy of Fine Arts. She is a member of Shift Gallery in Seattle, and her work is in the flat files of the Pierogi Gallery(NFsew York City) and the artist registry of White Columns (New York City).

Dylan Krueger

Dylan Krueger is a California-based designer and educator. He is the 2021-2023 Architecture Teacher Scholar at California Polytechnic University, San Luis Obispo. Previously, he taught numerous studios and seminars at California College of the Arts and The Southern California Institute of Architecture (SCI-Arc). While studying Design Theory Pedagogy at SCI-Arc, Dylan served as co-editor of OffRamp 14 and Offramp 15. He received a Master of Architecture from Southern California Institute of Architecture and a Bachelor of Science in Architecture from Temple University.

Practice Landscape

Practice Landscape works with the living environment inspired by a deep respect for the future, grounded in an understanding of the past. As designers, researchers, and gardeners, we reveal existing processes and carefully test new methods and practices. We specialize in ecological assessment, landscape strategy, plant inventory, landscape design, planting plans and research. We collaborate with clients who share a deep respect for the land and a commitment to ethical land management. We relish working with people and institutions across a spectrum of disciplines and scales and take seriously the role of collaborator. Practice Landscape was started in 2006 by Rosetta S. Elkin.

Lizzie Needham

Lizzie is currently practicing at HDLA as a landscape designer. Lizzie's passion for landscape architecture stems from her background in gardening, teaching in, and designing schoolyard gardens. She holds an MLA from the University of Virginia, and earned her B.A. in mandarin and environmental studies from the University of Wisconsin-Madison.

Mike Nesbit

Mike Nesbit is a fine artist based in Los Angeles. With a background in architecture, his multidisciplinary interests greatly inform his artwork, allowing him to explore areas between art and architecture with a focus on technique, repetition, and representation. He received a Bachelor of Architecture from the Southern California Institute of Architecture. Nesbit is a founder of the Non-Profit/Artist-Run Space, Maple St. Construct. Located in Omaha, Nebraska, Maple St. Construct is a gallery/residency program that looks to bridge the gap between Los Angeles and The Midwest.

Evelyn Saunders

Evelyn Saunders is an alum of the UVA's School of Architecture (B.ARCH, 2021). She holds a major in Design Thinking and dual minors in Historic Preservation and Government. She sees design as a powerful, immersive, and compelling form of communication.

Celina Qiu

Celina Qiu is interested in creating site-specific memorable spaces that call upon the ecological and cultural context of a place. With experience living in Hong Kong and Toronto, Celina is fascinated by how cities are shaped aims to find solutions to preserve urban ecologies and informal practices. She holds a Bachelor of Arts from the University of Toronto's John H. Daniels Faculty of Architecture, Landscape, and Design, and is currently completing her Masters of Landscape Architecture at UVA.

Kyle Schumann

Kyle Schumann is Assistant Professor of Architecture at the UVA, where he Co-Directs the Before Building Laboratory, and is Cofounder of design firm After Architecture. He has been named a University Design Research Fellow by Exhibit Columbus, Next Progressive by Architect Magazine, and made Cultured Magazine's inaugural Young Architects List. Schumann's research seeks to advance the accessibility of digital fabrication, leveraging democratized technologies and inventing and building low-cost ground-up fabrication and imaging systems.

Sasson Rafailov

Sasson Rafailov is a PhD student at UVA working at the intersections of philosophy of architecture and the history of design education in the 20th century. His scholarly writing is balanced by a commitment to craft in wood, ceramic, and stone, which he has pursued since beginning his studies in architecture almost a decade ago. The pursuit of craft in these materials is simultaneously a pursuit of spiritual fulfillment for the author.

Sarah Rivard

Sarah Rivard holds a Master of Architecture degree from UVA. After completing her Bachelor of Science in Architecture at Tulane University in 2018, she worked in Boston for two years on historic renovation and expansions of museums, higher education institutions, and a courthouse. Her thesis work takes a special interest in microplastic fibers, contamination, and the architect's role in the contaminated environment. ContaminantCraft is one component of her thesis, A Design Approach for the Plastisphere: The Micro, Meso, and Macro.

Samantha Rosner

Samantha Rosner is an artist, writer, and aspiring landscape designer. In 2017, she received her BFA from the Cooper Union where she studied film, painting, and media studies and she is currently pursuing her master's degree in landscape architecture at UVA (MLA '24). Through her landscape architectural graduate studies, she is weaving together her passions of photography, media studies, and landscape history.

Eli Sobel

Originally from Maine, Sobel has studied at the Gerrit Rietveld Academie (BA, 2017),The Maryland Institute College of Art (BFA, 2015), and The School of the Art Institute of Chicago (2014). Eli Sobel makes installations out of wood, ceramics, prints and photographs in which storage and appropriation are subject matter. He has shown within the United States, the Netherlands, Germany and most recently at SPACE Gallery in Portland, Maine. Currently he is a Path 3 MArch student at the UVA, 2024.

Elizabeth L Sweet, Sara Ortiz Escalante, and Raksha Vasudevan

Dr. Sara Ortiz Escalante is a scholar-practitioner, working at Col·lectiu Punt 6, a cooperative in Barcelona, Spain, since 2009. Dr. Elizabeth L Sweet is Associate Professor of Equitable and Sustainable Development at University of Massachusetts, Boston, and Dr. Raksha Vasudevan is a postdoctoral fellow at Teachers College, Columbia University. All three identify as feminist activist-researchers, and together have around twenty-five years of experience working with body map storytelling.

Theodore Teichman

Theodore Teichman is a Master of Landscape Architecture candidate at UVA focusing on commoning infrastructures of environmental and spatial justice. He received a Bachelor of Science and Arts with Honors from Carnegie Mellon University in Pittsburgh, PA in 2018 in an interdisciplinary research-driven program, locating a convergence of music composition and neurobiology, focusing on soundscape practices here and as Fulbright researcher in Serbia for 2018-2019.

Peter Waldman

Peter Waldman is a professor currently teaching at UVA. Educated at Princeton, and then a Peace Corps Architect in Arequipa, Peru, he became infected by the poetics and pragmatics of the construction site. For more than fifty years he has taught and practiced first at Princeton, then Rice in Texas, and finally commenced his Piedmont Condition in 1992 in the Oasis of North Garden where he grasped connective tissues first found in Mica Mines in Manhattan. He is a Fellow of the American Academy in Rome and the author of Lessons From the Lawn and Connective Tissues.

APPLIED
RESEARCH
+DESIGN